ADVANCE PRAISE

My wife was dumbfounded that I read the entire book in three sittings over just three days. You have no idea what my daily reading of world events consumes of my daily routine! I don't usually have the time or the inclination to read an entire book, but Rosie's story and the authors's ability to shift to the horror from the nostalgic was especially artful and powerful.

The Redhead of Auschwitz is a story of a heroic Holocaust survivor who lived through the worst obscenity ever tolerated by human civilization. Yet, the Redhead's own exquisite loyalty, her unyielding courage and indomitable faith inspires us to still believe in the decency of humanity. Hitler lost and the Jewish People out lived him proving, once again, that despite every effort to destroy us throughout the millennia, we remain an eternal people embraced by G-d.

—**Rabbi Meyer H. May, Executive Director, Simon Wiesenthal Center**

D1512986

Nechama Birnbaum has written a very n

account about her redhead grandmother's life growing up in Crasna, Romania and her experiences in back breaking work in a brickyard, Auschwitz, Bergen-Belsen, the Duderstadt ammunition factory, Theresienstadt and DP camps. Her testimony honors the memory of family members who were murdered by the Germans, and demonstrates how, against all odds, she survived.

"The redhead who promised herself that she is going home," leaves an incredible legacy of 5 children, 28 grandchildren, 120 great grandchildren and 7 great, great-grandchildren.

—**Alex Grobman, PhD**

The Redhead of Auschwitz was a difficult book to write but not so to read. Rosie Greenstein's granddaughter captured the experience of her grandmother and drew so close that she was able to write in her voice. The result is a powerful work that traces Rosie's experience from the lively family life of her youth, to the German invasion of Hungary, ghettoization, deportation, arrival, Auschwitz and the daily struggle for survival. No one survived Auschwitz without luck but Rosie is able to describe the many ways she defeated death by wit and wisdom, determination and an iron will. She was one of the very few who entered the gas chambers and returned. She was more valuable to the Nazis alive than dead. We follow her through the death marches to liberation and the return and catch the briefest glimpse of her life afterward. Each chapter begins with a verse from Psalms chosen with such great sensitivity that we see how Psalms can accompany us all the days of our life from the depths of anguish to the heights of joy, from the darkness of humanity to majesty of human kindness and our Creator. An important story told with grace and love!

—**Michael Berenbaum, Professor of Jewish studies**

THE REDHEAD OF AUSCHWITZ

A TRUE STORY

NECHAMA BIRNBAUM

aɪp

ISBN 9789493231801 (ebook)

ISBN 9789493231795 (paperback)

ISBN 9789493231818 (hardcover)

Publisher: Amsterdam Publishers, The Netherlands

info@amsterdampublishers.com

The Redhead of Auschwitz is **Book 17 of the series**

Holocaust Survivor True Stories WWII

CONTENTS

This book is dedicated to my mother, who is also a redhead, and the most courageous woman I know.
It is also dedicated to my daughters (who are redheads in spirit) and the best thing that ever happened to me.

"And he (David) was a ruddy with beautiful eyes."
1 Samuel 16:12

"'I will not die but I will live,'" says the psalm and continues, "'and I will declare the works of God.' Sometimes the refusal to die, the insistence of the holiness of life, is itself the work of God."
—Rabbi Lord Jonathon Sacks

PART I

1

CRASNA. MAY 10, 1944.

Why should they say
The nations
Where is their God?
Our God
Is in the heavens
Whatever He pleases
He does."

Psalm 115:2–3

The drums turn out to be the most life-altering sound I will ever hear, but when they first boom, I barely register the noise. They thud dully in the distance, a background noise to the story that is playing in my head. I know I am letting my mind drift and I revel in the freedom of letting it go. The stream laps next to me, the dragonflies hum, and the sweeping leaves of the weeping willow dance in the breeze, creating a soft orchestra of sounds that lull me into the space where nothing matters, and everything is good. But then, "Boom!" The sounds again. This time it registers. Drums? Why is someone pounding on drums in middle of the day?

I turn right to follow the sound and see two Hungarian soldiers march by. One wears a drum on a cord like a necklace and he pounds on it emphatically. The other carries a trumpet in one hand and a megaphone in the other.

"All Jews to the Town Square!" he shouts. "Attention! Attention! All Jews to the Town Square!"

It is those Hungarians again. They are always trying to assert their control over our small town, to prove they really have a stake in it. They don't. My village, Crasna, is on the border between Hungary and Romania and the two countries fight for us like toddlers fighting for a toy. I would also fight for my village. She is beautiful. Jagged mountains line the horizon like huge fortresses and the stream wraps around us like a moat wraps a castle. You would think the stream would protect us, but the Hungarians got us in their grubby hands four years ago. Since then, things have been a little different, but we are used to that now.

In the Town Square there are dozens of people milling about. It looks like the eve of a holiday, but instead of shopping at the small market stands, the people are crowded around a podium that is set up in front of the church. A Gendarmerie Officer stands on a small stage, holding a megaphone.

"Attention all Jews! Attention all Jews!" He is shouting into the megaphone. Most of the town is here, not only Jews. I see my younger sister, Leah, in the corner with her friends. I see my brother, Yecheskel, with a few of his friends from *yeshiva.*[1] I spot my mother's best friend, Kokish Emma, but I do not see Mama.

"I said attention!" the officer bellows.

The hubbub quiets down.

"All Jews must go home and pack a bag. Fill your suitcase with only clothes and food. It is very important that you leave all your valuables at home." He smiles. "All your valuables must be out for us to see. If they are not, you do not want to know the consequences. Go home and pack up, be ready to go very soon. You should start now. You will want to be ready." He puts down his megaphone and steps off the stage. The hubbub in the square starts again, but this time it has a buzz of confusion. I swallow hard as a feeling of nausea rises in my throat.

I walk home and Leah joins me as I enter our courtyard. Her eyebrows are lifted in worry and there is fear in her dark eyes. Leah is 17 years old, exactly 17 months younger than me, and at least 17 times smarter than me.

"What was that all about?" Leah asks as we make our way through the courtyard.

"I don't know. It makes me very nervous."

We walk into our apartment. Mama is there, holding a pot that she must have brought in from the outdoor stove. "Where have you been? What makes you nervous?"

"You did not hear the drums, Mama?" Leah asks. "They called all of the Jews to the Town Square. A Gendarmerie Officer said we have to pack our bags with whatever we have, and we have to give our valuables to the officers coming around."

"The whole town was there!" Yecheskel says, stamping his feet on the rug and brushing the arms of his jacket before he walks in. At 13, he is starting to turn into a man, but he is also still very much a boy.

"I can't hear anything with the stove clanking away like it does. I made us bread. I guess I will need to pack it."

"What do you think they want from us?" I ask.

"I don't know," Mama says. "It cannot be good."

Leah and Yecheskel and I look at each other with stunned expressions. Suddenly, without a word, Mama goes to the hall closet and takes down a suitcase from the upper shelf. She removes the dresses that hang in the closet and lays them on the table. There is a low ominous beat, the soldier drumming somewhere in the distance, and we find ourselves moving quickly to its rhythm.

"Put on the finer ones," Mama says. "We should be well dressed for wherever we are going. Oh, and take your cardigans." She hands us the rest of the clothes from the closet. Leah and I dutifully stack them on the table, then fold them and place them into the suitcase. I notice my hands are shaking. It feels so odd to be packing without knowing where we are going. An hour ago, we weren't going anywhere.

"Mama, your engagement ring!" I say. It is the only valuable that we have. My father bought her this ring when he asked her to marry him and even though he has been dead for 13 years already, I see Mama looking at the ring every day. I cannot imagine letting Mama leave the only thing that remains from our father for the Hungarians to take.

"My ring?" asks Mama, looking down at her hand. "They didn't mean I have to leave my engagement ring?"

"I think they did," says Leah. "They said, 'You do not want to know the consequences if you don't.'" Her voice is small.

Mama's eyes open wide. She swallows hard.

"They said that?" she asks.

Suddenly I am full of rage. The Hungarians took my mother's job and her house, but they won't take something as meaningful as this.

"Give it to me quick," I say, holding out my hand. "I will sew it into the shoulder pad of my cardigan."

Mama slips the ring off her finger and hands it to me. I take it and sit down at our sewing machine. Everything seems very surreal as I prepare to hide our only valuable in my clothing. I undo the stitching of the shoulder of my cardigan. Mama always told me to work faster, like Leah, and now, under pressure, I work just as fast and efficiently as my sister. I slit open the shoulder pad, stick the ring into the cushion and stitch the pad closed again. My lines are perfect, but Mama is not looking. She paces around the room, placing things in our suitcase with precision: flour from the cabinet, a stack of small towels, and the sheets from our beds all fit neatly inside.

"Go get dressed," she says, handing us our clothes. "Give me the clothes you are wearing now so I can pack them."

The dress is navy and off-white, made with the finest linen, ordered by Mama from England. The large pleats are razor sharp because I ironed them to perfection. My sister may be the talented seamstress in the family, but I can iron so perfectly that the pleats on our dresses could cut the skin.

I pull the dress up under my skirt and once it is fully around me, I take off my skirt. Then, I pull the dress up under my blouse, fasten the buttons, and take off my blouse. Leah and I hand our clothes to Mama and watch as she folds them and places them in the suitcase.

"Put on your cardigans," Mama says, gesturing to them and then drumming her fingers on the wooden table.

My heart beats frantically, as if it is trying to get out of my rib cage. I pull the cardigan over my shoulders. The ring, hidden within the right shoulder pad, feels like it weighs 1,000 pounds. Sweat pours from under my arms. "Mama," I say, "I can't keep the ring on me."

"Take it out, *Mamale.*"[2] She does not look at me. She drums her fingers louder on the table.

I pull the cardigan off and in a single step I am at the sewing machine again. I slit open the shoulder pad and pull out the ring. Without a word, I walk outside to the outhouse. The sun hits the diamond and makes a sparkling rainbow. I open the door to the outhouse and throw Mama's diamond ring, with its shimmering rainbow, down the hole with all my might. If my mother can't have it, the Hungarians can't have it either.

I do not know where my will to do this has come from, but when I go back inside and sit next to Mama, Leah, and Yecheskel, I feel a strange calmness. We wait.

The door is opened violently and two Gendarmerie Officers march inside with their rifles out. I have never had a rifle pointed at me before. I look at the hollow little hole at the front of the rifle, and the angry face of the officer behind it, and feel a swoop down to the lowest part of my belly.

"Go outside! Take your suitcase!"

Mama gets up and takes our suitcase and I watch in a dream-like state as she drags it out the door. The soldiers walk around our home, looking under beds and under the table.

"Nothing valuable in this rat room. We will check their bodies, though. Maybe they hid something there," they report to each other, and then, "Outside! Get outside!" they say to us.

I stumble out the door with my siblings. The two Jewish families with whom we share this courtyard, the Rosenbergs and the Brachs, are already there. A few other men and women have come outside to watch. One who borrowed eggs from us yesterday, and another whose kids I babysat for last week, but now I see they are smiling as the soldier pushes me with his rifle. I feel disoriented and full of shame.

"OK, stand up now together over here!" an officer says. He pushes Mr. Rosenberg with his rifle. Mr. Rosenberg stumbles forward. "Come here now!" the officer waves to Leah, Mama, and me. "Stand over here!"

We do as we are told. With the barrel of a rifle staring us in the face, we do not have much of a choice. Mr. and Mrs. Rosenberg stand next to each other. Their children quickly surround them.

"Listen carefully!" The officer who pushed Mr. Rosenberg is speaking. "We need to make sure that you do not have any weapons on you. That would be stupid of us, and we are not stupid. We are going to have to check some of you for guns." He walks up to Mr. Brach, who is holding open his hands to show that they are empty. "Oh, it is not you I am worried about, you small little Jew," says the officer. "It is the ladies I need to check."

Some of the boys who are watching us begin to laugh. The officer turns to them. "We need to check these fine ladies to see if they are hiding anything, don't we?"

"You bet you do!" yells a boy.

The officer puts his hand on the shoulder of one of the Brach girls, named Lutchie. She shakes under his grasp.

"Come here little lady," the officer says. "We have to make sure you carry no arms." He pulls her aside. Then he grabs her sister, Miriam, and pulls her aside, too. Then they lead the Rosenberg twins, Suri and Idy, across the courtyard, and then come back for Leah, Mama, and me. "We are going to search you now," the soldier nearest the Rosenberg twins says. "There better not be any guns, or worse, rifles!" At this the group that is idly watching starts to laugh. Hiding a rifle on us would be as easy as hiding a baby cow, and they know it.

"You can't do this," Mr. Rosenberg starts to say.

The officer whips around. "No? I can't? Watch me!" Then he turns back to the women. "Take off your clothes, young ladies!" No one moves. "I said now!" The neighbors watching us inch a little closer.

I freeze. I cannot believe this is happening to me. I feel like I am watching the scene through a fuzzy window. I have never been naked in front of anyone before, ever. Leah and I have never even changed in front of each other, even though we have shared a room and a bed all our lives. Even in our one-room apartment we have always instinctively known how to dress privately. The courtyard whirls around me like a crow, flapping and spinning. I hear laughter and shrieks and a baby crying. I see the hard, round shape of the tip of the rifle, which is being held by the nearest Gendarmerie officer. As if in a dream, I open the buttons of my dress. When the air hits my skin, it feels like I am being dipped into an ice-cold well. I hear more laughter in the background, but all I can think about is my arm, naked and exposed. I fumble with my buttons. A horrible shame washes over me as my dress falls away from my body and lands on the ground. I step out of it. There is a flannel scarf that I wear wrapped around my belly. Ever since I was a little girl, I have suffered from terrible stomach cramps which leave me feeling sick and weak. The scarf is the only thing that has helped, so I have always wrapped it around me before dressing. I slowly unwrap it.

"Hurry up!" someone yells from the background and a few boys laugh and shriek in response, "Hurry up, you Jew!"

"Did you not hear? We said hurry up!" An officer has his gun near my hip.

I flinch and quickly pull my undergarments off. I am shaking.

"Look at that, all the Jewish ladies naked. Ohhhh, look at them!"

"I never imagined I would get this lucky, all the Jewish ladies to look at."

"Ha, look at them now!"

The voices from the crowd are getting louder and my face feels flaming hot. The air around me nips at my bare skin. I only look at the ground.

One soldier comes over to me and puts his hands on my body. He lifts my arms and pats my underarms. He runs his fingers down my body and behind my ears. From the corner of my eyes, I can see a smirk on his face and that makes tears spring to my eyes. They hover there, but they do not spill over.

"Nothing on the redhead," he calls out. "Nothing dangerous on her." He moves to the next woman in our line. I hear more laughter. My body is out for the taking. It is not mine anymore.

When the inspection is finally over, we are allowed to put our clothes back on. I put on my beautiful, ironed dress, now creased and dirty.

"Follow us! Walk in a row!" orders a soldier, the fattest one of all of them.

"Bye now!" A man calls from the courtyard with a laugh as we walk away.

We fall in line behind the Rosenbergs and the Brachs, and we all follow the soldiers. Something tells me not to go, not to follow them —to stay right where I am—but as my feet move against the protest of my mind, I realize I do not have a choice. My choice fell away from me along with my dress. It is now in the hands of the soldiers who touched us.

They take us to the Town Square. When we arrive, we notice green buggies made from cracked wood with old horses hitched in front of them. All the Jews from our town are there, along with many onlookers. The Gendarmerie officers pile our friends and neighbors into the buggies, throwing suitcases over their heads. Suitcases and people pile up higher and higher. The onlookers stare at us as if we are the circus and add to the chaos with their jeering and laughing. Then I see that some of the onlookers are crying. I see Kokish Emma, her face is red and tears stream down her cheeks. Her husband holds onto her arm.

"Look what is happening to the Jews, they don't look too proud now, eh?" a man calls from the crowd.

The soldiers push us closer to the buggy.

"Ha! Look at that man sitting on top of his suitcase. He is hoarding! I am going to make him give it to me," another voice says.

"Jews will finally learn to share!" shouts another, followed by laughter.

I watch from near the buggies as people climb in and try to stuff their suitcases underneath their bodies to sit on.

"Look what they did to the Jews! Look what they did to the Jews!" a lady says. Her voice is full of shock, but also glee.

I take one last look around before I board the buggy. This was where I hailed the king, along with everyone else from our town. I can see the schoolhouse where I learned and danced and played. No one ever cared that I was Jewish. I spent my childhood in this very square, meeting friends and shopping for Mama. It has always been my home, but in an instant, it has turned into something else. Something I can't even recognize.

"Move along, move along!" A Gendarmerie officer pushes me roughly toward the nearest buggy with his gun. As I move forward, I suddenly remember something and turn to Mama. "I forgot to lock the door!"

The Gendarmerie officer laughs straight in my face. I smell his breath. It smells like meat and cigarettes. "Don't worry darling," he says. "There is no need to lock your front door now." He pushes Mama up into the buggy and she stumbles at her ankles. Yecheskel throws the suitcase to her, and she manages to find a place for it between two people who are already on board. I climb in just as Mama collapses down onto the suitcase, looking like she might faint. Yecheskel joins us on the buggy, then Leah.

"What is happening?" she asks Mama. Her eyes bore into Mama's, desperate to find answers there.

"The war really came to us," Mama says, shaking her head. "They are probably going to take us to work. We will work, and when the war is over, we will come home."

I hear her words, but they do not make sense.

Yecheskel nods. He holds someone else's suitcase above his head.

The wagon lurches and we start off, slowly moving away from the square.

"Where is your God now?" someone screams out from the crowd. "Where is your God who you are so proud of? Huh?" A few ladies laugh. Some people clap.

The last thing I see before I am carried away by old horses from the town I love, is a black camera in my face, and then a flash. A man has climbed onto the back of the buggy. He leans in and takes pictures of us with his camera. One picture, two, then three. Then he hops down and stands in the street, inspecting his equipment as if this is just another day. The wheels of the buggy turn forcefully as the horses heave forward, pulling their load behind them. I hold onto Mama and the waiting begins, as our transport makes its way to wherever we are going.

2

CRASNA. APRIL 1935. AGE NINE.

*"Let them praise His name
with dancing.
With drums and harp
let them make music."*

Psalm 149: 3

I am not the kind of girl people would think to see on stage. I have red hair, and some say that doesn't deserve the spotlight. My skin is pale and I'm usually half sick. That is why it means so much when my teacher picks me to dance in the school performance. Through dance, I have discovered a place where I can be myself more than anywhere else. Dancing isn't just for the stage—although to be perfectly honest, it is the place I like best to dance. Although the stage is a world of make-believe and pretend, the imagined flowers that fall at my feet as I take my bows are as real as the straight A's my little sister gets on her report card. Since my mother's work, feeding the students at the yeshiva, relies on her so much and she relies on her job to feed her children, she is never in the audience, but still, it is nice to hear the resounding applause when I finish my steps.

In my head, I am constantly aware of a rhythm that the entire earth dances along to. The wind itself is the choreographer, using the air to make music and movement happen. It pushes the current in the stream to make them ripple, whistle, and plop. It rubs on the strings of a violin, just taken from its case, even before being touched by the bow. It squeezes in and out through the throats of humans and animals. Musicians in the Town Square capture swift gulps of air into their lungs, and then force them down into the mouthpieces of their trumpets and tubas, until they rush out again, with a reinterpreted sound that bellows in the ears of anyone who is listening. I imagine a master conductor opening his hands and moving the wind one way or another, until the whole world is a swirling mass of dance and song. That is why, since my first dance lesson, it has always felt so natural for me to move my body and dance when music is played.

Even in our morning routine, I feel movement and rhythm pulsating through everything. Mama churning the milk into cheese (thump, thump, thump), Leah slicing the warm sourdough bread (sliver, sliver, sliver), and Yecheskel easing each foot into his shoes as I hold them (step/press, step/press). There is a dance as we set the table for our morning meal: plate down, knife down, fork down, sit! Take bread, smear cheese, have a bite, swallow! We quickly eat the hot bread, letting it slide down our throats until our bellies feel warm and full. There is a rhythm in the way we pile as many cucumbers as we can onto our forks and pop them into our mouths, while Mama keeps time with her pleading, "Won't you all hurry up?" There is a cadence to the way the door swings open just as we finish our meal, when the boys from the yeshiva who pay for Mama's homemade breakfast march in and sit themselves down to eat. It is in the way we kiss Mama goodbye, one by one, and walk to school: turn the corner, cross the bridge, drop off Cheskel, and then run!

I have always felt that finding rhythms and music in life is the best part of living, and today is going to be the best day of the school year—the day we have been looking forward to! Today we will finally find out which groups we have been assigned to for the Grand Performance! The performance is the highlight of the school year. Sure, we work hard and study every day, but the main event, around which everything else revolves—like the earth around the sun—is the festival in which we will perform. We are the only school in Crasna, besides for the *yeshiva,* so everyone has or knows a child in the school, and everyone will come to the performance. We had tryouts a few weeks ago, and then the teachers (who know exactly how to find the talent in each girl), placed us into groups.

When I get to school, there is a huge group of students crowding around the bulletin board. As I inch closer, reading the postings and looking for my name, my heart is pounding like a big bass drum. I find my assignment right where I hoped it would be, under the big letters that read: DANCE.

We suffer through an hour of arithmetic, and then we all disperse into our performance groups. I find the classroom where the dance group is meeting; it is quickly filling up with girls and boys from all different grades. The English teacher, Miss Elias, stands in front of us and claps her hands. "Girls and boys, welcome to your very first dance practice of the year!" A few older girls clap their hands in excitement. I feel lucky to be in the presence of all these grown-up girls.

"All of you have shown promise in the art of dancing," continues Miss Elias. "I am excited to help each of you find and hone your talent. We will practice every day. For me, dance is the most beautiful expression of what is deep inside, so while I can show you techniques, the real beauty of it must come from you. Therefore, today I will not be teaching you any of the specific steps we will learn for the festival. Today, you will play with what dance feels like to you." She motions to the drummer boy and his partner, a boy with a trumpet, who are both standing on the side of the stage. The drummer boy promptly starts to hit the drums with his hands. Boom, boom, boom. Thump, thump, thump. Miss Elias puts her hands to her chest and then opens them wide. "Dance!" she says. "The only rule is not to be shy. I want to see you all dance!"

The older girls start swaying to the music. Some twirl around. I close my eyes so I will not see anyone looking at me and I get up on my tippy toes. With my hands at my side, I swing around. The music gets faster, it pounds in my ears. A feeling inside my chest opens and spills out over my entire body. As I sway and twirl, something is born in that moment. The rhythm of life, and of dance, comes alive inside of me.

Once, my *Zaidy*[1] told me that there is a world where all the souls stay before they are missioned to come down to our world.

"Do you know what language the souls speak in that world?" he asked me.

"Yiddish?" I guessed.

"Souls don't have mouths, they cannot speak."

"So then how do they have a language?"

"The souls talk in the language of music," Zaidy explained. "They talk in beats and strings, in drums and harp."

"Really?" I asked, trying to imagine this beautiful language.

"Of course! That's why babies calm down when you play them music, they are remembering. That's why music speaks to us in a way that nothing else can."

When Miss Elias tells me to dance, I finally understand what Zaidy meant. If music is the language of the soul, then dance is the way my body speaks to those souls from here on earth.

"Move to the rhythm!"

I open my hands like Miss Elias, exactly as she did when she started dancing a moment ago. I twirl around and kick up my feet to the drums.

"Very good," Miss Elias claps when the music stops. "That was beautiful dancing!"

When we get out of school at the end of the day, I am still on a high from the dance practice. "Let's go play in the stream," I suggest.

"Race you there!" Leah says.

We run past the houses, the market with flour and chicken and eggs, the store fronts, and the church. We run down the hill so fast until we almost flip over. The sweet scent of grass and sunshine fills my nose and chest. The clouds hang low in the bluest of blue sky. We stop when we get to our spot in the stream where the water falls over the rocks in a rush from the mini lake. The bushes along the edge of the stream burst with little bouquets of white flowers that lean down over the stream. Dozens of butterflies swoop around the flowers. The trees whisper to each other through their leaves, and the birds sing as they hop from the branches to the rocks and then back to the branches again. The stream lets off a cooling mist that ruffles my hair. Our friends Gitta and Raizel are already playing in the stream. Leah kicks off her shoes and jumps in. "I won!" she announces. She is younger than me but aside from our race into this world, she usually beats me in just about everything else. I jump in after her and we play in the stream until the sun turns pink in the sky and spreads out like strawberry marmalade on white yogurt.

When we get home, there is chicken for supper. It is only one small piece of chicken for all of us, but Mama knows how to stretch it in so many ways, so we are never hungry. Next to the chicken there are potatoes—plump, smelling of apricot, and dripping from the chicken juices. There are vegetables cut up in a salad and farfel on the side. I cannot get it down my throat fast enough.

After dinner, Zaidy comes for his nightly to visit. Zaidy is Mama's father and really like my father, too, because we don't have our own anymore. He lives ten minutes away and he walks over every night to spend time with us. I don't love anyone more than him in the whole world.

"Where are my girls?" he booms as he bends down to fit through the door. Leah gets to him first. He picks her up in his arms and throws her in the air. He can lift anything with his big, strong arms.

"As for you, young lady," he turns to me with a stern face, "aren't you too old to be picked up by an old Zaidy like me?"

Before I can answer Leah is back down on the floor and I am almost touching the ceiling! "And my prince!" he says to Yecheskel, who giggles as Zaidy tickles him and holds him up high.

We sit down to have tea together. Mama brings out the steaming kettle and cups. Zaidy sits at the head of the table (after he checks the cabinets to make sure we have enough flour, oil, and eggs). He looks like a king with his long gray beard and deep blue eyes. A magical king, drinking a goblet of liquid gold.

"How was your day, Chaya Necha?" he asks Mama.

"It was good, the usual."

"I got to learn in front of the whole class today," Yecheskel says.

"My *Talmid Chacham*,"[2] Zaidy says.

"We started dance practice for the festival," I say.

"How was it?"

"Really good."

"I am sure you're going to be a great dancer."

I beam.

"Leah got full marks on her arithmetic exam," Mama says. "The highest in her grade, actually."

Leah blushes and smiles.

"My little smart granddaughter," Zaidy says to her, "I am so proud of you." He looks at his watch. "Oh, it is late. Got to get back home to *Bubbe*."[3]

I run to get his hat.

"Thank you, sweetheart," he says. He kisses us all and opens the door. We watch from the window as he makes his way up the street.

Mama takes out her book. Yecheskel sits down and practices his reading like his *Rebbe*[4] told him to. Leah and I get busy with the dishes.

"It's my turn to dry," I say.

"It is somehow always your turn," Leah says, but she dips the plates in the long wooden basin and starts scrubbing anyway.

"Not true, don't you remember yesterday I washed?"

"No, that was two days ago, but whatever."

I shrug and pick up the clean folded towel, wipe the plate dry, and set it on the shelf—dead center, just like Mama likes it.

And there is the rhythm again, the rhythm of a day turning to night. A day that opened with a burst of beats is now closing with the soft swish-swash of water in the basin and the light clink of the dishes as they are stacked. There is the rustle of pages being turned, the murmur of bellies that have been filled, and the ping of silverware as it is polished and put away. All the sounds that sprung open in the morning, and hustled, and lived, and were used all day long, are now being put sweetly back to bed. This is what I miss most when the music changes and nothing is the same.

3

THE KLEIN BRICKYARD OF CEHEI. MAY 10, 1944. AGE 18.

"Like for a friend
Like for a brother
I went about (for him)
Like a mourning mother in gloom
I bent over.
But when I limped
They rejoiced
And gathered
Gathered against me
Were the wretched
And I do not know why
They tore at me
And would not be silenced."

Psalm 35:14–15

I sit on the floor of the buggy and feel the wooden boards vibrating under me. I know I should be feeling something, but it is as if my brain is frozen. I see what is happening, but it is as if I am watching it happen to someone else. I watch my mother sit on the floor with Yecheskel's head on her shoulder. I do not want to remember seeing her undress. The faces of the people who watched us being shoved up onto the buggy flash before my eyes, but I close them and try to shake the image away. We had good relationships with our neighbors. I noticed that some of them were crying when we were put onto the buggy, but I cannot believe that others laughed. Were they faking their kindness toward us all this time? The more I try to understand what is happening, the more my brain feels like it will explode. I cannot understand that everyone from our little Jewish community is here on this buggy with us, looking worn and ragged. We haven't done anything wrong. We paid our taxes, we went to school, we made dresses for anyone who came to us. Everyone loved our dresses.

The vibrating of the boards beneath me smooths out to a whir and the horses come to a stop. The buggy door opens, and a group of Gendarmerie officers are once again standing before us.

"The Jews stink!" one of them says. Some children and older men needed a bathroom along the way, but of course there was none. They had accidents right here in the buggy, nothing else could have been done. I am used to the smell; it has become a part of me. It feels like we have been traveling for days, but I know it was really just a few hours.

"Get out! Get out!" another soldier yells.

We all get up and unfold together. I climb out of the buggy and land on top of the person before me. We scramble to find our suitcases. The Gendarmerie point their rifles at us. I shiver. I see some of my friends, but I do not meet their eyes. The soldiers surround us.

I try to look around and see where we are, but the horses and buggies have kicked up a thick red dust that swirls in the air. It stings my eyes and I feel tears welling up, but they are not enough to wash it away. If I open my mouth, I will swallow it, so I seal my lips shut. People swarm all around me—some are from the buggies, but many were already here. Finally, the dust settles and between the shoulders of the group I am standing in, I can see that we are in a field filled with bricks. I see a wooden sign that says, THE KLEIN BRICKYARD OF CEHEI. What are we doing in a brickyard? Ahead of us there are seemingly hundreds of people moving around with bricks in their hands. The women wear headscarves, and the men have beards. There is a factory building with a slab of cement jutting out from it on one side. There are a few wooden buildings without walls. There are train tracks running through the yard. I look up. We are in a valley and the hills that surround us are covered with Gendarmerie Officers with rifles pointing at us. We are trapped in the lowest place on earth. A rat scurries at my feet. I do not move as its hairy body brushes my ankle. The sky becomes an angry gray, and the air gets cold. The horses and buggies are led away. People start murmuring to each other, trying to guess why we are here.

"It is good to be away from our town during the war. We don't want to be there during the battle," someone says.

"Yes, they are isolating us away from the battle zone," another says. "All the towns from around this area are here."

"We just have to do some agriculture work until this is over, that is what the Rabbi said," another voice says.

"Mama, what do you think we are doing here?" Leah whispers.

"This is war," Mama says. "We will have to work a little but then we will go home. We just need to do as they say."

The soldiers are saying something to the people in the front of our group, but I cannot hear what they are saying.

"You need to find somewhere to sleep!" I finally hear a soldier say. I look toward the factory and the crudely built wood structures without walls near them, maybe we can sleep there? But they are already swarming with people. Night is setting in.

"Find someplace to sleep, you lazy Jews!" another soldier says.

I see people setting up makeshift tents. We watch as they pull material out of their suitcases and set it up so they can sleep underneath. We watch people moving out of our group, dragging their suitcases with them. Those who were already in this brickyard when we arrived start to build makeshift tents with their clothing. Some take places in the wooden building without walls. All around us people open their suitcases, take out blankets and clothing, and make tents.

We watch more people spread out across the brickyard. The men of each household start to make a tent while the women and children huddle on the ground.

"We don't have anyone to make a tent for us," Leah says.

"We don't need anyone," Mama says.

Yecheskel drags the suitcase a little closer to where another family is setting up their tent. We follow him. He sets the suitcase down and Mama purses her lips and unlatches it. She takes out a blanket and a sheet. I take out our dresses and hold the smooth silk to my face before I tie them together to make a wider cloth. Leah and Yecheskel find a long stick and hand it to Mama and she drapes a sheet over it. She struggles to keep it steady in the wind and Yecheskel runs to hold it down for her. Leah takes her rubber band from her hair and secures the sheet so that even though it flaps and tries to break loose, it stays on the stick. Our new home.

I am tired from the upheaval of the day. I just want to lay my head down in my warm bed at home and snuggle under the covers and sleep—and then wake up and realize this was all a bad dream. I am startled by a brisk voice.

"You can't be here," a soldier says.

"What?"

"You can't stay here," he says. He flings the sheet off the stick. It falls to the muddy ground. "Go on then."

"We are nearly done, sir," Mama says. "I don't see why we can't just finish up quickly and rest our heads here . . ."

"You don't have to see anything, you filthy dog!" He grabs Mama by her front collar. "How dare you talk back to me, Jew. I said you cannot stay here, so move before I move your bodies for you!"

I quickly grab the sheet from the ground and Yecheskel pulls the suitcase toward him.

"That's better," he says almost in a sweet kind of voice and my insides shake. He folds his arms and with a smile, watches us pick up all our belongings. We quickly walk away in a huddle with our tent on our backs. As we walk, we see other families being shooed away from their new makeshift homes. The soldiers seem to be enjoying themselves. "Move along, move along," I hear them saying from all around and weary men take apart their houses. My eyes tear up with anger.

"Why do they care where we stay? They do not! They just want to make us move."

"I don't know, just please don't make trouble," Mama says.

We come to a spot a little further away than most of the other people. We find more sticks and pile them up over our suitcases. Leah adds some of Yecheskel's shirts to the string of three dresses I made. When we are nearly finished, there is another soldier standing over us.

"Get on, get on," he says. He flicks his hand, shooing us like we are mosquitoes. "You can't stay here, go on now." I feel embarrassed. Why can't we stay here? My shame turns to anger. I ball my fists but then with absolutely no choice I start to take the clothing down and follow Mama as she walks on.

We find a third place and assemble our makeshift tent quickly. When we are finished, we look around and wait for a soldier to come and tell us we must move but the ghetto is blessedly quiet.

"Mama," I say, but I am too tired to finish my sentence. We lay down next to each other and even though I am exhausted beyond measure, I do not sleep for the racing of my heart. My head feels hard against the cracked, muddy ground.

In the morning the sun streams right into my eyes. I am in my bed at home. I am home! I am home! Then everything comes flooding back to me and in a moment of complete horror I remember, and I kick my legs as if I am fighting my reality, trying to pry its strong hands off my wrists. I reluctantly open my eyes. There is a soldier standing above our tent. He has a rifle in his hand, and he watches Leah who is curled up in a ball. Her hair is caked in mud, and she buries her face straight in the ground. I shake her awake. Yecheskel and Mama are asleep, too. The soldier jabs his rifle against Mama's head. She wakes up with a start and quickly stands up and straightens her dress.

"You all need to start working now," he says. "Report to the factory." He points to where a large group of people are already gathering. They are surrounded by soldiers with machine guns, as if we are dangerous and need to be kept in check. He turns around to leave but stops again. "And you cannot stay here." With one swipe he knocks down the branches of our new house and our clothes fall slowly to the mud.

Without a word, Mama picks up our clothes and blankets and puts them in the suitcase and latches it close.

"This war will be over soon," she says.

Yecheskel places his hand on her shoulder, and they walk together to the factory. Leah and I follow close behind. We reach the brick building. There are piles and piles of bricks on the ground just outside of the factory. Hordes of people stand around them. A Gendarmerie officer points to a pile on the dusty ground with his gun.

"Take these to the field over there." I look to where he points. It seems like there are miles between where we are and where I see people dropping loads of bricks. I have had nothing to eat, and my arms feel like jelly. I reach down to pick up some bricks and immediately fall on my knees over them.

"Get up you lazy redhead!" the soldier says.

I stagger up with my load. I take a step and stumble and then take another one as fast as I can. The bricks threaten to pull me to the ground. Sweat is pouring down my back. I walk as fast as I can. I cannot believe I am doing this. I finally get to the other side of the field, and I drop off my bricks. I barely inhale when a soldier tells me to head straight back to the factory and bring more bricks. I turn and walk back to the pile of bricks.

The sun rises slowly in the sky and beats down on us. The soldiers are on the hills that surround us. High up, in the fresh air, they follow us with their guns. We are in a well of dust. It is midafternoon when my stomach grumbles. I haven't had anything to eat since yesterday just before this nightmare started.

"I don't belong here," I whisper to myself over and over again.

There is a shrill whistle.

"Go eat now!" a soldier says.

I look around. There is no food. I notice people lining up by some open ovens in the far corner. I find Mama and Yecheskel and we wait in line to cook a few potatoes Mama has in her hands.

"Where did you get those?" I ask.

"I packed them," Mama says. "I have some more food in the suitcase, too. Don't worry."

It is our turn on the fire and Mama puts the potatoes down on it. They are barely on the fire for a minute when a soldier comes over to us. The crowd around the ovens starts to disperse at the sight of him.

"Move along!" he says. "You are done here!" He swats at us like we are flies.

I feel choked by his cruelty. "Get away from here, before I shoot you now! What is taking you so long?"

Mama grabs the potatoes, and we walk away as fast as we can. We find a quiet spot and Mama splits the potatoes among us.

"They are delicious, Mama," Yecheskel says.

She gives him a weak smile.

They are so hard to chew. I don't seem to have enough saliva to swallow them.

As we sit on the ground and eat our potatoes, a drizzle starts. I want to run for shelter, but I realize there is nowhere to go so we stay where we are.

Just as the rain begins to come down hard, the soldiers order us to work again. Rain is in my eyes, blocking my vision, and the bricks are so heavy; they keep slipping from my hands. Mud slops on my dress. I put the bricks down for a second to wipe myself off, but I grab them back up when a soldier raps on my back with a stick. My body moves but my brain stops working. I watch Yecheskel drag mortar double his size across the field, I watch Mama hunched over from the weight of the cement, slowly inching her way to the other side. I watch Leah putting the mortar on her back, not caring that her face is covered in mud. I see, but this is not how I really see them. I see my mother needlepointing with her friend, arguing over the latest novel they read. I see Leah braiding her beautiful brown hair. I see Yecheskel making us laugh. I can't see them for what they are doing now. I am in a dream. I went to sleep two nights ago as a regular 18-year-old girl, dreaming of marriage, but since then I have been stripped naked in front of neighbors and the soldiers, I have lost my home, and I am being forced to carry mortar across a rainy, muddy field. I want to talk to Mama, but the soldiers are all around and soon we all drift apart. The sun goes down completely but we work on.

"I am going home from here," I whisper to myself. "I don't belong here."

The rain lets up and I walk back and forth and back and forth between the place where I get the bricks and the place where I bring the bricks. I walk without thinking and then suddenly, in front of me, there is a little boy, and he hangs from the tree. I jump back. Two soldiers stand around him. They laugh as he gasps for breath, their fat bellies shaking up and down. He starts kicking and he cannot breathe. They laugh harder. His eyes roll back, and he faints. I want to hit them both and grab the boy but my whole body is shaking, and I am going to be sick. They are playing a game with a little boy. They have their guns ready by their belts. I back up and start running, but the bricks are still in my hands. I stumble and I see them splash water on the boy's face. He wakes up and starts kicking again and I pull myself up and walk away as fast as I can. When I get to the field where we are supposed to drop off the bricks I can barely walk. I try to get to the spot where the soldiers told us to put the bricks down, but I fall and drop them. I gather myself up and pick up the bricks and take a few more steps but I crumple down again.

"What's the matter, redhead?" a soldier calls to me. "You don't know how to walk?"

4

CRASNA. 1935. AGE NINE.

"The father of orphans
And the defender of widows
Is God
In the abode of His holiness."

Psalm 68:5

I was nine months old when I learned how to walk. Mama said my father was so proud of me, he would take me outside and watch me walk around for hours. One day I fell and hurt myself quite badly, and after that I refused to take another step. They tried again and again to get me to walk but I was a stubborn baby, and I did not want to. Every time I crawled Mama would say, "Silly child, you know how to walk! Silly child, you know how to walk!" Then one day Mama and *Tatty* [1] were out in the courtyard with me and I stood up, clutched my dress tightly for support and took a step.

"Silly child, you know how to walk," I said to myself.

Mama and Tatty laughed for a few minutes straight from that. Mama said I walked around for days, muttering to myself, "Silly child, you know how to walk," as if I couldn't believe I took so long to get up and walk again.

I love it when Mama tells me stories from my younger years because they all involve my father and, even though he is not here anymore, he is still a big part of our lives. Mama says I am an exact copy of my father. Maybe that's why it is sometimes hard for her to look at me. I have his red hair and blue eyes. Mama says my hair is hajszín szőke, blonder than red, but that's just wishful thinking.

I know my red hair is considered ugly, but I don't care because I have a part of my father that I get to wear on my head every day. Some people may think it is something to be embarrassed of, but to me it is a crown.

My father died when I was five years old and, being that I am the oldest child, I have the most memories of him. Leah was only four at that time. Pinchas, my little brother who died, was two, and Cheskel was still in Mama's belly so of course he can't possibly remember anything. Although, sometimes he mixes up Mama's stories of him as if they are memories from his own brain. I remember the day my father died clearly, like a flash of lightening in a blurry storm, and I know that the memory is fully mine. First, he was sick in bed and then they sent him to a hospital that was too far away for us to visit. I was playing outside in the courtyard one day and I saw Zaidy, Mama's father. He walked slowly to our house, and he was bent over a little. As he got closer, I saw that he was crying. I had never seen him crying before that. He did not have to say anything, I just knew. I ran all the way up the twisty steps to the *shul*[2] where my uncle was learning. He looked up over the *sefer*[3] at me and I said, "My Tatty died." He stood up and scooped me into his arms and ran down the steps with me to Mama.

My father was a teacher, but "Not just a teacher!" as Mama would say. He had students from all over the country. Sometimes he had students from places as big as Budapest. They would come and he wouldn't just teach them regular knowledge. He would teach them character, and how to be a person, and there is nothing as important as that.

Mama said that he used to set the table every morning before she got up.

"Why are you setting the table?" she would ask him. "That is a woman's job. Do you think I cannot manage it?"

"You are nursing a baby," he would say. "You are taking care of everything; you should have to set the table too?" And so, she let him do it.

Sometimes it makes me sad that I don't remember a lot of things about him, and that I must rely on Mama to tell the stories (which she does quite often, mind you). I feel bad when his face is blurry in my head. Fuzzy red beard, blue eyes . . . but very transparent and not fully formed. But I never forget how he made me feel. He used to take my hand in his when we went to the outhouse together to wash up. He let me hold the candle all by myself and he put his fingers to his lips and winked at me. I knew not to tell Mama, but my father thought I was big enough to hold a candle. I nearly burst with pride as the flickering flame warmed my face and made the dark room glow.

Once when I was on a walk with him, I jumped into a puddle. I was wearing my brand-new shoes. He took my hand and took me into the nearest shul. He took my stockings off and placed them out to dry. While we waited, he told me stories. The only rebuke I got was, "Your mother is going to kill us." But I was safe because I was with him.

Sometimes I feel sad that I do not have him with me anymore. Especially when my friend's fathers meet them unexpectedly in the street and give them a big hug, or when they pick them up from school and before setting off for home they take firm hold of their hand. In those times, when I feel like there is a little swirling hole in my heart, I think of a story Mama told me.

"You know Rosie, when you were born, I thought you were a little angel baby."

"Was I?"

"Well, that is what I thought. My friends who had become mamas all warned me that babies stay up all night. They looked so tired, with dark circles under their eyes, and I was worried that when you came along that I would be just like them."

"But I was an angel baby who let you sleep?" I asked, already feeling proud of my baby self.

"That is what I thought, until one night when you were a few weeks old. I woke up and I almost panicked! Your father's bed was empty, and you weren't in your bassinet! I stumbled to the kitchen, and I found you and Tatty sitting there. You were so tiny and peaceful in his arms. He read the Talmud as he swayed and sung softly to you, so I wouldn't wake up. When he saw me, he smiled and said, 'You caught me. Now go back to bed, you need your rest!' And so, I did. And to think that all along I thought you were sleeping through the night!"

When that lonely feeling wells up inside of me, I close my eyes and picture myself as a little baby in my father's arms. I imagine him holding me in the crook of his left arm and rocking me gently, our identical red hair reflecting the moonlight as it streams in through the window. Then, I don't feel so lonely anymore.

5

THE KLEIN BRICKYARD OF CEHEI. MAY 20, 1944.

*"You deliver us
Like sheep to be eaten
And among the nations
Have you scattered us?
You sell your people
For no fortune
And you did not
Inflate their prices.
You make us a disgrace
To our neighbors
The mockery and scorn
Of those around us."*

Psalm 44:11,12,13

"Things will get better," Mama says repeatedly. But they don't. They get worse. My brain cannot catch up to what is happening. Every morning I wake up and I realize where we are all over again. First, my brain says that I should be at work ironing the dresses that Leah sews, but then my body tells me that I must drag bricks like a workhorse. These are the longest days I have ever lived through, and somehow, one day just bleeds into another as if I am in a dream. Rumors circulate the brickyard as to what we are doing here. Some of the former leaders of Crasna, who were brought with us in the buggy, say we are here to work for the war effort for a few weeks. Eventually, they say, we will be able to go home. Some people say they were just evacuating our town and some of the neighboring towns, so they will not be bombed. I do not know what to believe. Mostly I do not have time to think. Before this, I actually thought that being a seamstress was the worst job in the world.

One morning, after a rainy night, we wake up tangled in blankets and wet, green mud. There is mud in my mouth and in the corners of my eyes.

"This war has to end soon," Yecheskel says. He brushes wet mud from Mama's back.

"It will," Mama says. "This cannot go on too long." She puts her arm around his shoulder and rubs it. He lays his head on her shoulder. "Come eat something before work," Mama says.

I open our suitcase and Mama comes to pick out something for us to eat this morning. Our bundle of food has gotten smaller, and I feel a nauseated nervousness as I look at the dwindling pile and Mama's shaking hand as she pulls out a loaf of bread and breaks off a small piece for each of us. She leaves only a tiny piece for herself. She looks like she has aged ten years in the ten days we have been here. The air is filled with dust from the bricks. We open our mouths to eat the bread, but instead we inhale the clay-filled dust. We all cough as it settles on our tongues and throats. Our fingers shake with hunger and the bread, what was once my mother's beautiful bread, is as stale as the bricks we carry. My heart pounds irregularly. In the past few years since the Hungarians took control of Crasna, we haven't always had a lot to eat, so I have known what it is like to go to bed feeling a little bit hungry. But I have never known hunger to this extent, the never-ending way it claws at your insides. The way it demands and demands something that you cannot give. Mama barely eats. Whatever little bit of food she packed she gives to us, and she knows it is not nearly enough. While I carry my bricks, I dream of the cakes Mama used to make, especially her *dobosh,*[1] and I wish I had them and could stuff them in my mouth right now—to feel the lightness of the whipped egg and the smoothness of the sugar that floats on top like boats on a stream. I want to pile them into my mouth and gulp them down until my belly is so full that the button on my skirt feels like it will burst. For the past few days my skirt has been so loose that it slips off me. I've had to tie it with a rubber band to keep it up.

"Get to the factory, you lazy rodents!" A Gendarmerie says to us. He has his rifle out, so we stand up at once and we walk straight to the factory before he has a chance to hurt us. I swallow dust as I walk. I am so thirsty, but I know I will not get a drink all day. Mice and rats squirm around my ankles.

"Take this pile!" a Gendarmerie tells me, pointing to a small mountain of bricks by his feet. "Take these to the field!"

I bend down to get the bricks and he hits me on the back. I pause for a second as tears spring to my eyes, but I do not let them fall down my face. A rat scurries off the bricks as I pick them up. The pile is almost as big as I am. It reaches my chin and down to my shins. I take a step, but it is hard to move because the bricks reach my knees and block them from bending, but I walk as fast as I can because when I walk slow it only gives the soldiers an excuse to hit me. I walk through the thin winding path that leads to the field where there are other workers building structures. I am not sure what they are building, in fact I am not sure they are building anything of importance at all, but I try not to think of that. The long path to the field has been worn into the ground by the people transporting the bricks and it twists and turns past many trees. Everything falls away as I focus on breathing and try not to choke on the dust. I take step after step even though the bricks are so heavy, and I am so hungry. I feel gutted.

Suddenly, I see a lady suspended in the air in front of me. I stare at her for a second. She is our neighbor, Mr. Waldman's daughter-in-law. She comes from a rich family in the town next to ours. She was always proper and polite, and I was jealous of how well educated she was. She screams a deep horrible scream, and I can't comprehend how such a sound can come out of a lady as beautiful as she is. She has been hung from the tree. She floats in a distorted way. Her hands are twisted backwards, her knees are at the most peculiar angle. She is inches from the ground but tethered to the tree.

She screams again, a hollow sound. Her body convulses from her belly and her scarf falls from her head. The soldiers stand around and laugh in her face. One lights up a cigarette for the other.

She cries out again and they laugh harder. She turns white and she faints. The soldier splashes her with water, and she wakes up and screams again. They laugh casually and let the ropes go and she falls to the ground with a splat. Her limbs are twisted, and she does not move. I vomit into the trees next to me and then I carry the bricks to the other side of the field where they belong.

When I get back to our little tent, I see Mama and I fall into her arms.

"I saw it too."

"What is happening here?" I sob. "Why is this happening?"

"I do not know, Mamale," she says. She strokes my hair. "God will help."

Leah runs into the tent. Her face is white. "Did you see that?" she asks.

We both nod.

She sits next to us, and Mama holds us both. "Go to sleep girls," Mama says after a while. "I will wait up for Cheskel."

I decide not to tell her I saw them do it to little boys, as well. None of us sleep until Cheskel comes in and we breathe a sigh of relief that he is unharmed.

The next day I see two more girls hanging from the trees by their hands. I know them from our town, and they are also from rich families. Maybe the Hungarians have something in for the rich ones. Nobody touches me. The women's faces are white and the pain looks like it is too much for them to bear. I see little boys hanging. We are a sick game for the Gendarmerie. Hanging us from the trees until we faint from the pain, then waking us up so we can feel it again. Screams echo in the forest.

Toward the evening we gather around the oven to cook our food. We meet Mr. Waldman, our neighbor. He looks grave as he runs his fingers through his beard.

When my grandfather died, Mr. Waldman let us stay in our house rent free. He knew we couldn't pay our bills. Mr. Waldman used to learn with Zaidy and every year, on the anniversary of his death, he threw a big party in his memory. Mamma made vanilla *rugelach*[2] that looked like they would dance right off the table.

His daughter stands next to him. She has her baby tied around her chest with a cloth. Leah and I stand on our tippy toes to see him.

"Ooooh, Hi Eliyahu," Leah says. She pinches his cheek lightly with her thumb and forefinger.

"He is getting so big!" I say.

Leah gives him a smile and he coos back.

"Oh, he is so cute!" we both say at the same time. His mother smiles sadly at us. I see the deepest expression of fear cross her face and she holds her baby tighter to her chest.

Mama and Mr. Waldman are conversing quietly. "There is a mint here . . . asking for the man of each household to report there . . . wives have to watch . . . then do the same thing to the wives . . ." Mama twists her fingers. "Men have been carried out of there on stretchers . . . full burns on his thigh . . . half dead . . ."

We keep looking at the baby, but I know Leah is trying to listen to Mama and Mr. Waldman.

"Maybe they won't ask us . . . no man of the house . . ."

We hear Mama's voice crack.

"They don't care, they just want to know where all the money is hidden," he says. "They will call me next, and I will have to hand over my entire life's savings to them. They know I am wealthy."

"Hopefully they will not call you," Mama says.

A few days later Mr. Waldman is called into the headquarters. Later, his sons carry him out on a stretcher. His eyes are closed, and his face is white.

After two days, he dies. A group of men and his sons bury him right here in the ghetto, on a little hill over the factory. His daughter with the baby wails as they lower him into the ground. Mama cries along with her. He was a dear friend of our Zaidy, and he helped us so much.

"I am going," Leah says to me one night as we stack up more sticks for our tent.

Mama is out of earshot.

"You can't leave, Leah, in case you haven't noticed, we are surrounded by soldiers with machine guns."

"Not out of this ghetto, silly, to the mint office. I'll let them interrogate me if they want to."

"Are you crazy, Leah? You can't! Not what after happened to Mr. Waldman!"

"So, what then? Eventually, they'll make Mama go and they will torture her. She is already giving us most of the food and barely eating anything herself. She won't make it. You can't make me change my mind. I've already decided, I'm going."

"No, you are not, Leah. Just leave it, maybe they'll forget about us."

"Does it look like they are the type to forget? Come on, Rosie. We can't let them hurt Mama."

"And I cannot let you walk into that awful headquarters."

"I am going and there is nothing you can say to change my mind."

I open my mouth to answer, but I know she is right. I feel sick to think of her walking straight into that office. I cannot look at her.

"Don't worry about me," she says. "I promise, I will be fine."

But of course, I worry. We finally settle down to sleep for the night. My muscles are burning, I can't lift my arms anymore, even just to scratch an itch on my foot. I am so tired, but I can't fall asleep. I just lie there, watching my family sleep on the ground, and I can't recognize us for the people we were just a few weeks ago. How is Leah able to sleep through this? She is going to march right into the headquarters tomorrow, maybe she will also be carried out on a stretcher, with burns on her legs. Would they burn her alive? They seemed capable of doing that, the way they hung that little boy, the way they killed Mr. Waldman. The worry swishes through my brain like sloppy water, sneaking into every crack and crevice. I pray nonstop, "God, let her be ok."

The next morning, I wake up and Leah is gone. I can barely breathe. After a few minutes I see her walking toward us. She is like an angel floating with wings above all the sleeping families on the floor. When she reaches me, I hug her to make sure she is real.

"I did it," she says smiling.

"Oh, my goodness, are you ok? What happened? What did they want from you?"

"They had a big pad and paper and they asked me where my family lives and where do we keep our valuables and if we are hiding anything."

"What did you say?"

"I told them we have a very big wooden basin that we washed the clothes in, and it is made out of walnut wood, so it is very expensive."

"And what did they say?"

"They started laughing!"

"You did not tell them about our sewing machine?"

"Nope! They are not taking my sewing machine."

Leah is a master seamstress. We lived very near to a fabric store and bought yard after yard of fabrics from there. With those fabrics Leah made the most beautiful dresses—for every woman in town, it seemed. With her skills, she kept our family alive.

"You are crazy! Did they hurt you?"

"No, they looked up our family name on the papers and obviously we aren't on the rich list, so they just told me to go."

I sat down, put my head on my knees, and took several deep breaths. There was a pattern. They tortured the rich people: hung them, burned them, killed them.

Mama stirs. "What happened?" she says, sitting up quickly.

"Nothing, Leah is so brave. She went to the headquarters and told them all about our valuables."

"Leah! I am you Mother! You cannot take responsibility like that! That is my job! Are you okay?"

"Do not worry, Mama. They only want rich families."

"Sick people," she says. "I'm happy you are okay, Leah, but do not do that again. Ever."

"I won't, Mama"

Watching my mother, I understand a little more about her love for us now. She has sacrificed everything for us. Every day she has set out to make it a good one for us, even though she had to do it single handily. I know she would not hesitate to offer her very life up for us. She has always tried to shield us from her own suffering. And she doesn't want us to shield her just yet.

"We are going to make it through this," Mama says. "You girls are going to be all right."

The soldiers come around and our moment as a family is broken up by their barks.

6

CRASNA. 1935. AGE NINE.

"Steadfast is my heart
O God
I will sing
And make music
Even with my soul."

Psalm 108:1

The morning of the school festival I get out of bed early. I want to get a head start on the milk. Mama needs me to watch Mr. Balan milk his cow, and then bring the milk home for us. I pocket the coins Mama has left for me on the table and walk slowly to his house. It is early so I don't have to run like most mornings.

I knock on the little wooden door and Mr. Balan answers.

"Hello young lady," Mrs. Balan calls from the stove. She is a fat, dumpy lady with a smile that is just as fat and dumpy. Mr. Balan is thin, and he wears a scowl.

"Good morning, Mrs. Balan."

"Will we be seeing you perform in the festival this afternoon?" Mrs. Balan asks.

"Yes, I am going to dance and read a poem. I had to memorize it. I hope I don't mess it up."

"Of course, you won't." she says. "We will be rooting for you in the audience. Your Mama isn't coming, right? She has to work?"

"That's right." I don't mind that my mother cannot be there. I have an innate understanding of what Mama must do to keep our family going—which is so much more than any other mothers I know.

"Well, at least she doesn't have to waste her time," Mr. Balan balks.

"Oh, don't be silly, Hendrick!". Mrs. Balan turns to me. "Mr. Balan marked the festival down on the calendar weeks ago. He can't wait for it. He pretends he has no time for it, and yet he is coming along with me to see it. Ok, don't want to keep you waiting. Off you go to milk that cow."

Mr. Balan and I go out to the backyard where the cow is waiting in her pen. Roosters and hens run around our ankles, squawking up a racket.

"Oh, shush! All of you," says Mr. Balan.

"Mooo!" says the cow, in response.

I giggle.

Mr. Balan places a three-legged stool under the cow, sits, and grabs her udders. He swiftly coaxes her milk into the bucket. He pours the milk into a glass bottle and hands it to me. Then he turns back to the cow to milk her some more.

"Thank you, Mr. Balan! It looks nice and creamy today."

"Off you go," he mutters, but I know he takes pride in his cow's milk. I leave the coins on a table outside of the pen.

I walk home carrying the bottle carefully. It is a soft spring morning, and the sun is starting to shine, which makes everything come alive. I have to hold myself back from dancing home. Mama hates it when I dance in the street. Plus, she would know if spilled even a drop of milk. Less milk means less cheese.

After breakfast, Leah and I walk as fast as we can to school. We dare not be late for the festival. We go straight to the auditorium. I feel a thrill as we rush right past the classrooms. No math! No spelling! No grammar!

The teachers greet us at the entry to the auditorium. They are dressed in their finest, with pretty lipstick on their lips. Even grumpy Mrs. Feder looks nice.

"Girls, boys, backstage please," they usher and herd us. "Find your places. Find your groups. We will hand out your costumes."

We move to the back of the stage and the harried teachers and assistants help us assemble into our groups.

Finally, it is time to start! I was chosen to read the poem at the beginning of the festival. I have been memorizing it for weeks. I pray that I will not forget my lines and embarrass the entire school. I wait behind the black curtains and as they open I blink and squint at the bright lights, but after a minute I see row after row of people sitting in the audience, until the end of the auditorium.

I stand before the assembly, open my mouth, and the words pour out like a flowing stream, sweet and clear. They swirl like a current following a riverbed, zigzagging left and right, undulating faster and faster. They gush as if in a torrid of rapids, then dabble like tiny waves nearing a precipice. When my words reach the edge, I take a breath and nearly stop, then tumble and rumble the words out again, as if they are pouring down over a waterfall. I speak of communism. I speak of equality for all. When I am finished the whole school claps in a thunderous rhythm, and my chest swells with pride and relief.

The play begins and I wait backstage with my dance group. We try to talk as quietly as possible but burst into giggles when we hear a girl onstage mix up her lines. Mrs. Felder has to run backstage to shush us.

Finally, it is time for our dance. We walk onto the stage in single file. The band at the corner of the stage starts to play and I feel music deep in my belly. My body slowly talks back to the music. The sounds lift me from inside my body until I am up on my toes. The violin wraps airwaves around me until I spin around. The audience disappears and becomes brighter all at once. I pirouette on my toes. Then, crashing cymbals and speeding violins fill me up until I explode. I lift my arms and leap high. I am flying. I am alive. I kick up one pointed foot and then another. I twirl slowly, then faster and faster until everything around me blends together into a frantic blur, but it doesn't matter because I am dancing from deep inside my soul. I lift my hands overhead again, and then drop down to the floorboards of the stage. I leap again, and again. I cannot stop. The audience claps and suddenly I feel as if I am one with them. There is no telling where they end and where I begin. When the music stops, I catch my breath and curtsy with my group. Candies and roses land at our feet.

As I curtsy again, I notice there is a man in the front row of the audience. I shiver. He is staring straight at me!

After two performances of the play, it is finally time for us to go home. On the way I pass by the fabric shop, as I have always done. Mr. Raizomovich has owned this fabric store for as long as we have lived here. Sometimes Leah and I stop in to play in the store, and he gives us scraps of fabric to wrap around our shoulders and pretend we are fine ladies from the city. The store has so many different and beautiful fabrics displayed on every wall. Rows and rows of material are propped up against the back wall—every color, every pattern. Today, Mr. Raizomovich stands in the front door and his face brightens when he sees me.

"Oh, good Rosie, it's you. I have been waiting for you. There is someone here I want you to meet, come inside for a moment, will you?"

Curious, I step inside.

The man who watched me from the front row stands in middle of the shop. From close-up I can see he is shorter than he looked from the stage, with a tall bowler hat and a big belly. He has a twisty mustache, and he twirls it slowly with his finger. Mr. Raizomovich puts his hand on my shoulder.

"Rosie, this man came all the way from Bucharest, do you know what that is?"

Of course, I know what Bucharest is, I think to myself. It is such a big city. Who doesn't know this? But I don't want to be rude, so I just nod politely.

Mr. Raizomovich continues. "He came all the way from Bucharest to bring fabric for my store. Do you know for who?"

I shake my head.

"For little dancers like you! He personally picks out the fabric for the costumes of his little charges and I told him, I know just the girl who he can make into a star." The short man looks into my eyes. "Let us see if you live up to your lovely neighbor's recommendation," he says. "Won't you please dance for me, darling?"

My heart began to pound. I have heard of people like him. Famous dance masters who turn little girls into stars. I can't believe there is such a person standing right in front of me, and he wants to see me dance.

Mr. Raizomovich turns on the radio and folk music streams out of it.

I curtsy.

"Look at that, a natural performer," Mr. Raizomovich says to the dance master.

The dance master claps his hands in delight. "Beautiful curtsy; now dance!" he says to me.

I feel nervous but I close my eyes for a minute and try to forget they are in the room, watching me. I let the music enter my heart.

When the song is over, and I am done, I smile and curtsy again.

The dance master rocks back and forth on his feet and claps his hands together like a child. "Boris!" he exclaims. "You were right about this one! Give me three months—three months—and I will make a great dancer out of her."

Mr. Raizomovich puts his hand on the dance master's shoulder, and says, "You did not believe your old friend. I may not be a talented man, but I know talent when I see it!"

"That you do," the dance master laughs. "That you do!"

Then they remember I am still standing before them.

"Go on Rosie," Mr. Raizomovich says, "I'll have a talk with your mother later."

I walk out of the store very straight and proper, trying not to smile. As soon as I know they cannot not see me anymore I start to run, and a huge goofy smile breaks out across my face.

I run into my house. I almost forget that Mama is still in yeshiva, cooking. I want to tell her right away, but I must wait and wait and wait. She finally walks through the door and before she can even get her coat off, the words burst right out of my mouth.

"Mama! Mr. Raizomovich showed me to a dance master, and I danced for him and now he wants to train me for three months and he will make a great dancer out of me. He said I am going to be a star, Mama!"

Mama looks at me with a strange expression, almost as if she is trying not to smile. She slowly takes off her coat and turns to hang it on the rack behind the door.

"Mama! Can you believe what I just told you?"

She turns back to look at me and she still has that funny look on her face. "Chana Rechel Greenstein," she says, using my full Jewish name, "if you even think of going off with that dance master, I will break both of your legs."

I look at her and my heart drops to my knees. I am not sure if she is serious or joking.

"I will talk to Mr. Raizomovich," she says. "That dance man won't bother you again."

The next day when Zaidy comes to visit he picks me up and twirls me around. "I will dance with you like this at your wedding," he says. "We will dance and dance and dance!" He puts me down and wraps one big hand around my waist and with the other he intertwines my small hand, and we waltz around the room, pretending it is my wedding. Mama claps along in the background. I laugh as I hold his arm and he twirls us around and around.

No one talks about the dance master after that and I try not to think of it myself, except for sometimes before I fall asleep at night. I close my eyes and imagine myself dancing on a stage far away, maybe all the way in America. A place where no one makes fun of girls with red hair, where I can be the girl I was meant to be. Where there are bright lights and big crowds clapping and me twirling in the middle of it all.

PART II

7

THE KLEIN BRICKYARD OF CEHEI. MAY 31, 1944.

"Fall victims
At your side
May a thousand
And a myriad
At your right hand
But to you
It shall not approach."

Psalm 91:7

One morning after Leah and I leave our makeshift tent, we walk to the factory and see a large crowd of people surrounded by the Gendarmerie. There are cattle cars on the train tracks behind the people.

"What are those for?" I ask Leah.

"Who knows?" she shrugs. "Come, we don't want to be late. We walk together to the factory and we each pick up a pile of bricks. I watch her perfect hands wrap around them. Hands that could turn any fabric into a couture dress. I cannot believe she is doing this now.

We drop the bricks at the far edge of the field and return to the factory for another load. Now there are more soldiers, and they are pushing and bullying nearly everyone in the brick area. There is mayhem and confusion as they grab arms and push backs. A few soldiers come up behind me, Leah, and some other girls who returned with us from the field, and they push us into the group of people being herded toward the cattle cars.

"Get on! Hurry up! Get in!" the Gendarmerie yell. They hit people from behind with their sticks. Women scramble to get in with their babies. Men young and old climb in, along with children. Right before my eyes, they become a mass of bodies being pushed and shoved as they vanish into the boxcar.

"Get on you little girl!" a Gendarmerie shouts at me. "Wait! First I need to check you for valuables."

He puts his rough fingers down my dress and checks my entire body. I am nauseated by his touch. I want to push him off me, but his rifle is on his hip and the ladies hanging from the tree flash before my eyes. Finally, he pushes me toward the crowd, and I become part of the mass of people as I am swept onto a cattle car along with them. I move through the open doors and stumble back onto Mama. She is here with me and Leah, and she tells us that Yecheskel is in the car too. She tries to hold me up, but the crowds of people pouring onto the car are like waves crashing into us and pulling us from one another. Leah gets pushed to the side, a little distance from me. We are in a metal, rectangular cattle car with no seats and no windows. More people are being pushed into this small space. I find a sliver of a spot to stand in, but then more people are pushed onto the cart, and a wave of arms and legs and backs hits me and pulls my torso one way, my legs another. I stumble backwards. The girl in front of me has her back to me. The crowd presses her so tightly against me that neither of us can move. I think I hear her moan. Her hair is in my mouth, and I struggle to breath. I try holding my hands up to block myself, but more and more people crash into me. There is no more space, if one more person is forced into this car, I fear it will burst apart. There is a slam of the door and the clank of a lock, and our only stream of light is cut off. I feel panic set in. There is not enough air in the car and the heat is thick and stifling. Sweat pours down my legs. The girl's hair is in my eyes now. I want to brush it away, but my hands are pinned to my sides by the people surrounding me. A baby starts to cry and then another baby follows. Soon all the babies on the cattle car are wailing together. My heart beats fast, I need to get out of here, but I am caged in like my heart is caged inside my ribs. The cars jerk forward, and we are on our way. As we move along, I pray for a breeze to seep into the car, but no air comes in. I feel someone's elbow in my belly and another's sweaty body on my back. We rattle through space, but to where we do not know.

"I need to use the bathroom," I hear Yecheskel say from somewhere behind me. I look around, there are no bathrooms, not even a bucket, not that we would be able to get to one anyway. I hope we will stop soon, but the car shakes along on the road, on and on and on. I hear someone shout, "She is dead right next to me!" My heart stops in my chest. The girl's hair sticks to my face, and I can barely breath. It starts to smell like body waste. I feel my cheeks burn with embarrassment. We rumble down the tracks, twisting and turning as the air gets staler and the smell even worse. Soon my mortification gives way to the agony of the need to relieve myself. I close my eyes and let myself go, wetness trickles down my legs and onto my ankles, a tear slides down my face, wanting to join the wet floor. What seems like hundreds of more hours pass and my feet burn from standing so straight for so long, my arms are tingling and numb. I am weak from hunger.

"My baby, my baby," I hear a woman whimper close to me. "My baby . . . she's dead." I try to cry out, but no sound comes. It feels as if there is no air left to fill my lungs. I am so weak, and so tired, my brain cannot not think anymore.

I fall asleep and then suddenly there is light sneaking through the cracks and my head is stiff and leaning to the right side. I wonder how Mama and Leah and Yecheskel are. They are only a few feet from me, but it may as well be miles away because I cannot get to them. I am pinned in my place. I am starving, my insides churn, and I feel like I will vomit, but I force whatever I still have in my body to stay there, and I swallow. I close my eyes again. The light dims slowly, and it is night. My knees ache and beg for me to give them a break. I close my eyes and, again, fall asleep standing up.

Mama's hand snakes around the people between us and suddenly there is bread in my hand. Her shaking hand squeezes mine. I hold the bread. I don't know where she got it from, but I know I cannot eat it. There is a little girl next to me and her face is green, and her eyes are closed and fluttering. I open her mouth and place a piece of bread inside. Her eyes shoot open. She opens her mouth for more. I place the rest of the bread on her tongue.

Finally, the train lurches to a stop. It is deathly quiet in the car. Then there is a clank and a click, and the metal doors are swung open. Light and sound floods the cattle car. I am not ready for the light. I need to close my eyes. A few soldiers stand at the door of the car. They look different than the Gendarmerie soldiers. They are taller and slimmer, with light skin and blue eyes piercing at us. I look beyond them. There are thousands of people on the platform. I don't think I have ever seen so many people in one place at one time. Children cry and mothers scream and, before I can try to take it all in, I am pushed off the train by the person behind me.

"*Schnell, schnell!*"[1] say uniformed soldiers standing outside the carts with guns in their hands. "Get out, line up!"

We are on a train platform. I am standing, but I feel only half alive. I am not hungry anymore. I feel the world spin around me. I hear gun shots and then thankfully Leah is next to me.

"They shot Perl," she says. "She couldn't get off the train fast enough. I think she is dead."

Perl Waldman is married to one of Mr. Waldman's sons. She had polio when she was a child, so she has always walked with a slower gait than the rest of us. But she is all grown up and married now, so she is ok—she cannot be dead. We find Mama. She clutches onto Yecheskel.

"Schnell! Move!"

We walk to where to the soldier points us. When he is out of sight Mama puts her hand on my cheek. She looks at me and then at Leah and a flash of raw panic crosses her face.

"Rosie, Leah. You are sisters. You need to stay together. Whatever happens, I need you to know the most important thing is to stay together. You need to promise me this."

"Of course, Mama," Leah says.

"I won't let her out of my sight," I say.

Mama nods her head. "My girls, I just want you to always, always have each other. Stay together! Nothing will make me as calm as knowing that you have each other. You must never leave each other!" She talks loud and fast with panic. "It was always my family that kept me going. Stay together!"

I take Mama's hand. "We will always be together."

Our words calm her a little.

Another train pulls up to the platform we are on, and like a factory line, the soldiers open the train car and rush the people out. Hundreds of people stream onto the already crowded platform. I watch a man help his daughter step off the track, she looks at him hopefully with her big brown eyes, and then a soldier kicks them apart. I hear shots. Boom! Boom! Boom!

A stick is in my back and a soldier is nudging me along. He does not look into my eyes.

"Get into line!"

There are five lines of people. Leah, Yecheskel, Mama, and I are side by side, each of us in a line, with a man I do not know next to me in the fifth line. A soldier pushes the man as we all inch forward. All I hear are shots, and screams, and snarling officers.

"Schnell! Schnell!"

Dogs bark loudly and run around and in between the people. I feel like the chickens in our courtyard when the dogs used to chase them.

Our row stumbles forward and I crane my neck to look to the head of the line.

There are little people around us. They look like elves. They are men but they look like children. Their eyes are huge, their heads are shaven, and they wear funny striped uniforms. They push us and move us along with their bony hands. Finally, after what seems like hours, we reach the front of the gate. There is a man sitting up ahead on a chair, like he is sitting on a throne. He has his finger up and he looks bored and lazy. One elf man brings the lady in front of us to him. He flicks his finger to the right and the elf pushes the lady to the direction of his finger. Another elf brings the next woman to stand before the cruel-looking man. He reaches his gloved finger into her mouth and pries it open. Then he flicks his hand to the left and the elf man holds the women by her shoulder and walks her to the left. Then it is our turn. I step up to him first. He lifts his eyes ever so slightly and runs them down my whole body. I shiver slightly and I am glad he does not look at my face. I wait. Then he points his finger to the right and the little man pushes me to the right. Leah is next and, in a moment, she is by my side on the right. Then comes Mama. The man barely looks up at her, and he lazily points to the left. An elf man moves Mama to the left. We watch Yecheskel step up to him. Right. He looks at Mama with fear on his boyish, perfect face and, very slowly, he steps over to join Leah and me.

"Yecheskel!" Mama cries. "My baby! My baby! They cannot take my baby away from me. He's my baby!" She puts her arms up in the air, but no one responds.

An elf man brings the next woman up to the man on the chair. He points to the left. People are piling up in front of Mama and also us.

"Come to me! Yecheskel!" Mama screams from behind them. She sounds like she is falling.

"Mama!" cries Yecheskel.

The people being moved to the left are swallowing her up and we can hardly see her anymore. Yecheskel looks around, right, left, no one is looking at him.

"Mama!" he cries again, and he runs to her side. More people join both sides and I stand on my tiptoes and crane my neck to try to see them. I find them, finally, and I see he has his arms tightly around Mama's waist and then more people are ushered to the left side, and they are blocked from my view.

Leah lets out a sob.

"It is ok," I say, "It is good that one of us is with Mama."

She nods and then she takes my hand, and we move with the group on the right.

8

CRASNA. 1931 AND 1936. AGES FIVE AND TEN.

"I proclaim as an obligation
God said to me,
My son, you are
On this day
I have given birth to you.
Ask from me and I shall give you,
Nations your inheritance
And your processions
To the ends of the earth."

Psalm 2: 7–8

Yecheskel was born three weeks after my father died. I was only five, but I remember Mama's blooming stomach as she sat on a low chair and cried for our father. Then I remember the brand-new little baby and Mama's tired but happy face. The whole town came to his *bris*,[1] it is not every day you see a child named after his own father. In our community, children were only named after the dead. I remember wearing my pretty white and navy dress. I remember Bubbe brushing my hair. I remember running around the shul with Leah and Pinchas eating rugelach, and no one told us to stop. The shul filled up with people. I remember the room going dark because there were so many people—they sat on the windowsills and blocked the sun. I watched their shadows flit around on the *Bimah*.[2] Mama stood in the corner with the ladies. Bubbe Heilbrun was on her right and Bubbe Greenstein was on her left. She held my tiny baby brother on a white pillow in her hands. He was the most beautiful baby, with caramel skin and perfect little eyes and nose. When I put my finger in his palm, he would wrap his entire hand around my finger and hold on tight. I remember Mama passing him over to my Zaidy Greenstein, my father's father. I remember Zaidy holding him in his arms and calling out: "and they will call his name in the Nation of Israel; Yecheskel Yaakov, son of Yecheskel Yaakov!" It seemed like the whole shul burst out crying at once. I did not cry; I was not sad. Yecheskel was our comfort baby. I don't remember Mama crying too much either. I was only five, but I remember her lying in bed, nursing the baby, and gazing down at him with a face melting with love. She let me, Leah, and Pinchas climb onto the bed with her and snuggle as she nursed him. Pinchas was almost two years old at that point and he was already talking in full sentences.

"Baby Cheskel, my baby Cheskel," he said, and he planted his chubby hands on Cheskel's tiny toes, the only place he was allowed to touch, and he bent down to kiss them. "My baby," he said matter-of-factly when he was done with his kissing, then he straightened his chubby legs out, wiggled his little tush closer to Mama, and let out a contented sigh. Oh, how Mama laughed.

"You're so cute my Pinchas," she said, and leaned over to smush his cheek. He looked back at Mama with eyes blue and wise, like he knew he was the big boy now.

Everyone came over to bring us food during that time. Our counter was covered with cakes, challah, and potato *kugels*.[3] People came in with worried eyes and big frowns. Their faces confused me. I knew my father had died but we were still a family. We had a beautiful new baby, a chubby toddler that said the funniest things, two sisters who were already big-girl helpers, and a Mama who took care of us no matter what. Imagine if Mama had died instead of Tatty. Now that would have been a reason to frown. But our Mama was here, and she was strong—and even at five years old, I knew we were going to be ok because we had her.

Sometimes Mama would let me watch Yecheskel while she put Pinchas to sleep. I could hear her singing to Pinchas in the background while I laid with Cheskel on Mama's bed, his deep, brown, teardrop-shaped eyes staring straight into mine. Even at the age of five, I felt a love so deep and perfect, I knew I would take care of him forever. But it didn't turn out like that at all. I tried to take care of my younger siblings but even though Yecheskel was the youngest of us all, he took care of us.

Five years later, Yecheskel is five and I am ten. We are sitting at the kitchen table. Mama is spooning out chickpea stew for all of us, but none for herself.

"Mama, take some of mine," Yecheskel says.

"Do not be silly," Mama says. "I am not hungry."

I know she is trying to feed us before herself. I also know she doesn't eat much since the day that Pinchas died.

"When I get older," Yecheskel says, with furrowed brows and the most determined look on his face, "I will own a big factory, one of the biggest factories in all of Hungary. I will be so rich, Mama, and I will buy you all the diamonds you want, and long fur coats. I will buy you a big house with a fireplace and as many books as you want. I will, you will see!"

"Oh, will you?" Mama says. She laughs a little. "Can you get me fine meats and chicken, too?"

"Oh, yes," he says. "Chicken and meat whenever you want. In fact, I will get you a cook to make it for you. You will not have to cook another day in your life."

"I am not sure I would want that, I love cooking," Mama says with a laugh.

"So, you can cook when you want. I will talk to the main cook and let her know you are allowed in the kitchen whenever you want."

Leah giggles. "Where does he get these things from?" she asks.

"You can laugh," he says, "but you won't be laughing when I am your rich brother, let me tell you that much."

"I won't be," Leah says.

"I will take care of you, too, Leah and Rosie."

"We better be nice to you now," I say.

He waves his hand like those kinds of things are beyond him. "And don't worry Mama," he adds, "I will also be a great Torah scholar. I will learn half the day. I will be both rich and smart."

Mama smiles at him. "Of course, you will my Yecheskel Yaakov," she says. "Now will my smart, rich son please go with my oldest daughter, Rosie, to the market to get me eggs?"

"Sure Mama," he says.

"Leah, watch over the factory while we are gone," I say. We all laugh.

We make our way the short distance to the market, past the courtyard and down Main Street. We get to the Town Square where the market is set up. There are stalls selling flour and sugar and salt. There is a stall with live chickens strutting around it, not knowing they will soon end up on the table of some lucky family. The trick with chickens is to find the fastest one that is moving the slowest, but we are not buying chicken today, unfortunately. There is a stall with all different kinds of beautiful flowers and when we walk by that stall the smell is intoxicating. The egg man stands by his stall and guards it as if any minute someone will come to rob him of all his eggs. I picture egg yolks flying everywhere from the fight that would ensue. The egg man is a huge man, his torso is round, and his arms and head stick out at a funny angle. He looks like a turtle from the stream. Yecheskel holds the carton for me while I bend down to pick out the eggs. I like to get the best eggs for Mama, and while they may look all the same to some people, I know how to tell the difference. I want the biggest ones and the ones with the most perfect shape. I pick up each egg and examine it and when I find one that satisfies my requirements, I place it into the carton.

"What's the matter freckle face, do you not trust my eggs?"

I can feel the heat rise to my face like a thermometer, and I know I am flaming red. "I do," I say.

"Then hurry up, freckle face! Hurry up, girl!"

I quickly pick the last few eggs and motion for Yecheskel to come with me. He gives the egg man a stare. "Stop that!" I whisper under my breath. "Let's go."

"What is wrong with freckles?" he asks when we are far enough from the egg man.

"Everyone knows they are ugly," I say.

"Why are they ugly? I like them."

"You are just saying that."

"I am not! They are like stars scattered on your face, as if your face is the sky when it gets dark."

"Well, they might look like stars to you, but they really are just one of those things that are considered ugly, even Mama says so."

"I think they are nice," he says. "But what do I know?"

A few days later, Yecheskel comes to me with a brown paper bag scrunched in his hand. "I have a present for you," he says.

"For me? Why did you get me something?"

"Just open it," he smiles, his eyes shining.

I take the brown bag and open it. Inside is a black jar made of glass with a white lid.

"Open it!"

"What is it?" I ask, removing the lid and looking at the smooth whipped cream.

"Freckle cream!" he says. "I went to the pharmacist. I said, 'You have to give me something for my sister's freckles.' He gave me this. He said it really works. You put it on twice a day, make sure to rub it all over including your neck. They should start disappearing in three weeks."

"Yecheskel, how did you afford this?"

"I have my money saved up," he says. "Don't worry about me."

"Thank you Cheskel, you didn't have to."

"I wanted to."

I put the cream on every morning and every night. Within three months there is not a freckle left on my face—and they never come back.

9

AUSCHWITZ. JUNE 1944.

"They divide my garments
Among themselves
And my clothing
Cast lots."

Psalm 22:18

The soldiers on the right side lead us to a big building. We enter single file, and I see that it is completely empty except for dozens of girls walking around, looking very busy. I look closely at the girls. I see they are just skin and bones.

"Take off your clothes!" a woman soldier barks at my section of the line. She looks as if she is only a few years older than me. She has blond, curly hair pulled back into a bun and she wears a blue blouse and a mid-length skirt. "Put your clothes in this pile!" She points to a pile of dresses stacked up one on top of the other.

"Now!"

I slowly move along in the line. I have been wearing the same dress since we left Crasna. It is very dirty now, but you can still see the fineness of it beneath the grime. The perfect stitching, the cut of the fabric. No matter how poor we were Mama always made sure to get us two fine dresses every year. I run my fingers over the sides of my dress. I slip my hands into the pockets and feel the silk pouch inside. A soldier woman is next to me, and she hits a girl behind me on the head with her rubber stick. The girl cries out. "You are not moving fast enough," she says.

I frantically open the buttons on my dress and pull it down. My hands shake and I try to take my undergarments off as fast as possible. I burn with shame again. I don't want to see everyone naked around me, but I can't help but look. The skinny girls gather our dresses as fast as we take them off and stack them into a mountain of beautiful clothing. Silk dresses flow and bunch up like flowers. Wool dresses hold stiff. Now we are in line with nothing on.

"Stand in line! Stand in line!" another soldier says.

We stay in line. The room is dark, and I shiver even though it is not cold. I am not hungry anymore. I was hungry in the cattle car; I was hungry on the line into this place; but now I am not hungry. I only shake from weakness as I stand in a line behind dozens of other girls to see whatever comes next.

We come up to a few chairs set in a row with some of the horribly skinny girls standing behind them. The line breaks in front of me and we sit down on the chairs. The girls hold small machines in their hands. Before I can think, the girl behind me takes the machine and runs it over my head. I gasp.

A huge clump of curls tumbles over my eyes and onto my naked lap. Off my head, my hair looks even more red, like fire, like blood. Suddenly, I think of the way I had wanted to put my hair in a low bun for my wedding. I was going to part it down the middle so the strawberry and gold highlights would disperse like the Red Sea splitting down my head. It was going to meet at the nape of my neck in a gentle wave of reconnection. Leah was going to sew an organza veil for me, and it would drape down my back in gauzy ripples. My hair would shine through it like the red sun shining through the clouds and all our town would come and celebrate with me. Instead, there is a small girl behind me, and she is placing a machine on my head until my hair is severed from me, along with my identity. Like in a weird dream, the girl starts to sing as she places the razor back on my head. "*Little boys with black hair*," she sings. My brother Yecheskel flashes in front of my eyes. He is learning in the living room, he is with me in the market, he is making Mama laugh after a long day.

"*Little girls with blonde braids*." My mother trying to dye my hair blonde, running with my friends down the hill toward the stream, their braids flying behind them like wings.

A huge clump of red hair falls past my face and on to my lap. The girl brushes it to the floor.

"*What was it was*." Dancing, laughing, working, living.

"*It is no more*." The Hungarian soldiers walking into our house. The way everything shifted and tilted.

"*It went away, in that time, in that hour*." Wisps of red, like fire, like blood, are all around me. Other girls are also getting shaved. The girl who shaves my head continues to sing, "*What was, it was*," and she puts the machine on my head again. Another thick lock of curls falls off my head.

"Stop!" I shout, but no sound comes out of my mouth. I watch in horror as my hair falls like wisps of blood. I cannot believe this is happening to me. I want to put my hands on my head to save my hair, but I am too scared to move.

"*It is no more*," she sings.

Another thick bundle of curls falls off my head, as if it has been executed. It falls to her song.

"*It went away*," she continues, and another bundle of locks falls.

"*In that time, in that hour*," she runs it over the other side of my head.

I can't stop this from happening. The razor hums on my scalp as they cut close to my skin.

"*Little boys in black hair*," she sings merrily. "*Little girls with blonde braids*," as another lock of hair falls to the floor in front of my eyes. It feels like something deep inside of me is being ripped off my head.

"*What was, was, it is no morrrre!*" With one last swipe she pushes the machine across my scalp and thousands of wisps of hair float down around me. She nudges me up and points to another line of girls.

Another skinny girl rushes over to sweep up the pile of hair around me. My hair on the floor has no life anymore. She picks up the red mountain of wisps and forms it into a ball. It looks like a bird's nest. She adds it to a basket in her hand. I feel like she is stealing something from me.

As I walk to the other line of girls, I see a piece of broken glass on the floor. I look down at it and a strange girl looks back at me. My heart jumps in my chest. It is me, my reflection. My head is naked. There is nothing on it but the thick skin of a stubby scalp in a weird oval shape. My ears stick out like little nubs on the side. My eyes are too low down on my face, my nose too big, my lips too wide. I was always told I was ugly because of my red hair but I knew it wasn't true, I was beautiful. But now without that red hair I am the ugliest creature to ever exist.

I promise, I whisper to the creature in the glass, *I promise you now, I will never touch a scissor to my hair. I will never cut it again.*

The weird creature nods back at me and I leave her there and walk to the next line.

More skinny girls are here handing out dresses. The women soldiers have sticks and they hit those who do not put their dress on fast enough. I see the young soldier from before lift her stick over her head and bring it down hard on another girl's shoulder. Images flash in front of me but they don't stay with me. I only see what is in front of me for a moment before it fades. A skinny girl hands me a little blue dress. It is made from one sheet of fabric. Even though I can't sew well, I can tell that this dress was put together in haste. Just one piece of fabric folded and sewn. I put it over my head. It is dirty and it smells like urine. I put my hands through the short sleeves. The dress falls over my chest. It is thin and there is a rip on the front and a rip up the whole right side until the top of my thigh. It does not reach over my knees. The smell of it makes me dry heave. It is dripping with filth. This is my new uniform.

"Out, out!" Another women soldier snaps at those of us who are dressed. I start to walk outside with the others, but the room is spinning around me. The ugly gray walls, the unclothed girls, the hair being picked up off the floor. I have not eaten in three days. Everything shifts to one side, then to the other, and then suddenly everything goes black.

10

CRASNA. 1935. AGE NINE.

*"And he (David) was a ruddy
with beautiful eyes."*

1 Samuel 16:12

Mama thinks that nut oils are the answer to my horrible red hair. My red braid has a lot of problems entwined into it. When I walk through the market, the old ladies who sit on chairs out front twist their wrinkled lips and spit their saliva straight at me. It lands on my shoes with a splat. It makes my face turn redder than my hair and I have to look at my nails to stop myself from crying. Looking at your nails can help you stop your emotions, mid-laugh or mid-cry. That is because Adam and Eve were made from the same strong material as our nails are, before Eve's sin of course, so looking at your nails can remind you how strong you can really be. That gets your feelings in check real fast. Mama tells me they are not spitting to be mean; they are trying to be helpful because they believed that spitting removes the devil that resides in red hair. When I was seven, or even eight, I would brush my hair out a hundred times at night just in case the devil was really living in there. By age nine I knew that it could not possibly be true. I know Mama never really thought the devil lived in my hair, but she still thinks that it is ugly, like the rest of our town does.

I have always thought my red hair was beautiful, even if no one else did. I love the way it looks like a strawberry from the garden and its flecks of shiny gold that sparkle in the sunlight. More than anything else, I love my hair because it is the hair of my father and even though he is not alive anymore, it shows me that he once was here, and that he left me his special hair color to remember him by. I get to wear a part of him on my head every day and that is worth however many spit marks I have to scrub from my shoes. And not that it matters, but I know one day I will move to America where all the movie stars have red hair, and no one will call me ugly then.

When Mama greets me with the nut oils to dye my hair, I pray it will not work.

"Rosie," she says, "I spoke to a man who opened a new stall in the market. He has lots of different serums. He gave me this for your hair and said that it will dye it blonde."

I eye the black bottle.

"What is in it?"

"Oh, nothing dangerous. It is just a mixture of nut oils, OK?"

I do not want to dye my hair, but she looks so hopeful about it, so I say yes (as if I have a choice).

"OK, come sit in the backyard. I set up a chair for you in a good spot. I have to run back to yeshiva to finish up the supper there so let us make this quick."

"Can I go play?" Leah asks. "I don't have to wait for Rosie, right?"

"No, you can go, but don't go into the stream without her there. It is not safe."

"Of course not," she says, and runs off. Her perfectly brown hair bounces behind her.

I sigh.

"It will only take a few minutes," Mama says. "Then you will be free to go."

We walk to the garden. I see she set the chair up far enough away from her radishes and cucumbers. I sit down and Mama puts a spare cloth around my whole body and my neck, so my uniform will not get ruined.

Mama stands behind me. "Come tilt your head back into my hands."

I lay my head back and feel a cool sensation as she pours some oil onto my head. She spreads it over my hair and then pushes it gently into my scalp with firm fingers. Water drips down my face, into my eyes, and onto my lap. I do not complain. I know it makes my mother happy to try and make me decent looking. She massages my scalp with circular motions and then takes a comb and runs it through my hair with the oil still in it. As Mama gently combs my hair, I feel my skin pull back and my eyes lift at the sides. Then she pours warm water from the wooden basin over my head and mixes in some soap to wash the oil out. She fluffs my hair with a fresh towel and brushes it, and finally ties it into a tight braid.

She walks around the chair to examine me from the front. She tilts her head and studies me. "I already see a slightly more yellow tinge," she says. "It is working. Off you go now, make sure Leah is OK."

I run my fingers over my smooth scalp and tight braid. "Thank you, Mama."

Before I leave to find Leah, I duck my head into the house and look into a small mirror that hangs on the wall. A young girl looks back at me. She has wide, almond-shaped blue eyes.

Rosie, I say to the girl looking back at me, *you are beautiful. You are so beautiful.*

I turn around and crane my neck to examine my braid. Whew. It is still as bright red as ever!

When I get to the stream Leah is already swimming. Her brown hair is wet and lily pads float around her shoulders. She lays her head back on a big gray rock that jut out in the middle of the stream and the water whooshes past, stirring up a white foam. On either side of her, branches heavy with leaves reach into the stream like animals taking a leisurely drink. Twiggy green bushes, lush with white berries, stretch like umbrellas over the branches and gnarly roots wrap around the shoreline. Wild grass grows tall all along the far side of the stream. Dragonflies flitter about, chasing each other gaily, as if they are playing a game of tag. The cool breeze flips around at the collar of my shirt.

"Come in, Rosie!" Leah calls. She cups her hands together, gathers up some water, and then splashes it all over my feet.

"You cannot do that to your older sister! And Mama said you must wait for me before you go in!"

"She won't know unless you tell," she laughs.

I take my shoes off and jump in right next to her, minding the rocks. The water cools my skin that was hot from the sun. Splash! My landing drenches Leah for a second.

"Got you back!" I say.

"Ha!" says Leah. She puts her hands on my shoulders and dunks me under. I wriggle out from her grasp and let my body drop down deeper in the cool stream, until I am beyond time and place, in a world where I can be completely myself. I love the complete silence of this underwater world. I open my eyes and watch orange fish and tadpoles swim around me.

"Hi fish," I mouth, letting my breath out, "hello baby tadpoles." My greetings come out in bubbles. I push myself upward and break the surface of the stream and take in a deep breath.

Leah and I swim and play in the stream until we are finally exhausted. We pull our bodies out of the stream, which is a bit of a struggle because our clothes are so heavy and clingy, still full of water. We lay next to each other on the grass under the sun. Mama does not like when we drip water all over her mud floors, so we must take care to dry ourselves in the sun before we go home. I look up into the sky and at the twisty branches, dripping with leaves overhead. The weeping willow by the stream is my favorite tree. It is humongous, a giant tree, with branches that stretch in every direction. Long, stringy vines hang down, and swing in the wind. I notice purple wildflowers in the grass right next to my head. Delicate lavender petals ring the bright, yellow centers at the top of each stem. In school, Reka told me that a flower can tell you if the one you love also loves you back. I pluck a flower from the ground.

"Leah, should I tell you a secret?"

"Yeah!"

"But you have to promise you won't tell anyone."

"I won't! Tell me."

"But then you have to tell me your secret back."

"OK, I will."

"I think I know who I want to marry."

"You do? Tell me who!"

I blush, suddenly embarrassed to have said it out loud. "It is one of the boys that come for breakfast." Lately I have been doing the dishes in the basin while the boys eat the breakfast Mama makes for them.

"His name is Yaakov."

"Yaakov? Which one is he?"

"The one with red hair."

"Oh him." She smiles. She looks proud and scared to know that I have a secret like that.

Yaakov comes most mornings for breakfast. While the other boys burst into our home, so full of energy, he is much quieter. He has a sureness about him, a confidence that shows he does not need to be heard. On the stage, I love to move and make noise, but in regular life I am quiet too, and his sweet silence attracts me to him like frogs to the water. It also helps that he has a head full of red hair.

"Who do you like?" I ask Leah.

"I don't like any of them!"

"You have to tell me! I told you, it is only fair. You promised."

"But I don't like anyone!" She grows very shy.

"Just tell me Leah, I won't tell anyone."

"OK, I like Mendy. Happy now?"

Mendy? Do I know Mendy? Yes, I think to myself, *he is the short one with the baby face.* "Leah, that's so cute," I say affectionately.

She laughs and turns away from me. I hold up a flower. There is only one way to know if Yaakov likes me back.

"He loves me. He loves me not. He loves me," I mutter to each petal as I pick them off, one by one, and drop them to the ground. My heart sinks: the last petal that remains lines up with my turn to say, "He loves me not." How can this be? I crumple the flower and pick another one. "He loves me. He loves me not. He loves me. He loves me not." I don't stop picking until I get to a flower that tells me what I want to hear, "He loves me!"

"He loves me!" I say as I pull the last purple petal from the yellow center. See? I knew he did.

11

AUSCHWITZ. JUNE 1944.

"Untruth they speak
Each man to his neighbor
A lip of smooth talk
With an insincere heart
Do they speak."

Psalm 12:2

I feel someone open my mouth and place something in it. My tongue circles it. It is a piece of bread. I open my eyes to look for who saved me, but by the time I can see, whoever it was is gone.

I stand up slowly, it is dark already. Nobody seems to notice that I fell. The women soldiers round up groups of ladies and shove them outside. We scramble to follow them. The soldiers use their sticks and put us into rows of five again. We march along on the muddy ground.

"Rosie! Leah!" Someone yells as we walk.

I turn around to see who is calling us but there is only a mass of faces in the dark.

"Leah, Rosie," the voice says again.

"It's Chanky!" Leah says. "She is also here!"

"Chanky!" I gasp. Chanky is our Uncle Duvid's wife. Uncle Duvid is Mama's youngest brother. He used to come over every *Shabbos*[1] to spend time with us.

"You are also here," she says, catching up to us.

We both hold onto her hand.

"Where's Duvid?"

"He is on the other side with all the men."

"Is Yitzchak Yehida with him?"

Yitzchak Yehida is Chanky and Duvid's son. He is two years old and amazing already. He has tight blond curls, big blue eyes, and a smile that is sweeter than Mama's milk-and-honey drink. He is so smart. Everything he says sends all the adults laughing.

Chanky's eyes cloud over.

"He's with my mother. I love him so much I can't bear even a few hours being apart from him. I miss him."

"Oh, Chanky don't cry," I say, "Yecheskel is also with our mother."

"He ran to her when that man separated us," Leah says. "Why did you leave him with your mother?"

"Well, we got to the line, did you also go through that selection line?"

We nod as Chanky continues.

"We got to the line, and I was with my mother and Duvid and there was this Jewish prisoner, like a skeleton, already at the head of the line, and he turned to me, and he was so frantic, and he said, 'You are so young and beautiful. You have to give the child to your mother.' And I protested, of course, because he looked so crazy, but then he pulled my baby's fingers from mine, and pried him out of my hands and handed him to my mother! And then there was the doctor in front of us and he pointed for my mother to go left, and for Duvid and me to go right. My mother said she will take good care of him until we see each other again and then she was pushed away by the next people in line. He wasn't even crying; he loves my mother, but I need him with me, especially in a time like this. I am just so worried about him!"

"It is going to be OK, Chanky," I say. "Your mother knows how to take care of him. You will see him soon."

"I hope very soon. I miss my baby."

We walk on. I see a long row of brick buildings illuminated by white lights on top of tall poles. They go on and on, one big building after the next. There is mud between each building. A gate surrounds the area and barbed wire swirls in big loops along the top of the gate. The soldiers bring us to a building that says "21" on it. It is long and red and brick. There is a woman standing outside the door, waiting for us. She is tall and strong looking. She has long black hair, thick eyebrows, and a square chin.

"I got them from here," the woman says to the soldiers. They nod at her and then walk away from us.

It is silent for a moment. Smoke bellows in the sky, its tendrils reach down and settle under my nose. I almost vomit. There is a thick stench in the air, like burning rubber. As the girls around me start smelling it too, they panic.

"What is that smell? What is that smell?" they shout.

Some girls start to cry.

"Why are you crying?" the woman says. "Stop crying!"

We ignore her. There is a wave of panicked cries again. "The smell, the smell, the smell!"

"Quiet!" the big woman barks. She raises the stick in her hand and smacks it down on a girl's shoulder.

There is silence.

"I am Eidy, I am the *Blockälteste*,"[2] the woman says. "I am in charge of this block, and you must listen to my orders at all times."

"Eidy," someone says. The woman's eyes are half closed, and her arms are wrapped around her body and the thin, blue dress like a hug. "Can you tell us what that smell is?"

Eidy looks at us with hard eyes. "Don't you know girls?" she says. "That smell is the smell of your mothers and fathers burning. It is the smell of the bodies of your sons and daughters, your nieces and nephews, your brothers and sisters, in the ovens. Don't you know this smell? Your whole family is burning. Look at the smoke. That is their remains."

"That can't be!" a young girl says.

"Don't be stupid," Eidy says. "You have nothing left now. They are all burning. You are alone."

Something is wrong with this woman. My Mama is not burning. My Yecheskel is too strong to let that happen. I am going to see them soon.

Leah looks horrified. "Did you hear what she just said?"

"You can't possibly believe her. She is making it up."

Quiet!" Eidy snaps. "We are going inside, and you must find a place to sleep." She speaks as if she did not just lie to us in such a horrible, cruel way.

People move forward as Eidy reaches for the door.

Leah stands glued to her spot in line.

"Come Leah," I say.

She shakes her head. "But did you hear what she just said . . ."

"Leah, she is out of her mind. Don't listen to her. I don't know why she is feeding us lies like this."

"Quiet!" Eidy shouts. "When I open the doors, you must all go inside and find somewhere to sleep!"

I am so tired I can't wait to lay down and descend into nothingness. Eidy opens the doors, and we step inside. It looks like a barn of sorts, but instead of stables for the animals there are rows and rows of bunks all made of wooden planks. The floor is a crude layer of rough bricks. I am hit by the grayness of it all. There are three levels of the bunk beds per row, and it goes on and on and on. I can barely see anyone's face, but I can make out the shape of thousands of bodies stacked one on top of the other, like books on shelves. Their heads stick out of the beds. There are so many people, it makes me dizzy. Then, the smell hits me. It is the smell of excrement and vomit and bodies that haven't been washed in months. I cover my mouth.

"Find a place for yourselves," Eidy shouts.

I look at the few rows of bunks that do not have girls on them. I don't see how we will all fit. We scramble like chickens. I reach the first open space I find and pull myself up on the plank. It is hard and I feel splinters pierce through my palm. There are already a group of girls on the plank. Leah climbs on behind me but there is no room for her, so she climbs onto the bunk right on top of me. I look at the girls on the bunk. None of them look familiar. They also have shaved heads, but they are taller and broader than me.

"Go to sleep!" Eidy shouts from the front of the room. "You are going to need it!" She goes to the door and walks out without so much as a backward glance at us. I shake from shock. The girl next to me puts her hands on my arms and steadies me. She looks at the girls on our bunk.

"We take care of the little one," she says.

They nod.

"Of course," another girl says.

I look around at the group of at least a dozen girls on the bunk with me.

"We are all from Satu Mare," says the one with her hands around my arms. "Where are you from?"

"Crasna."

"OK, little Crasna. We are going to take good care of you."

I try to smile but my chin quivers instead. "How are we going to sleep like this?"

"We are 15, I just counted. Let's do seven on one side, seven on the other and the little one will be in the middle of us."

"Thank you," I say. I am tired and my head is so heavy I need to lie down now.

The girls split up and seven lie down on my right, their shoulders overlapping; they are tied together like one flesh. Seven on my left do the same.

"OK everyone, lift your feet up so the little one can get comfortable," the one who hugged me says. There is no room but somehow the girls manage to lift their knees to their chins. They are a pile of skin and limbs. There is a nice space right down the middle of them for me to lay.

As I lay down, something Mama always said pops into my head.

"You've got to be careful girls," she would say. "You never, ever really know who the real person is. People are good at pretending.

They are sweet and nice and then when they don't need you anymore, who knows what they can do. You never actually know a person all the way. People know how to dress their souls up, put some makeup on. They can act polite when everyone is looking but you can never be sure."

I remember feeling sad at the thought that the world could be like this. But here, I was sure. Dressed in nothing but the same little dresses of rags, our souls are as bald as our scalps, we have nothing to wrap ourselves in, nowhere to hide. No money, no status, no pride. There are 15 women on this bunk with me. They smile so gently at me as I lie down that, regardless of the trauma of the day, I smile back. My Mama said that you could never really know but as the girls move over and squish themselves tight and lift their skeletal knees and bend them to their chests: I know. These are the most beautiful naked souls I have ever seen.

I am so tired I fall asleep right away, even in the packed position and with my stomach rolling into itself. But soon into my slumber I am awakened by the sound of Leah crying. I sit up in a flash.

"You can't come in here and take our space," I hear a voice say and then the thud of a kick on her body. I get up right away, no one was going to treat my sister like that. I pull my body up and peer into the bunk on top of me.

"Aren't you ashamed of yourselves?" I say. "She is a young girl. How can you pick on her like this? She just came here and already you are bothering her? We have to take care of each other."

They look back at me, but they don't say anything.

"If you don't stop, I will go straight to the Blockälteste and tell on all of you and I am serious!"

I am burning with anger. I do not care that they are all older than me and I am one and they are many. I am ready for them to hurt me, to scratch me, bite me, because when I look in their eyes, there is no human left in them. I brace myself for anything, but I am surprised. They listen to me. They nod and look away.

"They were all scratching me at once," Leah whispers.

I bend my head even further into her bunk and I wipe the tears off her face.

"I'm sorry, Leah."

"Thank you for that, Rosie."

"I better get back down before my neck twists off."

I fall back to sleep as soon as my body touches the wooden planks. All my bunkmates' feet are still up close to their chests, even in their sleep.

12

CRASNA. 1935. AGE NINE.

"A psalm
A song
For the day of the Sabbath."

Psalm 92:1

Friday is the best day of the week for me. On Shabbas, we go to school along with everyone else. Our friends who are not Jewish carry our book bags for us because we are not allowed to carry them on Shabbos, but we must still go to school (but we are allowed to go home from school early).

When we get home, Mama is sitting at the table in the kitchen, rolling out layers of flaky dough. The sign that she needlepointed hangs over her head. It says, "Never mix meat and milk together." with a picture of a cow needlepointed on it. There is chocolate cream in the bowl next to her.

"Yum! Seven-layer cake!" Leah says with delight. "Can I have a spoon of chocolate?"

"Leah, stop bothering Mama, she is in middle of making it," I say. "You are just like you were when you were two, bothering Mama to eat the cake before she can even serve it."

"I did not do that!"

"Oh yes, I remember. You whined and whined and whined for it, and Tatty was in bed and so sick, but he felt so bad for Mama—you were whining to her all day. So, he got out of bed to try and distract you, and Mama had to stop her cooking and lead him back to bed."

"Mama did I do that?"

"You were two," Mama says. "Tatty could not stand to see me getting stressed by you, especially when your grandparents were coming which was stressful in itself." She smiles, then adds, "But Rosie why are you bothering her about something she did when she was two?"

I shrug. "It is just funny that she keeps on doing it and now she is eight."

"I don't even want the chocolate anymore."

"Oh Rosie," Mama sighs, "go beat out the rugs, please."

I roll up the rug from the living room and take it outside. It is a mix of gold and turquoise threads, plus yellow threads like bursts of sunshine throughout the pattern. Mama made it together with her best friend Kokish Emma, who has a matching rug in her house. I lay it over a chair outside and beat it with a wooden stick until all the dust in it releases into little clouds around me and then evaporates into thin air. I lay it in the sun and go back inside to sweep.

Mama has finished her cake and she is now standing by the stovetop, braiding her challah. Her hands fly as she picks up the strands of dough and places them, one over the other, to make a braid. She flits to the cupboard and gets an egg, cracking it into a bowl and whisking it round and round with a fork until it is frothy. She grabs the paintbrush and brushes the golden mixture onto the braided dough in quick, sure strokes. She is a busy bee, my Mama.

"Thank you, *Zeeskeit*,"[1] she says as I sweep the floor.

"Of course."

Leah cleans the pots after Mama is finished with them and I take them from Leah and fill them up with water, which I heat on the stove. The water bubbles with a sweet sound because Shabbos is coming. While the water heats, I get the rugs from outside and put them on the clean floor. Everything is fresh and perfect.

"I get the bath first," I say to Leah.

She shrugs. No use arguing with the oldest. I carefully take the pot of boiling water and bring it outside to the bathhouse. I pour the water into the tub and add a little of the delicious silky soap. I get into the bath and relax into its warmth. There is a window high up in the bathhouse. High enough that no one can see us but the birds. I looked out at a twisting tree against the blue sky. I sing out loud and the trees dance to my song, like a big group of happy folk dancers. I laugh to myself and continue singing until Leah pounds on the door.

"Get out, it's almost Shabbos and you are taking up all the time!"

"OK, calm down, I am coming out," I yell through the thick, wooden door. I sigh as I get out. I get dressed and I feel sparkling and wonderful.

Mama has placed the food on top of the *blech*[2] on the stove and rushes to light the candles. We watch as they glow and then the mood is set, and we sing "Good Shabbos" as Mama covers her face and prays. On the table is the starched, white tablecloth that I ironed myself the other day and our only set of nice dishes. At the head of the table is a place for Uncle Duvid. This week it is his turn to come and spend Shabbos with us, since we do not have a father to make *Kiddush*[3] for us when he comes home from shul.

"Mama, we are going outside to play until the men come home from shul, OK?"

"OK, but make sure you come back in time."

Leah and I run out the front door. Yecheskel is already out in the courtyard waiting for someone to take him to shul and sure enough Mr. Birnbaum, Shmuel's father, comes along and offers him his left hand, with Shmuel already holding his right, and the three walk up the steps into Waldman's shul together. Gitta and Lily are outside, too. We sit down in a circle, carefully dusting the benches before we sit so as not to ruin our beautiful Shabbos dresses. A light dusk begins to descend upon us, and the world is purple and blue.

"Let's go to Goldbaum's again," says Gitta.

"No, they don't like it," says Lily. "He got really mad at us last time."

"We will hide really well, don't worry. I just want to watch," says Gitta.

We all look at each other and giggle.

"OK fine," Lily says.

We run to the Goldbaum house and find a spot in the bushes where Mr. Goldbaum cannot see us. We giggle into our hands as Mr. Goldbaum finally walks up the path to the house. The shades on the main window are not pulled down all the way. From our vantage point, we see him open the door and call out, "Good Shabbos, my darling!" We see Mrs. Goldbaum get up from the couch and smile at him and in a moment, she is in his arms. He puts his arm around her waist, and they intertwine their hands and waltz around the table as they sing the song that welcomes the Shabbos angels into the house. I watch his eyes staring straight into hers. She doesn't blink or look away. They look as though they are melting into one another, until their souls are fused together. I sigh. He spins her around. Even though we have seen this before we all watch with our mouths open. When they are finished dancing, she brings the bottle of wine to the table and that shakes us out of our reverie.

"Leah, we need to go home, we cannot make them wait for us," I say.

"Oh right," Lily says. We slowly crawl out of the bushes and run toward home.

Leah and I walk home together and thankfully get to the door just as Uncle Duvid and Yecheskel are arriving. Mama does not like waiting for us. I pray every day that Duvid will not get married soon. When Uncle Tzadok got married two years ago he stopped showing any interest in us at all and of course stopped coming on Friday night. When that happened, I cried and cried for hours straight.

Duvid sings the song that welcomes the angels to our home and Mama smiles and brings the wine and challah to the table and tendrils of smoke rise from the loaves. My mouth starts to water, and my stomach rumbles. We wash our hands and Duvid slices open the challah, and we cannot even touch it with our hands for the first minute, it is so hot. We dip it into the roasted garlic and oil. Mama puts out the loaf of gefilte fish with *chrein*[4] and mayonnaise and then we have the deep golden chicken soup. While Mama serves the main course, Duvid sings a Shabbos song.

> *"Blessed is the most high almighty*
> *Who gave rest*
> *For our souls' relief*
> *– from calamity and woe;*
> *And He will seek out Zion*
> *The outcast city.*
> *How much longer will be the grief*
> *For a sighing soul?"*

We manage to have room for the chicken and potato kugel that comes next. For dessert, Mama brings a beautiful apple strudel to the table and cuts slices for all of us. The apples are sliced so thin and sprinkled with sugar, and the dough is soft and flaky. She scoops homemade ice cream onto each plate and the creamy white vanilla melts over the flaky baked desert. Somehow there is always room in our bellies for apple strudel. Mama brings some nuts to the table, and we stayed up way past our bedtime cracking the nuts with the nutcracker and talking about everything and nothing at all.

13

AUSCHWITZ. JUNE 1944.

"I have kept faith
Although I say,
I have suffered exceedingly."

Psalm 116:10

I wake up with wetness on my forehead. At first, I do not know where I am. It is musty and dark and as my eyes adjust to the light, I remember. The events of yesterday roll around in my brain and I push them away. I look at the slats of wood above me and then at the seven skinny girls to my left and seven skinny girls to my right. They are all scrunched up so tight. I reach up to my forehead to brush the wetness off and I gasp as I feel my raw, flat scalp. I suddenly feel naked. My bare head is not meant to be in the open air. A familiar feeling of panic clutches at my throat. Another splat at my forehead and I look up and see liquid dripping from the wood above me.

I breathe in to try and slow my panic, but the smell makes me gag and want to throw up. I force my stomach to be still. One of the girls on my right stirs and then opens her eyes and sees me eyeing the puddle next to me.

"It is OK, little Crasna," she says, "must be some waste from someone above us." In horror, I wipe my hand on a dry spot on the wood next to me.

But there is no time to dwell on the dripping because there is a loud whistle as the door opens to reveal a faint gray light and a large woman in uniform. Eidy, the woman with the mean lies, has arrived.

"Get up!" she yells, as she claps her huge hands together.

The rest of the girls quickly sit up and our cramped shelf becomes chaotic as everyone pushes their way down to the floor.

Leah slips down from the bunk above me. She almost steps on someone's leg that is sticking out from underneath the bottom bunk. I didn't realize that the floor beneath each bunk was also considered a bed. The room is thick with bodies. It is gray and tight and there must be at least a thousand girls around me.

There are a few buckets of brown liquid in the middle of the room, we all walk toward them.

"It is our breakfast. Well, not breakfast, but what they call coffee. It doesn't taste like anything but mud, but drink as much as you can," one of the girls from my bunk tells me.

The mud coffee is sent down each line in bowls that we take turns drinking out of. I wait in line until the girl next to me reaches out and gets the bowl of coffee. She takes a quick gulp and then passes it on to me. My tongue is stuck to the roof of my mouth and my fingers shake in anticipation. I put the bowl to my lips. I have almost forgotten what it feels like to have liquid pass through my pursed lips and fill up my mouth like a spring. My throat is expecting a thirst-quenching liquid, but the spring tastes like mud, just as the girl said. I swallow it all the same and feel it travel down into my body until it sits in my stomach and makes it a little fuller. I place the bowl into Leah's shaking, waiting hands.

A tall skinny girl stands next to Leah. She looks like a five-year-old all stretched out. She has blond fuzz growing from her skinny scalp and huge green eyes. Her lips are the only part of her that look like they harbor some fat in them. Her hands hang limp at her sides and when Leah passes the bowl to her, she can't seem to lift her hands to grasp it. I lean in and take the bowl from Leah and bring it to the girl's lips. She sucks the liquid into her mouth. A few drops slide down her cheeks, but I nudge them back into her mouth with my finger. She looks like an injured deer and, in an instant, I know I am going to take care of her.

"What is your name?"

"Bailu, Bailu Turnover."

"I am Rosie Greenstein, and this is my sister, Leah."

Leah smiles faintly at her.

"Turnover?" Chanky says. "I know you from Satu Mare."

"No talking! Get outside and line up!" Eidy yells.

We listen to her and walk quickly out through the doors. It is spring but the sun is not out yet, and the predawn air is cold. Leah shakes like a floppy leaf. Our uniform does not come with underwear, and it is so thin.

"Line up! Line up!" Eidy says. She looks scared. "Get in line you crazy pigs, get in line."

"Those women with the uniforms are SS women," Bailu, who is still by my side, whispers to me. "They are Nazis. Better stay clear of them."

"SS, Nazis," I say.

"OK, shh. We have to be completely still now."

We line up in rows of ten. The sky is dark with no sign of morning and the ground is muddy and wet. I stand next to Leah and Bailu and I want so badly to say something more to Bailu, but just as I reach my hand out to touch hers, an SS comes clicking toward us. Everyone stands pin straight. I try not to shiver at the harsh stare of the stone-faced SS, and I look straight ahead. The officer walks up and down our row of people while the SS women count us. Eidy comes around and counts us, too.

My stomach pines for food and my legs feel like jelly but I do not move an inch. The sun comes up and the heat sets in and now it is hard to breathe but I do not move. My feet ache and I am so weak, but I do not dare move. Sweat pours down from my shaven head into my eyes and I try to blink it away. My legs can hardly hold my body upright, but I focus with all my might and clench my muscles into my bones to keep from falling down.

A solider comes down our row. He marches importantly. He counts us by the tens.

"Six!" he says as he passes me.

"Seven," as he passes Leah.

"Eight," as he passes Chanky.

"Nine," as he passes Bailu.

"Ten," as he passes the next girl who is even shorter than me. He pulls her out of the line and another SS comes and leads her to a group of girls waiting on the side. I wonder where they are going.

Time stops and there is an agony in where it stopped. My stomach grumbles and then it is quiet like it has given up. Every cell in my body shakes. I look around without moving my head. There are lines of girls in the short blue uniform in front of me. There are lines of girls on my right and my left. They all have shaved heads. They all stand pin straight. I do not know why we are standing like this. What has become of us?

Finally, it is finished. The Germans blow their whistles, and everyone splits up. Eidy comes over to us.

"Where do they go?" I ask, pointing to the girls pulled aside to the corner with an SS woman watching them.

"To the gas chambers," she says. "To die. No one comes out of here alive. There is no point thinking otherwise. Don't have false hope, do you hear me?"

Before I can respond there is an SS next to me. She wears a navy double-breasted suit and a skirt that falls just below her knees. She grabs me sharply by the back of my neck.

"Why are you standing here like a lazy pig? There is work for you to do."

She lets go of my neck and gathers the girls near me around her. Her face looks like someone pulled her skin down and let it hang there permanently. Her under eyes droop and so do her cheeks. They wobble with her anger.

"Follow me!"

When we get to work, I realize that not much has changed from the brickyard. Instead of bricks here, there are huge boulders of cement. More male and female soldiers stand near them and shout orders. My body knows what to do now. I take cement and walk across the field with it.

Eidy comes to the field to get us as the sun starts to descend. I cannot think anymore. The work here is harder because I have had nothing to eat all day. My heart beats wildly.

"Come!" Eidy says.

The soldiers hit us with their rubber sticks to make us go into neat lines. We are five in a row, five after five, after five. We march toward the barracks.

When we get to the barrack, Eidy leaves the room and then comes back with a brown loaf of bread. There is a little slab of margarine on the side.

"Some of this bread is for the morning," she says. "Do not eat it all now."

My limbs tremble. She hands out tiny slices of bread to each girl. She puts the bread in my palm and with shaking hands I put a piece to my mouth. I try to save the rest for later but then I shove the whole piece into my mouth at once.

"I will show you where the bathrooms are now," she says. I didn't need to use the bathroom all day because I didn't eat or drink anything.

We follow her outside and walk with her. A few buildings over from our barrack there is a long, thin, brick building. There is a row of holes to squat over, one after the next. There is no privacy, just open air where doors were meant to be. We wait on the line to do our bodily duties. As we are leaving, I see an SS walk in with a group of women. She is laughing to herself.

"These ones were doctors!" she announces to Eidy.

The women stare blankly.

"Isn't that true?" she demands.

"Yes," one of the women answers.

They do not look like doctors. They look like skinny prisoners like me.

"Well, respectable, fancy doctors," the SS says between bursts of laughter, "now you can clean the toilets. Go on!" The doctors' faces turn white. The SS pushes one doctor with her stick, and she falls into the toilet.

"Clean the toilets, you doctors!"

The doctors walk to the toilets with their heads down.

"That is right! Take your fancy hands and pick up whatever is in the toilet and bring it outside, then come back and do it again until there is nothing left to remove!"

A few SS women walk into the building. "Come see the doctors and their new job," the first SS says. They look and laugh. The doctors peer into the toilet holes. Their faces are red. The SS fold their arms and watch the doctors stick their bare hands into the sludge, gather the running brown feces, and bring it outside. I gag.

The SS women giggle and laugh.

"Not so proud now, eh?" one calls out to a doctor who has feces running down her dress.

"Come!" Eidy says. "It is time to go back."

I turn away from the doctors and follow the girls back to our barrack.

When we reach our sleeping quarters, there is finally nothing to do. Eidy retreats and few of us gather to talk.

"There is a gate that connects us to the men's camp," Chanky tells us. "I want to go see if I can spot Duvid and Yehida. Maybe they will look for us there. Do you want to come with me?"

"Of course," I say. "Leah, Bailu, come."

We walk out of the barrack. The ground all around us is mud, not a patch of grass to be seen. The sun is beginning to set, and I cannot believe it has only been one sundown and one sunup since we arrived.

"Be careful," Chanky says as we approach the gate. "It is electric. Don't touch."

The gate is about 12 feet tall. There is barbed wire along the top with little sharp points jutting out across it like the thorns on a rose bush. I realize that this gate with its spikes and electricity has us trapped in here.

A girl walks by us.

"Watch the gates," I say. "They are electric." She ignores me. She has a desperate look on her face. She walks straight to the gate.

"Stop!"

She keeps on going, ignoring me. She reaches her arm out as she walks and grabs onto the thin electric line on the fence. She wraps her bony fingers around it, like she is clutching for her life. Her entire body convulses. She shakes rapidly and then she is still. She is dead in front of our eyes, still holding on to the gate.

Chanky lets out a surprised moan.

"Ohhhh," Leah whispers.

"Oh, my God," I say. I cannot believe what I have just seen.

We all stand there frozen for a few moments.

"Maybe that is the only way out . . ." Leah says.

"Don't you dare say that! We are going home from here!"

We turn and walk away from the dead girl.

14

CRASNA. 1935. AGE NINE.

"And it is like a groom
Emerging
From his bridal chamber
It rejoices
Like a powerful warrior
To run the course."

Psalm 19:5

It was June when Pinchas died and for a long time it ruined spring for me. He was six years old. I used to love the spring, when the weather was warm enough to play outside for hours, but not hot enough to make you cranky and tired. I always loved the smell of flowers blooming and grass that has just been cut. The spring air seemed so alive and full of possibilities. But then Pinchas died in June and the June that came after it brought fresh air that smelled just like the day he died, and I was scared the season would bring something bad again. And all the Junes after brought the same feeling of doom.

Mr. Raizomovich had made a special market booth to show off his fabric at the merchandise fair in the Town Square. He used wood planks in his booth and left them out in our courtyard when he was

88

finished with them. We were happy to have something new to play with. Pinchas was always such a good boy, but he could play quite fiercely and scuff his shoes, so Mama told him to take off his shoes before he played rough, so he did. I remember him carefully unlacing his shoes and putting them aside before running around on the wood. He giggled and laughed and jumped, his red hair bouncing up and down. Then he screamed. Mama came running outside.

"What happened?" she said. She held her arms out for him.

"I stepped on a nail!" he cried.

Mama held him tight as he buried his face in her chest and she rubbed his hair and shushed him while he cried. When the foot got flaky and pussy, she took him to the doctor, but it was too late. He got an infection, and he died a few weeks later. Mama said he was calling for our father when he died. It made me happy to think that at least they are together now. But ever since then, Mama stopped having a smile on her face.

Until one June, two years later, when something wonderful happens and her smile returns.

"Girls," Mama calls to us, motioning for us to join her at the table where she is making a *kokosh*[1] cake. "I have something to tell you."

"What is happening? Tell us!" Leah says. We scoot over to the table.

"I am only telling you because I have to tell someone, it is still a secret so don't you dare tell anyone until it is official!"

"Of course not!" I promise.

"What is the news?" Leah asks.

"Someone is getting engaged," Mama says.

"Not Duvid, right? He is so young," I say.

"No, not Duvid."

"Whew," I say in relief. (We needed Duvid in our life back then.)

"You?" I blurt out.

"No, not me," Mama says.

Zaidy has been trying to get Mama to get married again for ages. She always refuses. He finds the nicest men that want to marry her, but she won't even agree to meet them. It makes Zaidy very sad, but Mama says she will never love someone like she loved our father.

"No silly!" Leah says. "It must be Chana."

My jaw drops as Mama nods. I thought it would never happen. Maybe because Zaidy always says our *Tante*[2] should have been a boy because she is so smart. I have always thought in my head that she looks like a boy, too. I can't imagine Tante Chana married.

The next day we go to Zaidy's house and Chana stands next to a skinny man. He looks nice. She has a big smile on her face but thank goodness she does not act shy like my other aunts did when they met us after they got engaged. Chana is practically normal. Mama puts her kokosh cake on the table and gives Chana a big hug and kiss. My uncles all come in with their wives and soon the house is full of people.

"Now I am the only single one!" Uncle Duvid says.

"Don't rush, you're 17, sweetie," Mama teases.

"Who is rushing?" Duvid says. He blushes a little.

Zaidy comes out from the dining room and in his hand is a bottle and a bunch of little glasses. He pours everyone a glass and hands them out and says, "*L'chaim!*"[3] and clinks glasses with everyone. His face is beaming. Tante Chana is engaged!

From that day on, there is an excitement in the air. We have a wedding to prepare for! Mama has dresses made for us. They are so beautiful I want to wear mine as soon as they are ready, but of course we must wait for the wedding. The dresses are a deep navy blue with a big pleat in the front and a white collar with a navy stripe. Even though they are starched they are still so soft. Mama said they are what is called a sailor's outfit.

The morning of the wedding I get up before the sun. "Leah," I whisper, "today is the day."

She groans. "Go away, it is still dark."

"But today is the wedding."

She smiles, slowly remembering. "Still, go away until the morning," she says, and rolls over and goes back to sleep.

When Mama wakes up, we eat breakfast like it is any regular day. How can we pretend everything is normal when we have a wedding today? Is the farmer still milking his cow? Are the stalls in the market still being set up? How can today be the most exciting day in the world for me but not for anyone else?

"Can I get dressed now?" I ask, jumping up and down.

Yecheskel laughs.

"You are acting Yecheskel's age," Mama says. "You have to do your chores first, and you know that." But she is smiling a big, huge smile and it is a very wonderful thing to see her face like that.

Finally, finally, it is time to get dressed. I smooth my hand over the starched navy pleat. I cannot wait to see Chana's gown. The seamstress has been working on it for months, but it is a surprise, so today I will be seeing it for the very first time.

"Let's go," Mama says, wrapping Yecheskel's *peyos*[4] around her finger until it forms a perfect curl.

"Let's go!" Leah says.

"One minute, let me put the flowers in your hair," Mama says.

She takes a bundle of baby's breath from the vase and wipes them dry. She is wearing lipstick, I notice. I love when her lips look so pink and pretty like that. She snaps some of the fluffy ethereal flowers off their long stems and sticks them into Leah's hair and mine.

"Now off we go," she says, and she opens the door for us.

We walk to Zaidy's house together. We pass by our neighbors wearing their regular day clothing and doing their regular day things and it boggles my mind how this is possible; they're going about their regular life while we are on our way to a wedding!

When we step inside, we see that the house has been transformed. Chana sits on a chair in the living room. It is covered with white lace and gathered by the edges. Her gown is of white lace, too. It travels down her body and onto the floor, and gathers at her feet like a perfect, flowing stream. There are flowers floating on it like lily pads. She wears a white veil like a crown on top of her head. She beams at us when we walk in.

"*Mazel Tov!*[5] Chana," I say, and I am suddenly shy in her presence.

"Mazel Tov," she says as she gives me a big kiss on my cheek.

Then it is Leah's turn to give her a hug. She gets a little tangled in the big gown.

"Here's the *Kallah!*"[6] says Zaidy. His hands are outstretched, and he is smiling so wide. He bounces on his feet.

I have never seen him so happy as this.

"Oh, what Kallah charm!" he says as soon as he gets one look at her. He holds up his hands. "What a beautiful bride!"

"Oh Father," Chana laughs.

Gypsies come in, one with a violin, one with a harmonica, one with the banjo. They start playing, and people clap their hands along with it. Leah and I look at the table, heavy with so much food laid out on it. We look at Mama, and she laughs.

"Oh, go on girls, eat whatever you'd like." We don't need to be told twice. We run to the table. There are little mini cream cakes, big fluffy sponge cakes, and little pieces of herring with crackers underneath. They all look up at me. I choose a little orange cream cake and popped it in my mouth. The cookie collapses in a crinkle and the cream melts in my mouth. Orange and lemon sparkle all over my tongue!

The music gets faster. Leah and I twirl around and around. More and more people fill up my grandfather's little house. Just when you think there isn't room for one more, another person pops in and the house somehow expands. The ladies are all dressed up and go to be with Chana in the living room. The men stay with Mendel, the groom, in the dining room. The music gets even faster. Zaidy and Mendel's father each take Mendel by the hand. The men from the village walk behind them, clapping their hand as they move to the living room to greet Chana. I run next to Chana so I can watch. Mendel walks up to Chana who clutches Bubbe's hand. Chana looks like she will explode from happiness. Mendel whispers something in her ear, and it looks like it takes her by surprise because she throws up her head to the ceiling and laughs as he reaches behind her and pulls her veil over her face.

We walk outside to the *chuppah*[7] under the velvet sky and stars that surround us. Mendel walks down the aisle with Zaidy flanking him on one side and his father on the other while the gypsies play their music. Chana walks down with Bubbe on one side and Mendel's mother on the other and everyone stands up as she slowly makes her way down the aisle. Mama has tears in her eyes and her lips are whispering something. Chana stands next to Mendel; someone reads a whole bunch of words and then he steps on the glass.

"Mazel Tov!" everyone shouts, and they are married!

Later, it is just our family eating the meal inside. We all get a chance to dance with Chana, besides for Yecheskel who falls asleep across two chairs. After I dance with Chana, I take Leah's hand and we spin round and round. The music makes me giddy, and I wish we would lift off our feet and fly around the room. The room moves around me in quick succession as we spin: the gypsies dancing with their violins in the corner, the desserts laid out on the table, Chana dancing with Bubbe, Leah's face. They all flash in front of my eyes. Suddenly Leah tugs too hard and we fall to the floor in a heap of giggles.

After most of the guests have left, Zaidy dances with Chana and then takes Mendel's hands and placed them on Chana's shoulders. Mendel looks a little lost at first but then he slowly leads Chana around the room. They stare into each other's eyes and Mendel looks at Chana with such tenderness, like she is the only person in the world.

Mama laughs a little. "Life goes on. I wouldn't believe it, but it does."

And we stand quietly and watch Mendel dance with Chana all around the room as their new life begins.

15

AUSCHWITZ. JUNE 1944.

"As for the heavens
The heavens
Are for God
But the earth
He has given to mankind.
The dead can't praise God
Not any who descend into silence.
But we will bless God
From this time
Until eternity
Hallelujah."

Psalm 115:16,17,18

The next morning, I wake up to the sound of a shrill whistle. Women tumble out of their bunks and step over each other to get their coffee. I slip off my plank and look in the upper bunk for Leah. I watch her open her eyes and I see yesterday being remembered on her face. She pulls herself down and we join the line for coffee. We walk toward the middle of the room where Eidy stands with a bowl in her hand.

The barrack is dark brown, dungeon like. Skinny girls walk all around me.

"I cannot believe this is really happening," Chanky says as we wait for the big bowl of brown liquid to be passed around. I don't know how to answer her. We watch silently as the group of girls walk toward us to wait in line for the coffee. I spot Bailu walking slowly, as if she is in a dream.

"There's Bailu, Bailu come stand with us," I call out to her.

"I meant to tell you this yesterday, but I forgot," Chanky says. "I know Bailu's family from Satu Mare. They were the richest ones there. Bailu never had to work a day in her life. This is probably more horrifying for her than for us."

"Then we have to take care of her," I say.

"We will."

"Come Bailu," I motion to her like she is a kitten that needs to be coaxed.

Still in a trance, Bailu slides herself between us. When the bowl of coffee comes around, I put it to her lips.

"*Zeilappell!*[1] Roll call! Get out!" Eidy says. To be honest, she looks more scared than us. I think she may get beaten if she doesn't keep us under control.

Like yesterday, we stand outside for hours. The soldiers click around us on their heels and count us again.

"One, two, three, four, five, one, two, three, four, five." There is a humiliation in being counted like we are livestock. Some girls collapse to the ground, and they are dragged to the side. Later I see them stuffed into a truck.

After roll call ends an SS uses her stick to form us into different rows of five.

"Get in line! Get in line!" she says. In the back of my mind, I wonder if she ever gets a headache from all her screaming.

"Follow me! Faster!"

She leads us until we reach a clearing with huge boulders of rock in the middle. More SS women and men stand there watching. Other groups of prisoners that arrived before us are already working on the rocks.

"Listen up you pigs! Take these hammers and make small stones out of these big ones and put them in the pile over there. Your time starts now. Schnell! What is taking you so long?"

She grabs one girl and thrusts her forward toward the boulder. The girl stumbles and the SS woman slams her head against the rock.

"Schnell!"

We run forward to the boulders and pick up the small hammers that litter the ground. The sun is high in the sky now and it blinds me. Sweat pours down my bald head as I lift the hammer above a boulder and smash it down. It does not budge. An SS woman comes up behind me and slaps me on the back.

"Work harder, you weak little girl. We only want girls who can work."

She shifts the gun on her side. I take a deep breath, lift the hammer until it is behind my shoulder and crash it down onto the boulder. A thin, hair-like crack appears. I look to see if the SS woman is watching. She is already hitting someone else. I sigh and bring the hammer up until it is behind my shoulder again. I slam it against the crack and it splits a little more, but just barely. I do it again and a piece the size of my finger flies to the ground. I pick it up like it is a diamond and I fold my dress to fit it inside. The day feels like it is 130 degrees and there is not even the slightest hint of a breeze.

Hours later we are still beating the boulders down into pebbles. The SS women have left us, probably to get lunch. My stomach feels gutted. I look to see who is standing around me and realize we have formed a little circle of the girls from our town. Lily Leiberman and her sister Raizy stand next to me, and Gitty Shtein crouches next to her. Chani Raizomovitch picks up stones next to Leah, and Raizel Sternweitzel hacks at the boulder while sweat pours down her bald head and face. These are my childhood best friends. I stop my hacking and study their faces. They look so different without hair; it is hard to believe they are the same people. Raizy looks older without her black bushy hair that formed a cloud of tendrils and frizz around her face. Her dark almond eyes look bigger now, but her lips are still red and full. Gitty is not quite as tall as Raizy and she is more willow-like, but she still has several inches on me. Her hair was straw blonde but now it is nothing. She is still as beautiful as ever. Lily has her hands on her wide hips. Chani looks funny without her long brown braids which used to hide the ruddiness in her cheeks. Her cheekbones jut out wide and high as she bites her lip over and over again. They are all still tall, still broad, their shoulders wide and their hips strong. I am a good head shorter than them and the girl from my bunk was right, I am a *muselmann*[2] already.

Lily puts her hand on my shoulder. "Do not be so sad, Rosie," she says. "We are going to heaven from here."

Lily was always the most religious one of all of us. I look at her. The other girls look at her, too, and they nod.

"It is OK, you know, it really is," Lily continues. "I somehow feel like I am going home. I am not scared anymore. This was a journey, and it was wonderful, but now it is over." She really does look calm as she picks up the rocks around her feet. "The whole purpose of this world really is for the next world, you know. This world is the corridor, before the palace. We are supposed to prepare ourselves in the corridor, so we can enjoy the palace. It is what our sages taught us. The next world is for eternity; this world is so fleeting."

"I am happy to get to see what comes next. What kind of world it will be for us," Gitty says.

"We are probably going to be in the highest level of heaven," Chani says.

"Of course. we are," says Lily. "You know that anyone who dies just for the fact that they are Jewish, goes up high."

"It is going to be beautiful," says Gitty, "real peace and tranquility, and we will be next to God."

The sun is in my eyes and on my back. Sweat pours from my body. I want to open my mouth and let the sweat drip into my throat, it is so parched. I look up at the cloudless blue sky and then at the tall, strong friends from my hometown and at their ruddy cheeks.

"Heaven," Raizy sighs. "We are going to heaven from here."

The sky billows with black smoke.

"You can go to heaven from here if you want," I say, "but I am going home from here."

They look up at me. "Rosie, what are you saying?" Lily says.

"I'm saying you can go wherever you want, but I am going home from here. After that we will see where I go but I am going home from here."

They are all quiet for a minute. "You are dreaming," Gitty finally says. Lily pats my shoulder like I am a child. I shrug her off.

"I hear your theory, Lily, I really do, but I am going home from here. We'll see about heaven afterwards."

Lily shakes her head sadly. She looks up at the sky. The billowing has stopped and now there are floating black tendrils of smoke. "Be realistic Rosie, I don't think anyone goes home from here. It won't be a bad thing to die, you know that."

"I am going home!" I almost yell. And then I lower my voice. "Leah, we are going home from here."

They look at me as if I am crazy. But I know, I am going home from here.

After this I do not see my friends again.

16

CRASNA. 1937.

"How great are your deeds God
Exceedingly profound are your works.
A boor cannot know
And a fool
Cannot understand this."

Psalm 92:5–7

When I turn 11 and Leah is almost ten, Mama brings us to a seamstress to learn from her. We work for her for free, and in return she teaches us the basics of sewing and dress making. Leah turns out to be not only a genius in math and geometry but a genius in dressmaking as well. She sits down at the sewing machine and the seamstress gives her a big piece of gray fabric and tells her to make a dress. Leah sits as still as the pins on the pin cushion, then murmurs to herself, "22x16, 17x55, 33x4." She bends over the sewing machine and gets to work without another word. Within days she has made a beautiful dress. Leah has magic hands. She is the princess who spun gold from hay. Me, not so much. I look at the fabric and a hopelessness comes over me. How am I going to take this huge piece of material and turn it into a tailored dress? It would be easier to swim to America, or maybe learn to fly. I fumble with the gray fabric. I try to make the right calculations. I prick myself with the pins. When I am finally finished and I try on the dress, it won't go over my head because I have made the neck hole too tight. The seamstress assigns me the ironing. There is a huge iron in the corner of the room, and I must heat coals to make it hot so I can use it. The iron is bigger than me and I must drag the whole thing over to the clothing. When I am done, I am sweating but also glistening with pride because you have never seen more pin-straight dresses as the ones that have had the good fortune to pass under my iron.

Our apprenticeship with the seamstress ends, and we get our first job with the Kellers.

Benny Keller was once a student of my father. Now, Mama has a job as a cook in his house. His father is a doctor and his mother hosts grand parties. One day Mama comes home from working for the Kellers and sits Leah and me down to talk.

"I know you girls are so young, and I don't want you to have to work too hard, but this is an offer I do not think we can refuse."

"What is the offer?" Leah asks.

"Mrs. Keller complimented me on my dress when I came to cook in her kitchen today," Mama says, smiling at Leah, "so of course, I told her my daughter Leah made it for me."

"Ma," Leah groans.

"Nothing to be all modest about, you have a talent," Mama says firmly and Leah blushes.

"OK, so what did she say?" I ask.

"She was completely blown away that Leah could make such a dress as this at such a young age, so before I left, she said she was thinking about it, and she would love if Leah can come to her this whole summer every day and make all the gowns for her daughters and herself for the wedding!"

"Oh, my goodness! Like one of the famous seamstresses that come to town before a wedding?"

"Yes, can you believe it? She said she would pay you very well."

"Wow!" Leah says. "But what about Rosie?"

"I told her that Rosie can iron better than anyone I know, and she said she definitely needs that for the wedding and all the parties afterward. So, she invited Rosie too. This is going to be fun for you! She has a beautiful big house and oh my goodness, you should see that library, it is out of this world. Books from wall to wall, floor to ceiling."

The Kellers are excited to see us, and I am excited to be part of the exclusive team that will help to make the wedding grand.

"I knew you would be good," Mrs. Keller says as Leah copies the dress Mrs. Keller wants for herself on her sketchpad. "I am going to look like Anne Chevalier," she sighs. "You can start now, 7:30 is dinner, please join us.

"We can't go to dinner," I say after she leaves the room.

"Why not?"

"Because they don't keep kosher here."

Leah rolls her eyes. "We can't not go every day, that would be rude. Let's just sit there with the family and eat vegetables and fruits."

"That's a good idea."

All summer long we stay inside the sewing room and sew dress after dress. Each one of Mrs. Keller's four daughters needs a gown and then seven new dresses for the week of parties after the wedding. I help Leah with the easier stitches, and I iron everything to absolute perfection. One day, just before we are to leave for the night, Mrs. Keller shows us the library.

"It is like I am in a dream," Leah says when we walk in. Mrs. Keller laughs.

"My girls don't even like reading. Enjoy it."

I look around at the walls. They have built-in shelves of cherry wood and are filled from top to bottom with books. There are two ladders, a big arched window with a soft window seat, and three huge dark-red armchairs around a fireplace with a cozy fire burning in it. We immediately set about finding books! Leah takes *War and Peace* and I take *Anna Karenina*.

We walk home that night with books in our bags and *leu*[1] to give to Mama.

No one is as proud as me when I run to my mother with it. This is the best thing about working for the Kellers. When there is bread on our table it is because of me and Leah.

In my spare time I read the books from the library. I don't understand most of them, but I love the books and their stories. I love the way a whole life was sucked into the letters and when I read them, the story pushes itself from the letters on the page, up into the air, and into my head. Each character is a life that could almost have been and with that, truths, dreams, love, and hate. Zaidy tells me that the Talmud says a person must think the whole world was created for him. Even if he was to be the only one born, ever, God would have created this whole magnificent world just for him. When I read of the lives of other people, I understand this a little better. Each life is so full of revelations and beauty, it seems worth it to me to have the whole world for each and every individual person.

We take Tolstoy and Dostoyevsky. We get lost in the pages and when we are finished, we lend the books to Lily, Raizy, Gitty, and Chani. Leo Tolstoy is unanimously our favorite author. His books are thick enough to last us till the next job we have with the Kellers, and it certainly takes us long enough to get through them. I love the books but to be completely honest, I did not understand all the themes in the stories. I enjoyed the love, but I did not like the betrayals.

It is Lily Lieberman who suggests we start a literary group. We meet in her garden on every Shabbos afternoon. Lily puts out watermelon and sometimes there are even cookies.

We sit in her garden on the wooden bench that her father made, around the wooden table with the white tablecloth covered with the needlepoint dragonflies. Lily holds the book. She is the smartest of us and she leads the group. She is probably the only one of us who really understood what the book was trying to tell us, but we do our best to join in.

"So, *War and Peace*," Lily says. "Have you all read it?"

We nod our heads.

"OK, shall we discuss our thoughts on the themes? There were so many," Lily says.

"I liked the part where Pierre says that you have to believe in the possibility of happiness in order to be happy," Raizy says. "That spoke to me. 'Let the dead bury the dead but while I'm alive I must live and be happy.'"

"I loved that too," Lily says. "Sometimes I question the right to be happy, while so many are at war. But we must always try to be happy."

"It is so wonderful how they loved," I add, "so romantic!"

"Makes me want to get married and start a family," Raizy says.

"Me too," I say. We smile.

"Let us hope it is not as complicated for us as it was for them," Gitty notes. We laugh. I finger the tablecloth and imagine it as a silky white gown.

"Although sometimes there is no peace without some war," Lily says.

"I wish it did not have to be like that," Raizy replies. "Why cannot there only be love?"

"That would be nice."

"Why couldn't God create a world like that? He is God! He can do anything."

"There are probably many answers to that," Lily says. "But I do like what Tolstoy said. Where is it? I folded the page."

"You can't fold the page! It is the Kellers book. I told you!" Leah exclaims.

"Sorry, I will smooth it down."

"It is not the same."

"What is the quote?" Raizy asks, trying to divert the tension.

"Here it is, 'We can know that we know nothing. And that is the highest degree of human wisdom.' Tolstoy wrote that right here. I liked that a lot. As much as I try to understand, I know I know nothing. It's too big for me," says Lily.

"My father said we are like an ant on a leaf, contemplating why there are some bumps on the surface that we have to go over," Chani says.

"I like that," says Lily. "Did you know there are millions of stars in the sky, all bigger than the earth itself? We are smaller than an ant in comparison!"

I did not know that. But my mind is still on Natasha's love and in front of my eyes the tablecloth turns into a beautiful couture gown.

17

AUSCHWITZ. JUNE 1944.

"Is it for the dead
That you will work wonders?
Will the lifeless rise up
And offer you praise?
Will we recount your kindness in the grave?
Your faithfulness when we are destroyed?"

Psalm 88:10–11

I float in the sky. There is a pair of red shoes on the ground that I want to wear, but I am floating high in the air above them. I keep stretching my legs down to them, but as soon as my bare feet touch the ground, they immediately push off and I float back up again. At first, I enjoy the hopping and floating sensation, and I lift my hands and flap them like a bird as I fly up and down. Then I begin to get frustrated as the pair of shoes gets smaller and I fly further away. I will myself downward and point my big toe toward them. My toe brushes the shoes and I try to hook them onto my foot but too quickly I am up in the air again. I float higher and I see there is nothing but hard ground and the red shoes for miles. I push myself down but this time I do not even reach the shoes before I am pulled back up like a puppet. I thrust my nose forward and aim my body downward with my arms stretched out in front of me. I know if I can just reach the shoes, I will be able to stay on the ground with them. Inch by inch, I dive toward them, but my body does a swoop like a "U" and before I can get them, I am back up in the air.

Tears sting as they well up in my eyes.

"Don't cry," says a voice next to me. I look to the voice and realize I am not alone. The higher I get, the more people there are, and I forget about the shoes for a minute and look at the thousands of girls all flying upwards above me. One girl reaches down and offers me her hand.

"Don't cry," she says again. "Come with us. It is all going to be OK."

I look at the faces of the girls. They smile as they float upwards. They look happy and suddenly I am happy too, and a deep feeling of peace glows inside of me. Then I look down and the shoes are a tiny red blip on the endless, hard ground and my happiness turns to panic. The shoes! I must get back to the shoes! I turn from the girl and with one last frantic dive, I plummet my body down to the shoes again. There is something in my eyes as I zoom back down, and I look up at the girl once more. She is still smiling but there are tears flowing from her eyes. They are big tears, each one rushing like a river and they crash like waves onto my face. I ignore her as I will myself to swoop down just a little further, and I finally touch the shoes and grab hold of them.

I wake up and there is something dripping on my face again. Eidy the Blockälteste is blowing a whistle. The room is dark and thick with the horrible stench and the brick walls seem to be crumbling around me. The girls on my bunk still have their feet scrunched up to their faces. They sleep like this every night to make room for me. I am dizzy from hunger. I get up slowly and see Eidy pulling girls roughly from their bunks.

"Get out for Zeilappell!" she says. We rush from our beds. We make our way to the bowl of coffee. I walk with Leah and Bailu. We are pressed together by the many shaven, skinny girls walking next to us. There are so many women around me with shaved heads and dirty dresses and skin, they swirl and tumble in front of me. We are like a pile of ants on a crumb, all crawling over one another. The dungeon-like walls close in a little more and I feel like I am suffocating in the middle of it all.

"Leah, when I get out of here, I am moving to a mountain without one other person there besides me," I say. I imagine a mountain with a small little house on top and miles and miles of fresh air and empty space.

Leah does not answer. I take a gulp of coffee from the bowl and pass it on her. She drinks and then passes it to Bailu who passes it to Chanky.

"Schnell!! Schnell!" The SS women enter the barrack and push us outside. We stand in lines, straight like soldiers. The SS walk around us with cold, hard faces. We are their prisoners. They occasionally grab a girl from one of the lines and laugh as they shove her to the side.

"You know where this one is going," one calls out. Another one laughs and pushes the girl to the ground. I shut myself off. I don't feel the sweat under my armpits and down my spine. I don't feel my pining stomach or my aching feet. I stand straight as a statue, and I don't feel anything at all.

They finish counting us and next we are divided into groups.

An SS woman stands in front of us. She towers over me. My head only reaches her chest. Her legs are thick like elephants, but her waist is small. Her face is scarred like someone etched lines into clay and her eyes are small and blue.

"You will come work where I show you," she says to us. We follow her to a swamp-like field. My feet get more stuck with each step. There are other women there and they all have their bodies bent over huge blocks of mortar. They move the mortar to the other side of the field and then people on the other side move it back. An SS kicks a woman who is moving a little more slowly than the others and she falls to the ground and stays stuck in the swampy muck.

"Move these," the SS says to us. There is a massive pile of mortar in front of her. We all go to pick one up.

"Get them to the other side of the field," she clips, "and fast." She takes out her stick and slaps it down on a girl's back. She laughs as the girl stumbles forward and slams her face into the mortar she is carrying. She whips her again. "Get up and move it!" There is glee in her voice.

I pick up a mortar. It reaches from my knees to my chin. I start to walk. My breath lodges in my chest. Each time I step down, the swampy ground holds my foot fast like a suction cup, and I must twist and struggle to pull it up again. I finally reach the other side of the field and put the mortar down. I find Leah.

"Come with me," I say.

"Where?" She has a brick the size of half her body in her arms and sweat pours off her bald head. Her face is red.

"We will not survive if we do this. We are going to drop dead. We have no food or water in our bodies, and we cannot schlep the mortar in this heat. Just come with me, we are going to hide."

She looks around at the SS men watching us with their guns over their shoulders. "I am not going anywhere besides for where they tell us to go."

"Leah, you won't survive here."

She shifts the brick to her back and bends over. "I am not running away."

I walk her to the end of the field and then I check to my right and left. No one is looking at me. I run.

One of the girls in my bunk told me that every day there is a different barrack that does not have to go to work. There is a rotation system. I am going to find the barrack that is not working today. After a few minutes of running, I turn around. I expect to see someone chasing me, but I am alone. I slip into a barrack. It is empty. One down and dozens more to check. I quickly leave the empty barrack and weave in and out between the buildings until I find the one that is full. At last, I find a thousand girls laying on their planks. They do not look up at me. I go to the corner and lay there until I see the light from the cracks in the wall begin to fade.

When I get back to my barrack it is already dark outside. I am numb from exhaustion. Eidy is inside and she passes around a bowl. This time it looks like they are serving soup along with the bread.

The soup looks like mud. One of the girls from my bunk stands next to me. I do not know her name and I do not ask. She has kind, dark eyes.

"The soup causes the diarrhea," she says to me. "It is so tempting to eat, but I am telling you, it is not worth it in the end. You fill up now but end up hungrier later. They put dirt in it, that's why." I watch the bowl of dirt get passed around and girls who look like skeletons open their toothy mouths wide and inhale it in. They gulp loud before they pass it on.

"Thank you," I say to my friend, as I pass the soup on to the next person before I can be tempted to drink it. Eidy then passes around a hard piece of dark bread to each girl and a small piece of cheese. I look down at my cheese and bread. My hands shake with anticipation. I am about to put the bread in my mouth when I suddenly think of Mama. We are sitting at our breakfast table, and it is heavy with fresh bread and cheese and a tomato basil salad.

"Don't forget to eat your cheese," Mama says to me, Leah, and Yecheskel. "It will keep you full in school, way fuller than the bread will keep you. There is something special about cheese."

We laugh and stuff the cheese laced with spicy peppers down our throats. It works. Later, while everyone is eating the school lunch, I have only my little bowl of fruit. I am not so hungry because of the cheese.

I turn to the girl next to me. "Would you like to trade my bread for your cheese?"

"This moldy cheese you want?" she grabs my bread from my hand and puts her cheese in its place. "I'll trade with you any day."

"Thank you." I fold the cheese and peel off a tiny piece and place it on my tongue. It tastes delicious.

After we eat, I start walking to my bunk with the rest of the girls, but Eidy comes to me and puts her hands on my shoulders before I can get there.

"You," she says. "I need someone to clean the crumbs from my room. Come with me."

I look around. I wonder why she chose me over the other thousand girls around me, but I do not ask her any questions.

I follow her to her room which is just a corner sectioned off with a few blankets. She opens the flap of the blanket, and we go inside. Her corner has a little bed, a small wooden table, and a rug on the floor.

"I cut the bread for all of you here. It makes a damn mess. Clean it." I look down on the floor and I see there are big crumbs of bread scattered all over. I am pleased Eidy chose me from everyone to do the job for her. I bend down on my hands and knees to get the crumbs while she sits on her bed and watches me.

"You know, all the other Blockälteste have boyfriends here..."

I look up to acknowledge her, but I am too hungry to talk, and the crumbs shine like diamonds in the corners of my eyes.

"... but I do not. I am a Rabbi's daughter, did you know? I am too good for boyfriends."

"You are," I say, turning back to the crumbs. My mouth begins to water. My stomach is flat, my limbs are fast becoming only bones, without any flesh on them. I pine for those crumbs. I pinch them up with my weak, skinny fingers. They are going to waste, I don't think Eidy would mind. I want to open my mouth and lay my belly on the rug and lick them up like a dog. I open my mouth. I cannot do it. I will not eat crumbs from the floor like an animal. I will not! The crumbs look up at me. They glisten. As I pick them up with my weak, skinny fingers, I swallow the saliva in the back of my throat. I gather them up and put them in the garbage pail. I may be hungry but there are some things worth more than food, clothing, and shelter. I have my dignity.

Eidy watches me shake the crumbs into the garbage.

"You can go now."

I get to my bunk, and I can barely say good night to Leah because I am so exhausted, so I weakly smile at her. She tries to smile back at me but her mouth quivers instead.

"Good night, Rosie," she whispers.

I get into my bunk with the other girls. They lay down quickly and all lift their legs to their chests again.

"Don't worry, stretch your legs out, we will all take turns doing the same," my friend says.

"I used to always sleep this way anyways," says the girl whose curled-up toes are inches from my eye. "This is comfortable for me."

I know it isn't, but I smile gratefully anyways. The girl on my left strokes my head before she lays down and I suddenly feel a strong pang. I have always shared a bed with Leah and now even in this horrible, squished, wooden slat, I am happy to be sharing a bed with these kind women. And with that slightly comforting thought, I drift off to a hungry sleep.

18

CRASNA. 1937. AGE 11.

*"For not eternally
Shall be forgotten
The pauper
Nor shall the hope
Of the afflicted
Be doomed
Forever."*
Psalm 9:18

The day before St. Nicholas Day, Teacher Dumitru calls me over after class. I stand by her big wooden desk with my hands behind my back and wait to hear what she wants from me.

"The school community has put together holiday presents for some special families in town," she says. With a very broad smile she reaches behind her desk and pulls out a package wrapped in brown paper and hands it to me.

"Thank you," I say, as I take the parcel from her. I leave the cold school building and meet Leah out front. She has a package, too.

Mama opens the packages as soon as we get home. Blue velvet fabric spills out from within the brown paper wrapping.

"Look how beautiful this is," Mama says. She fingers the perfectly stitched corners and runs her hand over the soft fabric. The blue dulls and shimmers along with her hand strokes. It is anything but beautiful to me. I know exactly what it is, it is charity, and I want nothing to do with it. Sometimes poor people come to our town to collect money for themselves and when they do Mama always invites them in for a hot or cold drink and she always has some money to give them. One time Mama heard the neighbor say, "Don't go to that house, there is a widow there with no money," and Mama got so upset! She ran out of our house after the pauper and put money in his surprised hand. "No one will take away my opportunity to give," Mama said. But apparently, she did not mind taking either. Leah makes us dresses out of the fabric.

When she is done, they are beautiful but just looking at them makes me feel cranky. Mama hums as she hangs them up in our closet.

"You can both wear your new dresses tomorrow," she says.

"You did a great job with the dresses," I tell Leah after Mama leaves our room. "But I hate them. They are charity. I wish they would burn."

Leah shrugs her shoulders. "I think they are very pretty."

She just does not understand.

The next morning, I put on the dress and go into the kitchen.

"Look at this beautiful dress," Mama says when I walk in.

I feel like I am wearing a cloak of shame.

"I wish this dress would burn," I say to Leah, low enough so Mama cannot hear.

A few days later Mama sends me to get milk from Mr. Balan. I get back frozen to the bone and place my shivering body in front of the stove to try and warm up. Suddenly there is a weird sensation in my stomach.

"You're on fire! You're on fire!" Leah screams.

"Oh my! I'm on fire!" I barrel through the door and throw myself belly first onto the ground and the fire muffles out with a whimper. I roll over and Leah runs out to help me. She stops short. We look at each other in awe.

"I guess I better watch what I say," I mumble.

"You think?" Leah says with her mouth hanging open.

We look at each other with stunned faces for a minute and then we both start laughing. My dress has a huge hole in the middle. It is completely burned.

After that adventure, when we are almost finished with dinner and I am feeling very comfortable and honorable in a very old dress, there is a knock on the door.

"Zaidy!" I say.

He hugs us and then sit down at the table.

"I was thinking," he says after taking a giant gulp of the tea Mama made him. "Perhaps one of you wants to come and keep Bubbe and me company tonight?"

"I do! Mama, can I, please?" I turn to Mama and try not to jump up and down. She smiles.

"Please, please, please! Leah got to go last time!"

Leah does not argue with me. She does not love going to Zaidy and Bubbe's as much as I do. She probably wants the bed to herself, anyway.

"Oh, all right," Mama says, "But don't forget to do your homework."

"Of course, we won't forget," Zaidy says, and he winks at me because sometimes we do forget when we are too busy playing games.

"Yes!" I run to get my school bag.

Mama puts in an extra pair of underwear, my pajamas, and my stockings.

We leave the house, hand in hand, and step out into the cold air of the courtyard. We hear animals howling in the distance. The trees whisper good night and the stream laps slowly along. I love the night; it feels like a secret world I am finally getting to be a part of. On this night, the town seems empty, like we are the only ones out in the whole wide world.

"My Rosie," he smiles down at me.

"My Zaidy!" I swing our hands back and forth.

"You know I am so proud of you, right?"

"Really? Me?"

"Yes, you. You are meant for great things my baby."

I feel my heart swell up and almost pop.

"I don't do anything special."

"You are special for who you are." He puts his arm over my shoulder and pulls me close. "I am just so proud to be your Zaidy."

My heart swells up and spills up and over to my face where it plants a big smile.

"I love you, Zaidy."

"I love you too, Rosie."

We reach his house and we both skip up to the steps like we have always done. Bubbe is waiting for us in the kitchen.

"I see she agreed to come," she says. As if anyone would have to get me to agree!

"Can you believe how lucky we got?"

"How is Chaya Necha managing today?"

"She's good, thank God."

"Day by day," Bubbe says. She looks sad for a moment.

"Day by Day," Zaidy says.

Bubbe isn't my real grandmother because my real grandmother died before I was born, so this Bubbe is my grandmother instead of the old one. She is nice enough, but not nearly as fantastic as my Zaidy, and sometimes I look at her and shake my head and think, *How in the world is my Zaidy married to this lady?*

Zaidy sits down at the table and pulls some paper out of his pocket, places it on the table, and smooths it. I sit down next to him, help him place tobacco on the paper, and roll it up into a tight cigarette with the tips of my fingers.

"What a perfect roller," he says. "I wonder who taught you?"

"It was you! You taught me!"

"It was me? Wow, I must have been a good teacher then!"

We both laugh.

When it is time to go to sleep Bubbe says I can sleep in her bed with her. I wash my hands and face in the bath house out back, then I change into my nightgown. Zaidy is doing his learning in the dining room. I run to give him a kiss before I go to bed. He kisses my head and carries on with his learning. His voice is strong and sweet, and he sings along to his learning.

"*Amar Abaya . . .*"[1] he sings. The whole house glows warm from his singing. I wonder if there is a more beautiful sound in the world. I run into Bubbe's bed and snuggle down into the sheets and blankets. It is much softer and bigger than mine. Zaidy's voice goes high and then low and then stops sometimes to murmur something in a low voice and then goes high and low again. My eyes start to close but I want to stay up and hear him sing more. I feel myself drifting off, and then I am fast asleep.

I wake up and it is still dark outside. I hear Zaidy moving around and through the slits in my eyes I can tell he is dressed already. He comes to the bed and picks me up ever so gently and says, "Shhhh," as my eyes flutter a little. He places me softly in his bed so I can have the whole bed to myself, and he smooths the covers over me. He kisses me on my forehead. The kiss flies straight inside of me and lights me up with a gentle glow, like a steady fire. He tiptoes out of the room. "Amar Abaya . . ." the singing starts again, and I am warm and safe and in a cocoon of bliss as I drift off back to sleep.

When I next wake up, the sun is streaming in through the windows. I jump out of bed and quickly get dressed. Bubbe is in the kitchen making oatmeal. The sweet smell of cinnamon fills the whole house.

"Here is our girl!" says Zaidy, and he skips over to me.

When we are done eating, we go outside together. Zaidy walks me to my house, so I can walk to school with Leah.

"Good morning, Mr. Greenstein!" says a man as we walked past him. "I see you have a guest this morning."

"Oh, only the most special one," Zaidy says, and I beam. "Have yourself a very good day."

"Good morning, Mr. Greenstein!" says another woman as we walk past. She has a baby in her arms and squawking chickens at her feet.

"Good morning, Mrs. Hanganu!" Zaidy says, and he tips his hat. I feel like a princess walking with the king who everyone wants to run up to and greet as he strolls through his kingdom. When we reach our house Leah is waiting outside. She runs over to give Zaidy a hug.

"Homework is in here," I report to Mama, and I pat my bag as she joins us outside.

"Good," she says. "And now you better get going before you are late to school."

I blow Zaidy a kiss goodbye. He waves and off to school we go.

19

AUSCHWITZ. JULY 1944.

"What profit is there
In my blood
In my descent to the grave.
Will dusk thank you
Will it recite your truth?"

Psalm 30:9

I wake up to a crash of thunder and for a minute I am back at home in bed with Leah, and we are under the warm comforter. Then when my hands grasp for the covers to pull them up over my shoulders and onto my cheek, it all comes back to me in a sinking moment. I am in a barrack with a thousand other women. I don't have a warm comforter. I do not even have a blanket. My bed is a wooden plank with 14 other women. I have scratches all over my body from the wood surface and breakfast today will be muddy coffee again, instead of oatmeal. I close my eyes and wish for it to go away.

The door slams open and Eidy marches in with a flashlight in her hand. She shines it on all of us.

"Get up! Get up!" she shouts. "Everyone out! Zeilappell!"

I take Bailu's hand on the way to get our coffee. She looks worse and worse each day. She is only 17 years old, and she looks as lost as a child.

"Bailu, do you also work dragging the mortars back and forth? You must run away with me. You will not survive doing that."

"No," she says. "I work in the factory. We make weapons."

"So, you need to run away Bailu. Come with me. Every day there is a different Barrack that doesn't have to work. They stay in their bunks. Do what I do. Go to work each morning but slip out right away and run back to the bunk."

"I can't, I have a set station. They will know if I am not there. They will beat me like they beat my friend when she was a few minutes late." Bailu shakes at the memory of her friend.

"Stop talking! Get out!" Eidy yells from the middle of the room.

I look out the door. The rain is coming down hard and heavy and the sky is a deep black hue, covered with gray rolling clouds. I wear only the thin dress they gave me. It has a rip all the way up my right thigh. I have no underwear on.

We walk to the door and step outside and immediately I am hit by the impact of the rain. The ground gurgles and flows like a muddy river. I don't have any shoes. The SS men are outside, and they have strong black coats on with their collars up. Their boots reach their thighs, and they hold umbrellas in their leather-gloved hands. My dress is like a soaked-through paper cloth. We line up without a word, just like we did yesterday and the day before. The wind whips through us and I struggle to stay standing. The SS men walk around us and count.

"One, two, three, four," the SS says as he walks by me. Someone falls to the ground. He steps on her, so she is pushed further into the mud. I try not to shake from the cold. The rain slams down on our bald heads and floods my eyes but I look straight ahead, and I do not wipe my face. Snot drips down my nose as the rain turns to hail and angry shards of ice hit my numb cheeks, each with a pinch of their own. The SS seem to smile from under their umbrellas as they count each girl slowly and deliberately. They are dry and we are wet rags, but I do not care.

After they count all of us an SS stands in front of us and says,

"The numbers are not adding up correctly, we must count again." He is almost laughing as he says this.

I lift my eyes up slightly to the sky. It is dark gray, but I am almost certain the sun is up already because of the hours that pass while we stand here. The sun is here, and we cannot even see it. I look down and watch the gushing lake frantically rush past my bare feet, down the hill it goes with an urgency that could easily knock me over. Even the water wants to get out of here. I am numb from my head to the tips of my toes. I stand straight as a board and the Nazis circle us again.

Hours later it is finally over. Everyone is accounted for. The rain gives up and the sun peeks out from behind the weary, gray clouds. The sky is the face of a woman who has finally stopped crying, drained but calm. I don't think or feel as I march with everyone else to the fields to work, but when we get there, I remember where we are. I pull Leah's shoulder.

"Please come with me, we are going to hide."

"Don't you know what they will do to us if they catch us?"

"I know what will happen if I stay here and work."

"I cannot do it, Rosie."

"But we will never survive like this. We need to go home, and we cannot go home if we work this hard. We will drop dead!"

She shrugs and picks up a block of mortar.

"I am too scared," she says.

I turn away from her and run toward the barracks. I dart behind buildings. There was a rumor yesterday that Barrack 14 would not have to work today. I run past the buildings until I find 14 and I slip inside.

"Who are you?" someone says as I walk inside.

I look up and see a small girl calling to me from her plank.

"I am Rosie Greenstein."

"What are you doing here?"

"I am running away from work."

The girl climbs off her plank to stand next to me.

"Where are you from?"

"Crasna."

"Oh, I am from Zenta," the girl says. "Crasna, I have a friend who has a cousin in Crasna. What is your mother's name?"

"Chaya Necha Greenstein."

"I know! Maiden name is Heilbrun?"

"Yes! How did you know?"

"A girl was just talking about her relatives in Crasna. She is in this barrack. I will take you to her."

I cannot believe it.

We walk down the Barrack together. She takes me to a tall girl sitting on the floor.

"This is Rivka Heilbrun," the strange girl says. Then she leaves us.

"Who are you?" the girl named Rivka asks.

"I am Rosie, Rosie Greenstein, I think you are my cousin. My grandfather was a Heilbrun."

"Rosie? I heard about you. My father is Avraham Chaim. Who was your grandfather?"

"Yehida, do you know him?"

"Oh, of course! He was my father's brother. Come sit next to me."

I sit down on the floor next to her.

"I have a *chossen*[1] waiting for me at home. He is our cousin, too."

"Wow! That is exciting. What is his name?"

"Yitzchak. Would you like me to tell you about him?"

"I would love that!" She is suddenly quiet, so I prompt her. "What does he look like?"

"He is very handsome." She smiles. She is beautiful. "He has blond hair and blue eyes. We met a couple of months ago. I did not see him before they took us here, I wonder where he is."

"Probably here."

"I hope not."

"I hope not, too. But tell me more about him."

And she does so until it is time to go back to my barrack for supper.

"It was so good to meet you," she says to me, giving me a hug. Her body is sharp with bones and nothing else.

"You too, Cousin Rivka. I will see you again."

But I do not. Not ever after that.

20

CRASNA. 1937. AGE 11.

"The heavens declare
The glory of God
And His handiwork
Is proclaimed by the sky."

Psalm 19:1

There is a storm that rages all night long. I hear it a few times. It wakes me up in my sleep and I look out the window and see the trees thrashing and white snow slamming down to the ground. Then I get back into bed and snuggle under my covers, grateful that it is not the morning yet. I wake up to Yecheskel calling out to us.

"Rosie, Leah, Mama, come quick!"

We all rush into the main room. He stands by the window, his hands and face plastered to the frosted pane. We run to join him at the window, excited, already knowing what we will see. The whole courtyard is white and sparkling. The rooftops, and streets, and even the garbage bins have been painted silky white. The sun has not yet fully risen and there is a secret calm in the atmosphere. It looks like God took a blanket from heaven and draped it over us to tuck us in. The blanket is sparkling with a million little diamonds, and no one has gone out to ruin it yet. We all stand there for a moment together, looking out at the quiet yard.

"It is like the manna from heaven," says Yecheskel.

Mama smiles and tousles his hair. "Except this manna won't keep you full until lunch," she says, the first to snap out of the wintery daze we are all in. "Which brings me to this: Rosie, go watch Mr. Balan milk his cow and bring back some milk, and Leah, you can set the table."

I don't mind going out into the cold morning. There are snow prints to make!

By the weekend, the lake is frozen over completely, the weeping willows are draped over it like protective mamas, and it has finally been deemed safe enough to skate on. Leah and I take Yecheskel to the lake and we start skating right away. We do not have fancy skates like some of the kids around us, but the ice is so slippery that our regular shoes work just fine. Raizy Waldman even lets me borrow her skates for a little while. They are white leather with laces that go all the way up. She insists that she likes skating with her shoes, but I know she really just wants to share with me. We go round and round the lake, faster and faster, and the crisp air rejuvenates me with every turn. Only when the sun starts to set, and the wind gets a little violent, do we remember we have a mother and a home to go to. We trudge back to Mama's, through the snow, together. When we get inside, we take off our boots and soaking-wet socks and try to wiggle our purple toes back to life.

"Oy! Look at your freezing hands," Mama says to us. She takes Yecheskel's hands into hers and rubs her hands back and forth over them until he says his hands have warmed up. Then she does the same to Leah and then to me. My hands start to get their sensation back from her warm, older-looking hands.

"Can we put the fire on?" Yecheskel asks.

"Sorry *sheifala*,[1] it is too expensive today. We need to save the gas for when it is really cold."

Yecheskel's face falls.

"Come, I will warm your toes up, too," Mama says, and she rubs his feet in her hands.

After the weekend it is time to go to school again, even in the snow. I put on my big boots and wrap a scarf around my face. Leah lags behind as we make our way down the street. I want to eat the cool, crisp air.

"Wait up," Leah calls.

I turned to her, and she throws a snowball in my face.

"You! I am going to get you back!" I pick up a fistful of snow.

She shrieks and ducks, and I chase her all the way to school. Helen, a friend in my class, stands in front of the school gates.

"Isn't this the best?" she exclaims.

"You know what the best part about the snow is?" Reka asks, as she catches up with us.

"That I get to do this to you?" Helen says as she drops a handful of snow down Reka's back.

Leah giggles.

"Oh! Cold! Cold! Cold! Cold!" Reka shrieks as she laughs hysterically. She squirms like a snake to get the snow out from under the back of her coat. "And what is so funny?" she asks and picks up more snow and aims it at Leah's face. We all laugh at once.

"No seriously," Reka says. "The best part of snow is that it means St. Nicholas is coming."

"What's so great about St. Nicholas?" I ask.

"What is so great about St. Nicholas?" Maria joins in. "What is so great about St. Nicholas?" She shakes her head and rolls her eyes at the question. "For one, when St. Nicholas comes, he brings chocolate. That is pretty great."

"Lots and lots of chocolate," adds Helen.

"He puts it in our shoes," says Reka.

"When Chanukah comes, we get money," I say.

"Uh huh," confirms Leah. "Lots and lots of money." (That part isn't *entirely* true.)

"Well, we like chocolate," says Helen.

I like chocolate too.

That night after supper there is that familiar rat-tat-tat on the door and Zaidy walks in. There are snowflakes glistening like stardust on his beard.

"Zaidy!" I say. "You came in the snow!"

"I am not made of sugar," he says. "I don't melt."

He sits down at the table and takes out his paper and tobacco. "However, I might freeze if I do not warm myself right now."

I sit down and he nudges the paper to me with his gloved hands. I roll it perfectly, just like he taught me.

"Very good," he nods his head. "You must have had a very good cigarette-rolling teacher."

"You, Zaidy, it was you!"

"Was it really?" He laughs.

"Zaidy, St. Nicholas brings all the girls in my class chocolate," I blurt out.

"We don't care Rosie, remember?" Leah says.

"I am just saying, is it bad to say that he brings them chocolate?"

Zaidy looks at me. I hope he isn't upset that I said that. He loves Chanukah so much. I love it, too. I love watching him light the Menorah by the window and I love singing the songs together with him. I love playing dreidel with him even though he cheats every time and lets us win all the coins. I don't want to make him think that I don't enjoy the time with him. But still, chocolate . . .

"Hmm, chocolate?" Zaidy says.

Leah and I nod our heads.

"He puts it in their shoes," Leah says.

"Hmm," Zaidy says. He strokes his beard. "Maybe St Nicholas will drop by here once he is in the neighborhood, anyway. I would suggest leaving your shoes out."

A few days later when I slip my feet into my shoes there is something blocking my toes. I stick my hand into my shoe and pull out a silver-wrapped foil package. Leah puts on her shoes.

"Ah!" she says, shocked.

She bends down and pulls the same thing out. We look at each other and our faces break out into similar grins. We unwrap the foil and a light brown, creamy square of chocolate sits in our palms. A warm feeling slowly washes over me. I break off a piece of chocolate and put it into my mouth. Leah does the same and her eyes widen with glee a moment later. The chocolate is like a river of sweet creaminess but, unlike candy, it has a deep undertone that grounds it. It melts in my mouth.

The next day when Zaidy comes I give him an extra hug. "The first Jewish Nicholas," I whisper in his ear.

"I have no idea what you are talking about," he says, and he smiles. He kisses me on the forehead, and I can still taste the chocolate on my tongue.

21

AUSCHWITZ. AUGUST 1944.

"Even though I walk
In the valley overshadowed by death
I will not fear evil
For you are with me.
Your rod and your staff
They comfort me."

Psalm 23:4

Each day is hotter than the last. Every morning we stand barefoot on the cracked, muddy ground for hours, sweltering under the blistering hot sun. Sweat pours down my face, and my body feels scorched and dry. The stench in the barrack is unbearable. Sweat upon sweat on thousands of bodies. One night, I wake up and there is a wet stain of feces next to me from the bunk above. My whole body is caked with the grime that is on me and all around me. Suddenly I have had enough. I cannot stay dirty for one more second. I sit up and pull myself up until my head peers into the upper bunk. I find Leah squashed halfway under a tall girl. I reach my hand in between them and push my sister. She curls herself smaller.

"Leah, it is Rosie. Get up."

"What?" She tries to sit up and she knocks her head in the board on top of her.

"Come down with me."

"What is it?"

"We have to wash ourselves, or else we will get sick. There is disease everywhere, we need to get clean."

Leah doesn't smile. "Why are you worrying about cleaning yourself now? Why does it matter now?"

I look at her face, it is smeared with dirt and mud. "Because it does. The last thing we need now is to get sick."

"You can go shower. I am going back to sleep."

I take her hand. Three tiny black bugs crawl over her wrist. "Come with me!"

"Rosie, I am tired. Please let me sleep."

I have no choice, so I leave her. I slip out of the building.

The camp is eerily silent. There is a white beam of light that circles around and over the tops of the buildings. My heart beats fast as I take a step toward the big outhouse buildings. I hear my feet padding on the ground, and they seem to echo through the whole camp. I almost turn around, but then I think of the girls who have died from disease, and I step forward.

There is a single SS patrolling the grounds. My heart beats fast as he shines his flashlight back and forth. The white beam goes up and over the big, brick buildings. I am the only thing alive outside besides him. I am like a walking ghost. He is coming toward me. I hide around the corner of the barrack. He passes and I exhale. I wait a few more minutes until I see that he is far enough away, and I step out again. If he sees me, he will shoot. I walk slowly to the bathroom. Everything is perfectly still. I finally reach the bathroom and heave a sigh of relief.

There are rows of toilets all lined up, and each is oozing with body waste. On the other side there are six sinks in a row. I turn one of them on, nothing happens. I try the next one. The fifth one finally works. Cold water leaves the faucet in a trickle. There is a bowl of lye next to one of the toilets. I've had my eyes on that lye since we got here.

I take my filthy uniform dress off and put it in the sink. I get it as wet as I can and then I take a few flakes of the green lye and sprinkle it on top of my wet uniform. I get my hands wet and massage it in, then let my soapy dress soak. Next, I work on my body. I spread the lye over my skin, and it burns for a minute but then I splash water onto it with cupped hands and the stinging subsides. The water is cold, but it is a relief against my sweaty skin. I rub the lye in roughly and spread it around over my body. I watch the water turn brown at my feet and my skin turn to peach again. When I am finished with my body, I wash my little dress out and hang it from the faucet of the next sink to dry. I must keep myself awake and alert, so while it dries, I hum quietly to myself. Finally, the uniform is dry enough to put on. I get dressed. I sneak back through the camp. I duck behind buildings when I see the white beams heading toward me. I slip into bed and fall asleep before I close my eyes. I am still in the reeking barrack, and I am still lying next to a pile of feces, and I am still sharing a plank for a bed with more than a dozen other girls, but I am clean, and I feel better than I have in weeks.

I start going to the outhouse building every few days. I scrub myself as hard as I can. I don't always have the fortitude to wash my clothing and wait for it to dry, but I always wash my body until there is not one spot left on me. Each time, before I leave the building, I look in amazement at the streams of running feces that overflow from each toilet hole. In the dirtiest room in the world, I am scrubbed clean.

One day, Bailu comes back from work stinking of benzene.

"Bailu!" I say as she walks toward me. I can smell her from a mile away.

"What?"

"You stink of benzene!"

She shrugs her slight shoulders. "We work with benzene in the factory."

"But why do you smell of it so much now?"

She looks down at her feet. I follow her gaze. Her long knobby legs are wrapped in rags that are dripping with oil.

"They make me feel warmer."

The summer is coming to an end. We can tell by the slight chill in the air at night. She is so skinny she can't warm up.

"Give them to me I will clean them for you."

"I don't want to lose them."

"I will give them right back, just give them to me."

She stares at me. "No."

I sit her down on the floor and unwrap the rags from her legs. She tenses up but she doesn't fight back. When I was younger, I used to put on dance shows in our town. I would get all the younger girls dressed up in leftover scraps of fabric from the fabric store. I used to wrap their legs like Bailu's legs are wrapped but with soft, brightly colored swatches of fabric—not stiff, dirty rags dripping with flammable oil.

"Bailu, tonight I am going to wash these for you, and I will give them back to you good as new, do you hear me?"

"Give them back to me."

"I promise I will."

She looks longingly at her rags.

That night I slip out of the bunk as quietly as possible. I check the door and wait for the white beams of light to pass me. I walk through the deserted camp to the building with the toilets. There is no one for miles besides the lone guard with the flashlight and the beams of light that crisscross over my head.

I reach the bathroom safely and breathe a sigh of relief. I get to work on Bailu's rags, then I scrub my body. When I am done, Bailu's rags are starched clean. The next morning, I sit her down before roll call and wrap her legs up again. She admires the clean rags.

"There's no oil on them," she says with wonder.

"You see? I take care of you."

"I know," she says, and we walk outside together for roll call.

22

CRASNA. 1936. AGE 10.

"He who fashions
Together their hearts
Who comprehends
All their deed."

Psalm 33:15

The spring comes with the splintering of ice as it breaks up and melts in the river. Cool water drips down the sides of the mountains and runs into the stream, making it hum and gurgle and so deliciously cold. Spring comes with the circus marching through our town. It is all anyone can talk about at school.

"There were elephants and tigers the size of this whole courtyard!" Reka says. "The elephants lifted their huge feet high to the sky but the woman riding them did not fall off! And then there were these gymnasts, they are called trapeze artists, and they could fly!"

"Fly? How could they fly?" I ask.

"They stood high up on a little platform on a pole, like higher than that window on the second floor, holding the trapeze swing, and then they flew down hanging by their fingertips from the swing, and then they let go and summersaulted through the air and the person on the other trapeze caught them just in time!"

My stomach drops just to think of it!

"Tell her about the juggler!" Hannah says to Reka.

"Oh! The juggler stood in the middle ring, but he did not juggle balls, he juggled huge, sharp knives!"

I gasp!

"Then the knives caught on fire!" Hannah says. "In the middle of his juggling act they just burst into flames!"

"And then he ate them!" Reka exclaims.

"And you should have seen how the girls walked on a high wire all the way up in the sky. A string thinner than a strand of your hair. The whole crowd held their breath because if she fell, she would die, but she did a perfect walk across."

"I have to go see it," I say.

"Your favorite part will be the dancing for sure," says Reka. "It was so beautiful."

"I don't think Jewish girls can go to the circus," Hannah says.

"You are right, I did not see any Jewish girls from our school there," Reka says.

I know she is right, Jewish girls can't go to the circus. Yet there is a pull in my heart, and I can't think of anything else I want more than to see the circus perform. I think of the circus during class when I am supposed to be listening to arithmetic. I think of the circus as I am washing the dishes. I think of the circus as I get out of bed the next morning and then when I get back into bed that night. I need to go!

I do not bother asking Mama. I can just imagine the stern look she would give me. But I can't get the circus out of my head. I take a chance and go to visit Zaidy.

When I walk into the house he is sitting at the table.

"Rosie, to what do I owe this visit?"

I sit down in the chair next to him. "Zaidy, I need to talk to you about something," I swing my legs back and forth.

"Anything, my Rosie," he says.

"I know I am not supposed to want to do this, but I do. I really, really do."

"That is often the case," he says, and he smiles.

Before I lose my nerve, I quickly blurt it out, "The circus is in town, Zaidy, I really want to see it."

He looks at me and at first, I think he is upset with me, but I can't help my feelings. I am being pulled between the desire to be good like everyone else and the desire to see the dancing and the costumes. I look up at him and my heart pounds. He smiles slowly and I feel like he sees right into the tug of war that is going on in my heart. He puts his hands into his pockets and takes out a few bills.

"This should cover the entrance fee," he says and puts the money in my palm.

I did not realize it would cost money to get in!

"You are such a good girl, my Rosie, enjoy yourself, Mamale."

I wrap my arms around him and give him a huge bear hug. He hugs me back and pats my head and I revel in that moment of being completely and wholeheartedly understood.

I go to the circus by myself, and I watch the whole thing from beginning to end. I love the dance numbers, and I memorize them in my head so I can perform them when I get home. I love the girl walking on high wire and the flying trapeze artists. I do not like the poor animals parading around, although they do look funny, and the man who tames the lion makes me sad. When I get home, I dance the dances from the circus over and over again. I jump around the courtyard clicking my feet and spinning.

"Why did Zaidy let you go to the circus and not me?" Leah grumbles.

"You didn't ask." I twirl around her.

She sticks her tongue out at me.

I sing the songs louder and try to get her to dance with me.

"I am going to study," she says.

"Oh well," I say, and I dance away from her.

Suddenly, I have an idea to make Leah feel part of it.

"Leah," I say. "Let's put on a circus of our own. Just with the dancing part." She comes back to me.

"How can we do that?"

"I will show you, come with me."

I take her to Raizy Fishman's house. Her father has an egg business, and he always has wooden egg crates sitting next to his house. I knock on the door.

"Hello Rosie and Leah," Raizy's mother says.

"Hi Mrs. Fishman, Is Raizy here?"

"Raizy! Your friends are here," Mrs. Fishman calls.

Raizy comes running to the door. "Hi," she says. "Mamma, I am going outside, OK?" We walk to the courtyard.

"So, Raizy and Leah," I begin. "I have a plan. Do you want to be part of our very own circus?"

"Oh yes!" exclaim both girls at once.

"But you still have not told me how we are going to do it," Leah says.

"With egg crates! We will build a podium."

"That's a good idea," Raizy says.

"Can you ask your father?" I ask.

"I will, as soon as he gets home."

"And Leah, you can help make the costumes. We will teach a dance to all our friends. Then we will make a show for the town."

"Our very own circus!" Leah shouts, clapping her hands.

Raizy's father lets us take the egg crates, so we shlep them to my courtyard and pile them up to build a podium. Then we gather all the girls who are interested, and I teach them a dance, step by step. The night before we are to perform, we go around knocking on doors and inviting people to come. We set up benches and chairs for everyone. Leah makes beautiful little outfits from extra fabric that looks like colorful paper. The skirts are short and so I wrap the paper fabric around each girl's legs as matching tights. So many people show up. They sit in the audience, and we perform for them, and when we are finished, they stand up from the benches and clap and clap.

Our performance runs for a few weeks. Then we get bored of it, and it slowly peters out until we forget about it altogether. Summer comes and the circus moves to another town. I forget about the burning desire I had to see it. I forget about the elephants and the man who ate fire, and the dancing girls who kicked up their feet; but I never, ever forget how my Zaidy made me feel.

23

AUSCHWITZ. SEPTEMBER 1944.

"The lord will support him
On his sickbed
When you have transformed his
Entire restfulness
In his illness"

Psalm 41:3

The mornings and evenings grow colder. There are no trees around us or grass on the ground, and I do not know for sure, but I think the worst of the summer heat has passed us. Now, when we stand in Zeilappell, we shiver but try to stay still so we will not be taken away. Everyone around me is getting skinnier by the day. I do not recognize Leah anymore. Her once beautiful almond eyes now bulge out of her face. Every part of her body is pointy from her bones. Her cheekbones jut out, I can see the outlines of her pelvic bone and hips against her dress, as sharp as a scissor. Chanky also is a skeleton. She used to be beautiful. I remember being jealous of her when Duvid got engaged to her. She was never a skinny lady. Her hips were full, her face plump with life and possibilities. Now it is like she has been sucked dry. I must look the same to them. I try to fathom how this can be happening to us, but my brain is too hungry to think. I can only think of my mother and what I will say to her when I go home and see her again.

One day, Eidy tells us there will be another selection. "They are just checking if anyone is sick and sending them to the infirmary to get better."

"I wouldn't mind going to the infirmary," Bailu whispers to me, "there is probably less work."

"Who knows what goes on there," Chanky says.

"It cannot be worse than here," Leah says.

"Or it could be," I say.

"Outside to roll call!" Eidy says.

We walk outside and line up for roll call. Bailu stands next to me, and it looks as if she is disappearing into the wind.

"Follow me, you lazy pigs!" an SS woman yells. She has a wide face and small, blue eyes, and her blonde hair is in a tight ponytail at the nape of her neck. She walks as fast as she can in her straight wool skirt.

We walk for some time until we reach a field.

A few men in striped uniforms stand there. They are gaunt and bald like us.

"Line up! We said, line up!"

We all stumble into a line.

"Take off all your clothes now!"

The men stand and watch with their hands behind their backs.

"Get undressed, I said!" the SS woman says to the first girl in line. She fumbles to remove her dress, but before she can get it off the SS smacks her stick into the girl's temple, and she crumples to the ground.

"That is what happens when you do not follow instructions fast enough."

We all take off our clothing quickly and stand naked and waiting in the open air. We are a row of living skeletons, our hips protrude, our stomachs fold in like hollow trees, anyone could count our ribs.

"Now, there is nothing to be worried about. These men are doctors here, and they will conduct a checking of your skin. If you have any boils or skin marks that indicate sickness you will be pulled aside so we can take you to the infirmary to be treated." The SS woman gestures at the doctors. "Come now to check them."

The doctors walk around and examine us. They walk around each of us and run their fingers up our backs, and they pinch and prod and look up and down for boils. I know I do not have boils on me. I am healthy. Slowly a group of girls forms on the other side of the field. They put their clothing back on and sit or lay on the ground and wait. A doctor comes to me, and the SS woman stands back as if she thinks I am contaminated already. The doctor looks me up and down and he touches my cheeks and opens my mouth and looks at my tongue. Then he goes behind me and he runs his finger down my back and stops at a bruise there. I know it is not a boil, it is only a scratch from the wooden bunk last night.

"Is she sick?" the SS asks.

Please do not say I am sick, I think.

"Yes, she is sick," the doctor says.

The SS backs further away and she points for me to go to the other side.

I do not move.

"You heard him. Let's go!" Her chin wobbles as she points to where the other sick girls are waiting. Leah stands very still by my side.

"You heard me!"

I do not move.

Leah gives me a slight nudge.

"I am not sick," I say. "It is just a scratch."

"MOVE! GO!"

I stay planted to the ground where I am standing.

She hits the doctor with her stick. "Make her go!"

The doctor picks me up under my armpits and moves me to the other side.

I stand with the girls who have been deemed sick. I look at their yellow complexions and sunken red eyes. "I do not belong here," I say to them. "I am not sick."

They shrug. "Who cares if we are really sick or not, we will get more food in the infirmary," one girl says.

"Yes, maybe that is true, but I am not sick, so I do not belong here. I know what I am, and no one can tell me otherwise." And with that I run back to the other side. I stand next to Leah.

"Rosie! What are you doing?"

"I am not sick."

The SS woman comes back, and I try to avert my eyes, but she recognizes me.

"What is she doing here?" she screams. "You!" She points to the doctor. "Take her back!"

"I am not sick!" I say.

"The doctor says you are sick, so you are sick!" In an instant, she brings her stick down on my shoulder. I fall to the ground. Leah screams. The stick slams down on my stomach. I cannot breathe. "Get this girl to the other side!"

The doctor picks me up by my armpits again and drags me to the other side. I kick him the whole way. The minute he puts me down I turn and run back to Leah. I stand next to her for a minute until the SS sees me again. By now her whole body is shaking with fury. She slaps my cheek with her stick. I fall to the ground, and she brings the stick down on my back. I am in pain, but I do not care; I am not going to the other side. No one is going to tell me I am sick when I know I am healthy. I try to get up and she bashes her stick across my face again. My ears ache and buzz.

The doctor comes to drag me away again.

I run right back.

"Why are you doing this to me?" Leah says. She has tears in her eyes. "Just let them take you to the infirmary. They will give you some food and medicine and then you can come right back."

"I am not sick, Leah! And no one is going to tell me I am when I am not."

"Who cares? This is not worth it."

Before I can answer the SS woman spots me again and she pulls the doctor over to me in a fit of rage.

"Get her away from here!"

He drags me again, but I wriggle from his arms and run back to Leah. The group of sick girls watch me with their mouths open, but I do not care.

"Why are you being so stubborn?" Leah asks.

When the SS sees me, she starts to walk toward me and I brace for her beatings or for the doctors to drag me again, but then she rolls her eyes and walks away.

"Ha," I say under my breath.

"You are so stubborn," Leah says again.

"It is the red hair."

"What hair?"

"Very funny."

"Next time can you please just do what you are told?"

"Not if it is something that I know is not true."

Leah shakes her head, but we never see the sick girls again.

24

CRASNA. 1937. AGE 11.

"He sends the springs
Into the streams
Between mountains
They flow.
They water every beast of the field
They quench the wild creatures' thirst.
Near them
Birds of the heaven dwell
From among the branches
They give forth song."

Psalm 104:10–12

Zaidy comes over after supper one evening, and from the minute he walks in, he is coughing so much that he can barely talk.

"Tatty, this is not OK, did you go to the doctor?" Mama asks.

"You sound just like Bubbe," Zaidy says as he sits himself down at the table. "Yes, I went to the doctor months ago. He said it is just a cough." He coughs into his handkerchief again and soon he is hacking uncontrollably. The handkerchief turns red. Leah and I look at each other in wide-eyed panic. I feel nauseous. I know something is not right, but I do not want to think about it. "Come Yecheskel and Leah, we need to clean our room now."

"But we just cleaned it this morning," Yecheskel says.

"Now it is messy again," I say. "Come."

Leah and Yecheskel follow me to our room. We sit on the bed together in silence. We hear Mama's low voice from the dining room.

"It is okay to go see the doctor, you know. I will take you there tomorrow. We will go to a good one in Bucharest."

"No, do not take off work, Bubbe will go with me."

"But you will go?"

"Yes, I will go," Zaidy says. He sounds so exhausted; his voice does not go above a whisper.

When we come out of the room Mama and Zaidy both smile at us, but we know their smiles are not real.

"Who wants to come sleep by me tonight?" Zaidy asks.

No one says anything.

"Oh, don't look so serious, you three. You look like someone died! It is just a silly cough." He wheezes and I watch as his chest heaves, and I realized he is skinnier than I have ever seen him.

"Come on! Cheer up! Who wants to sleep by me tonight? Leah, I think it is your turn, right?"

"Can I go?" Leah says to Mama.

"Yes, sure, I will pack your bag."

The next day, Zaidy brings Leah home and kisses us all before we go to school. We hear him tell Mama that he is going to go to the doctor in an hour.

"He was coughing the whole night," Leah says.

"It is just a cough. Coughs are not a big deal."

"I could barely sleep."

I shrug, "Let's talk about something else."

Zaidy comes back from the doctor late that night and Mama says we should go to sleep while she goes over for a little while to hear the report. When she comes home, we all pretend to be sleeping, but we hear her crying in her bed, and Leah and I lie on our backs and hold hands and don't say a word. It is hours before any of us fall asleep.

At breakfast, Mama's eyes are red as she stirs the oatmeal and makes the salad. She gives us a tired smile. No one says anything for a little while, but then Yecheskel says, "Why is everyone so quiet today?"

Mama sits down and motions for Yecheskel to sit on her lap. She tousles with his peyos and sighs.

"The doctor says Zaidy is very sick." Her voice is even and strangely calm.

"So, did he give him medicine? Just give him medicine," Yecheskel says.

Mama shakes her head. "Yes, they will give him medication at home. But he is very, very sick, and you should know that."

My heart drops to my knees. Tears spring to my eyes without warning. In the back of my mind, I somehow knew this was happening but hearing Mama say it out loud makes it too real.

But he is my strong Zaidy, I think. *Nothing really bad can happen to him. He will get through this, and we will all be ok.*

We go to visit him after school. He sits in his chair in the study and swivels to look at us when we come in.

"Oh, why do you all have such worried faces?" he asks. "You look like you saw a ghost."

We smile sheepishly because we realize we are standing there with open mouths, and he does look a little like a ghost.

"How are you, Tatty?" Mama asks as she bends down to kiss him.

"I am fine. Or I will be as soon as my grandchildren come and give me a hug."

Leah, Yecheskel, and I rush to give him a hug.

"Oh, I am only a little bit sick. I won't crack in half if you hug me," he says, and he pulls us all in for a bear hug.

"Come sit down for supper," Bubbe says as she whisks through the study and shoos us all to the kitchen table.

We eat supper and try to act normal, which we almost succeed in doing, until Zaidy coughs up blood on his napkin and we become deathly quiet again.

Zaidy stops coming over to our house after supper, and instead we go to him. Within a few weeks he is too weak to get out of bed and he officially stops working at his job as a *shochet.*[1]

Every free minute I have between school and chores, I spend with Zaidy, even though it is terrifying to see him rapidly get sicker and sicker. My Zaidy has always been there for me, now I am going to be there for him.

One day, I go to the house and Bubbe points to her lips as soon as I walk in.

"He finally fell asleep," she says as if we are talking about a baby. "He needs his rest now so please be very quiet."

"Can I go sit with him? I won't make a sound." She nods and walks with me to his room.

Zaidy lies on the bed with a thin sheet covering his thin body. His breathing is labored, and it comes out in wheezes, as if he is trying with all his might to suck air in through a tiny straw. I stand completely silent and look at my grandfather lying in front of me. He is the father I didn't have, the sun of my world, he is the deepest love I have ever known. I put my hand on his large frail hand and after a few moments he gives me a tiny squeeze and I know he knows I am there. I stand by him and hold his hand until Mama sends Leah to call me home.

When I get home, I take the Romanian newspaper that came that morning and cut out every last joke from the humor section. My Zaidy is sick, but I am going to cheer him up.

I go straight to his house after school with the balled-up newspaper clippings bulging from the pockets of my cardigan. When I get to the house I go straight to his room. The shutters are closed, and the room is dark, and it smells like the inside of a shoe with a sharp zing of alcohol trying to cover it. My tall, beautiful Zaidy lies on the bed, and I watch his chest rise and fall, slow and deliberate.

"Hi Zaidy," I say, as I sit on the chair next to his bed.

He turns to me, and his face is twisted in pain, but he tries to smile.

"Zaidy, I have such good jokes for you," I say as I unwrap the balled-up jokes from my pocket. I smooth them out neatly on my skirt. "Now here's the first one: Why did the Romanian stop reading at night? To give his Bucharest!" Zaidy has a shadow of a smile on his face now. "Aha, so you liked that one, Zaidy—I have more!"

"So, tell me then." I flatten the next paper.

"A man walks into a bar with his pet bear and says, 'Do you serve Hungarians?' 'Yes, sit down, what would you like?' the bartender asks. 'A beer for me and two Hungarians for my bear.'"

Zaidy wheezes a laugh. "You know, my grandfather was shot by the Hungarian police, so I like that one."

"How about this one? A man walks outside in middle of the winter in Bucharest and calls up to the apartment building in front of him, 'Close the window, you are making me freeze!'"

I take out the next one and unfold it.

"Did you save all the jokes from the newspaper?"

"Only the ones I thought were funny."

"I am in for a nice evening then," Zaidy says, eying the paper balls like a mountain on my lap.

"Yes, you are," and I continue reading him all my jokes until they are done.

He falls asleep a little while after that, so I bend down to give him a kiss on his cheek. I kiss him softly so as not to wake him up and it feels so wrong treating him so delicately.

Each day, I buy as many newspapers as I can afford, and I cut out every funny joke. After school I run straight to his house and sit by his bed and read him all the jokes again and again. Even when he stops responding, I read him the jokes. I still think I can see a smile on his face. I know that laughter is the best medicine and if the doctors can't give him medicine that works, I will fix him with jokes, until I have my Zaidy back.

One day as Leah and I are leaving school, we see Mama waiting for us by the front gate.

"Zaidy?" I ask.

"They took him to the hospital," she says.

Leah starts crying right there in the street, but I don't move a muscle on my face. The hospital. But they are going to cure him there with big medications and he will snap back just like that. He has to.

Only two weeks later, I am at the funeral of my Zaidy. We sit together: Mama, Yecheskel, Leah, Bubbe, and I, and the whole bench shakes from our sobs as if it is crying along with us. All my aunts and uncles are there, and the shul is packed with everyone we know. Jews, non-Jews, people of all ages cram their way into the little shul. Everyone cries but I cry from the deepest part inside of me. It is as if I have been gutted open and every part of my soul heaves out in pain. Tears stream down my face, and I am a little bit embarrassed by the sobs and moans I make, but I cannot help it. The coffin lays in full view, and I cannot believe my Zaidy fits in it. I almost expect the wooden lid to open and his tall frame to saunter out and ask everyone why they are in shul in the middle of the day.

The Rabbi gets up to speak. He stands at the podium and starts to cry.

"We lost a great man today," he says, "a man that could not find a bad thing to say about anyone and who always had a reason as to why someone may have done things in a certain way. He was quite creative, I tell you." A few people laugh, but Mama sobs even harder. "He always had a kind word, a beaming smile, a listening ear—and when you walked away from Yehida, you walked away with a vibrancy in your step, a happiness in your heart, and a hope for the present and the future. We lost a giant of a man, and he will be sorely missed in this world."

Lost. It seems like a funny word to use. I lost my keys to the house, or my math book, but now also my Zaidy who was really a father to me. I search for him in the same way you search for something you need desperately, and you know just where it must be, but when you look in your pockets again, all you get is the lining and your hands fumble in the gaping, spiraling emptiness. I moan again and Mama rubs my back. I am grateful to have her there because I still feel surrounded with love even through all the pain.

After the funeral, and after Zaidy is buried, we all gather in Bubbe's house and Mama and Chana and all my uncles sit in low stools on the floor. No one talks for a few minutes. The kids run around outside. Yecheskel joins them and it is weird to hear them laughing and it is weird to see my grown-up uncles crying. I want to give Duvid a hug. He is only 18 and has lost both of his parents already. At least I have Mama.

"How could this have happened?" Chana asks. "He was so young."

"The doctors said his lungs were so shriveled and black, it was a miracle he made it so long," Bubbe says.

Duvid looks at her sadly. "This does not feel like a miracle," he says as he puts his head in his hands.

I am only 11, but I know it was a miracle. Every second that my Zaidy lived was a precious, beautiful miracle.

After the seven days of mourning, everyone goes home. We go back to our regular life, but it is like we are pretending. I feel flat and empty. It is weeks before I stop looking at the door after dinner, waiting for his tall frame to fill the doorway.

"Ahh, a taste of *Gan Eden*,"[2] he used to say as he tasted Mama's *cholent*,[3] but no one is in his place now as she spoons out the stew. I eat with a dullness in my chest and tears in my eyes. Sometimes I just go to my bed and cry with my face in the pillow.

Slowly, life goes on, and one night I open my bedroom window and the frogs and the birds are singing their beautiful songs, and the stream is dancing along to them. I realize that even though I am still sad I am also happy again. I can almost hear Zaidy singing along with the frogs. I think of all the people that are not here anymore; my father, my brother, my Zaidy—and I wonder why I am the one to be found right here, listening to the world sing its sweet song. Even though I have no answers—and sometimes the sadness in my heart feels like it will pull me down and bury me—I still feel a strange and beautiful peace in where I am right now, and I know that everything is going to be OK. I look at the water and the hills and the flowers and I feel I am one with them. My body overflows with love and sadness and joy, so on this night, as I open the window, I join the river and the frogs, and I sing.

25

AUSCHWITZ. OCTOBER 1944.

"I will not die
Yet I will live
And I will recount the works of God."

Psalm 118:17

We stand outside yet again in Zeilappell. The weather is colder. I cannot believe it was spring when the soldiers came into our town. It feels like a million years ago. We stand pin straight in the cold and try not to let the wind shake us.

After we are counted an SS woman stands in front of us. "Everyone! You are going to take a shower. Take off your clothes, leave them here."

Another SS walks around with her stick and starts slamming it down on girls' bald heads. "Get undressed!" She orders. Her hair is in blond bottle curls at her neck. She wears black shiny shoes and a double-breasted suit.

The skeletal girls around me pull their dresses over their heads.

With a sinking feeling, I also pull up the thin, hole-ridden fabric dress and take it off over my head. The cold air nips at my chest.

"Schnell, schnell!" The SS woman spits at us. She looks at us and laughs.

"Oscar!" another SS woman calls out. "These are taking a shower today!"

The SS men from the other side of the field turn around. Their eyes widen with excitement when they see girls pull their clothing off.

"Thank you for the tipoff, Irma," one of them says and they laugh.

They walk toward us as we undress. They smile to each other. Two of them slap each other's hands. I look down at the ground as my entire body tingles with mortification along with the cold air.

The SS woman steps in front of us. She is dressed in a blue, wool suit. She has pantyhose on. "Come on!" She says with laughter in her voice. "Get into lines you animals!"

If only we had the dignity of animals. At least animals have fur on their bodies.

"March!" she shouts. We march after her to the showers. Lines and lines of girls. The SS laughter rings in my ears. The air is like sharp ice around me.

We walk into the building with the showers. There are SS men standing next to shower heads that come down from the ceiling. They have rubber sticks in their hands.

The SS woman who brought us here pushes us closer together in line. The first girl in the line looks at the water.

"Jetzt![1] Schnell," the SS man says. She inches in and then, it is as if she is hit with either fire or ice, and she jumps back. The SS takes his stick and shoves it into her mouth. He holds her like that under the water. She screams and blood falls from her mouth and turns pink from the water. He holds her like that for a long time. She looks like the stick will choke her. Then he pushes her aside and she stumbles away.

The SS motions for the next girl to go under the stream of water. She hesitates. The soldier's face becomes alive with fury.

"Hurry up!" he yells. "I do not have all day!" He slams his stick into her stomach and pushes her under the water. She shrieks from it, but he holds her there.

148

The next girl also hesitates, and the same thing happens to her.

Rosie, I tell myself. *Listen very carefully. The water is probably ice cold. You have two choices. Either go in right away and do not get hit with the stick or be scared and wait and then be pushed in anyways and on top of that get hit with the stick.*

The line inches up and my turn comes. Without a split second of hesitation, I step under the water. It hits me like shards of ice and fire together. It is so cold, it burns. My entire body feels under attack. I cannot breathe. But then it is over. The SS nudges me out with his stick, and I am free. I shake violently.

The little Jewish workers called *Häftlings*[2] are giving out new uniforms at the other end of the room. I am excited to get something other than my little blue dress with the rip up the side. A Häftling hands out packages to everyone. I go to her to receive my package. It is a perfect brown paper cube. Inside there is a pair of rough wooden clogs and a blue dress which is folded perfectly. I open the dress and take a look. It is covered with small black dots. The dots are moving. It is infested with lice.

I look around. Everyone is getting dressed. I have no choice. I put on the infested dress. My newly clean skin is now covered with tiny crawling bugs.

The lice are everywhere. The barrack doesn't smell nearly as bad as it did in the searing heat but now it is crawling with lice. It looks like the room is moving on its own. Sleep, our only precious escape is now broken every few minutes from the incessant inching of the lice. The shoes turn out to be nothing but another source of pain. They make walking even more difficult because everything sticks to the wood and we end up shlepping all kinds of debris around on our feet.

A few days after the showers, the SS men line us up in fives after roll call. There are two girls to the right of me and two girls to the left. We are rows and rows like this. Five, five, five, behind five. We walk for a while with no idea where we are going. We reach a line of even more girls lined up, waiting. The SS shoves us into line with them and we do not know what we are doing there. Finally, we inch up and I see what is going on. Up ahead, sitting at tables, are a few groups of the same skinny prisoner girls who shaved our heads. When a girl from our lines gets up to the table, one of the working prisoners grabs her arm and pokes at it with a wooden stick with a flash of metal at the tip. They seem to be writing something on each girl's arm, but I can't see what they are writing with. When I get closer, I gasp. They are holding needles in their hands. I rub my arm. They dip instruments that look like needles straight into a hot flame, burn the numbers into the skin, and then rub a green rag over it. I watch each girl flinch a little as the marks are burned into their flesh. I hold Leah's hand.

"Why are they doing this?" she asks. "What are they writing?"

I squint to try and see. "I think they are writing numbers on each girl's arm," I say.

As we get closer, I examine the prisoners writing the numbers. The one at the head of our line grabs a girl's wrist and pushes up her sleeve. She moves her hand up and down, barely moving her wrist. I look at the girl's arm. She has big, uneven numbers lining her forearm.

I look over at the prisoner girl at the next table. She seems calmer. She does not look at the girl in line in the eye, but she gently pushes her sleeve up and slowly writes small and even numbers. Her arm looks much prettier than the other one. I am not having those big numbers on my arm. Without thinking, I run to the line next to me. An officer shouts but no one shoots.

It is my turn to get tattooed. I reach my hand out to the prisoner. She takes my arm without looking at my face and carefully jabs numbers into my arm. Tears spring to my eyes but I do not cry out. Then she dips her rag into green ink and rubs it over the holes in my arm. I look down at my arm. A-13488. They are small and perfect.

Leah steps off the line after she gets tattooed and stands next to me.

I see her numbers are like big scrawls on her arm.

"Why did you run out of line, Rosie?"

"I wanted neat numbers," I show her my arm.

"Neat? Neater numbers? Is that what you are thinking of now? Who cares? You could have been killed for that!" Her voice is thick with anger and fear. "Was that worth it? Are you crazy, Rosie? Was that worth it??"

I look down at my arm and then look at the people around me. They walk dazed, as if they are already dead. No, I'm not crazy. I know now, I know deeper than the sinking souls of the ghosts around me, I know.

"Yes, it was worth it, Leah," I say. "It was worth it because we are going home! We are going home from here! We are going home from here. It was worth it because we still care. Do you hear me? We still care, Leah!"

Eidy leads us back to the barracks. I itch from my new lice-infested uniform. The lice seem to jump off from the dress and embed themselves in my skin that is stretched thinly over my bones. Before I go to sleep, I lift my arm up to my eyes. The skin around the numbers is red but I see the small black numbers clearly, A-13488. They are pretty and neat. "You are going home from here," they seem to say.

When we stand in Zeilappell the next morning, they call us by our numbers. It takes even longer now because they draw out saying each number. When they get to me, I sneak a glance at my number. A-13488. It is printed perfectly on my arm, and it gives me comfort to see it. Soon I know my number in my sleep. Sometimes we are asked to recite our numbers and the girls who do not say theirs fast enough are beaten. The SS actually laugh while they do this. I memorize my number and if they shake me from sleep and demand it, I will be able to say it. I will spit it out faster than they can ask me for it: A-13488.

26

CRASNA. 1940. AGE 14.

"My father and my mother
Abandoned me
But God brought me in"

Psalm 27:10

Things seem to go downhill after Zaidy dies. We did not realize how much he helped us with money, and when he is gone, things just get tighter. From the big things (like the money he gave us every week), to the small things (like the flour he put in our cabinet when we ran out). It all adds up, and we find ourselves hungry more often than full, but we are OK. We have each other. We have everything that we need.

Things are also changing around us, but it is happening very slowly, and we are too close to it to notice. It is like when you don't realize how tall your brother is getting because you see him every day. But then Yecheskel is taller and there is something different about our town. Something in the air.

Then Hungary takes over. After a nice number of years under Romanian rule, we are taken over by Hungary again. But Mama says this has happened before and we will be fine just like in the past. We go together with everyone else to welcome the Hungarians in. The first thing they do is they shut down the yeshiva. For everyone else, it is upsetting to lose a school so close by for their sons, but for us, we are losing the food on our table. Mama was the full time cook at the yeshiva and now that it is closed, she is out of a job.

A few days after Mama loses her job, we come home to find her sitting at the table with a letter in her hand.

"Who is it from?" Leah asks.

"It is from Aunt Chana," Mama says.

"Oh, how is she doing? We haven't seen her in so long! Since she moved to the city with her husband, she has only visited a few times."

"Last time was when Zaidy died," I say.

"I know, well, it is hard for her to travel with three little kids," Mama says. "But that's why she is writing actually. She could use help with the little ones."

"Can we go visit?" asks Leah. "I love babies!"

"Well, Chana says she can really use an extra set of hands now that Yaakov is so busy with the business." Mama looks at me. "Rosie, she wants to know if you want to go live with her for a little bit so you can help out."

"I would love to, but for how long? Do you think I am not going to miss you?"

"Of course you will, but you would be fine. You would go for a few months, and we would take it from there. Hopefully by then I would find another job and get back on my feet."

"Can I go too?" Leah asks.

"Yeah, can Leah come?" I chime in.

"Chana doesn't need two extra people to feed, just one. And Uncle Lipa wrote to me last week to say that he would love to have Leah for a little while."

"Why can't I go with Rosie to Chana?" Leah asks.

"Or why can't I go with Leah to Lipa?" I ask.

"Because neither of them needs both of you," Mama says.

I want to cry. I do not want to leave Mama and my home. But I hold back my tears. Mama already looks so devastated from telling us we must leave; I do not want to make it harder for her.

"Chana could really use your help, Rosie, and maybe you can do some sewing for her, too. I am sure you will love being around your favorite aunt for a bit. And Leah, you will love it at your cousin's, and it would be boring here with just me and Yecheskel, no?"

No, I want to say.

"It will be fun," Leah says. "I am excited."

"Yes, me too, I love Chana," I say. "And we will be back before we know it."

I arrive at Aunt Chana's house by horse and buggy. When I get off at my station the first thing that hits me is the noise. There are cars! They rumble past me, beeping and swerving at the corners while people cross the street quickly to avoid them. Mothers motion for their children to hurry and people barely glance at each other. I watch them open-mouthed.

"Rosie!" says a little voice.

"Wosie!" says another little one.

"Welcome, Rosie!" Chana says as she pulls the kids back from jumping on me. "Rechel Chava, give your cousin Rosie a hug. Yehudis, you too." Rechel Chava smiles shyly. Yehudis wobbles over to me first and gives me a hug.

"Aww, you are so sweet," I say, and I pat her little curls.

"Rechel Chava, go give your cousin a hug, too. Remember I told you she was coming?" Rechel Chava ignores her mother and just stares at me. "She is never shy, enjoy it while it lasts," Chana says. She reaches over the kids and gives me a one-handed hug and a big kiss on the cheeks. "It is so good to see you, darling, you must be starving and exhausted. Come to the car. Mendel is there with Devorah, she fell asleep, and I didn't want to wake her. She is so cute I can't wait for you to see her!"

Uncle Mendel is in the front seat. He smiles at me when he sees me. "Hi Rosie! We are so happy you are here." He gets out of the car to put my little suitcase in the back.

Chana opens the side door and Rechel Chava jumps into the car by herself, then Chana picks up Yehudis and puts her in. The baby sits in a special seat.

"Say hello to baby Devorah," Chana says.

"Oh, my goodness, Chana, she is beautiful!"

"A little fatso, no?"

"Her cheeks are bigger than her whole body!"

I get in the car next to the sleeping baby. Mendel sits in the driver's seat and starts the car. I look out of the window as everything moves passed me. There are big stores all in a row, each with something different in their front window. Monstrous pieces of meat hanging in one, a dress on a mannequin in another, hats of all different colors in the next, and then we are going too fast for me to make out any more of them. I am mesmerized by how fast and smoothly we are moving.

We pass by a few streets of houses, each one with a little square of grass in front, surrounded by lots and lots of cobblestone streets. Then we turn the corner and there are big buildings lined up next to each other. The car slows down in front of a gray, brick building.

Devorah wails suddenly from her car seat.

"Shhhh, shhh, my love," Chana says.

Devorah cries even louder.

"Do you mind shaking her seat a little to rock her?" Chana asks. "Oh, look Mendel, a spot over there!" I feel dizzy as Mendel quickly swerves and backs up next to the sidewalk. I try to rock Devorah, but she screams even louder. Chana jumps out of the car, opens the door, and takes Devorah from the car seat.

"Here, take the baby. I will get the girls," she says.

I take the baby and hope I will not drop her while Mendel takes my suitcase from the back of the car.

"It's a lot to take in," he says.

"Yes, I will get used to it."

"You will, the kids will love you. Thank you so much for coming to help us here."

"Of course! I love Tante Chana."

He smiles and looks at Chana shepherding the kids across the street. "She is something else," he says.

When we get inside, Chana serves supper and I eat more that night than I have eaten in a week. I am so tired from the trip that when Chana shows me to my room, I fall right to sleep without a single thought in my brain.

When I open my eyes the next morning, I hear loud beeps instead of birds, and I remember where I am. I am so tired; the night was punctuated with Devorah's wails and Mendel and Chana puttering around the house shushing her. No wonder Chana is so tired all the time.

Chana is already pouring something from a box into bowls when I come down to the kitchen. Rechel Chava and Yehudis sit by the table. Yehudis throws pieces of the brown mush down from her seat.

"Oh no, Yehudis!" Chana says. She bends down to pick it up and kisses Yehudis's little toes on the way. Yehudis giggles.

"I think you are done here," Chana says, and she lifts Yehudis up in her arms and hugs her. Devorah cries from her bassinet in the corner and Chana runs over to rock her.

"Shush my little baby, Mama loves you," she says.

"Can you hold her for a few minutes? I need to get Rechel Chava dressed," she says to me.

"Sure," I say, and I pick Devorah up and hold her awkwardly in my hands.

A few minutes later Chana comes back with Rechel Chava all dressed, and her hair pulled back, and she puts down a bowl in front of me.

"Sit here, give me the baby."

I sit down gingerly and try not to get the milk that has spilled on the chair onto my skirt. I only brought two skirts with me, and I don't want to have to wash one already on the first day. While the kids play for a bit, I have a chance to properly look around. Chana has her own oven right in her kitchen and two sinks, not a wooden basin like we have.

"It's a little different than Crasna here, no?"

I laugh. "Very different."

"You will get used to it fast like I did. Anyways, I was wondering if you can take the children to the park when they get bored of playing, which will be in about three minutes? There is one a few blocks down; they will show you where to go and if you would want to take them on a walk now, that would be amazing. Heaven knows I could use a nap."

"Of course, I can."

"You are such a doll, my little niece." She puts Devorah in her stroller and as soon as she is in it, she immediately opens her tiny mouth and lets out a shriek so loud I cannot believe it came out of her little lungs.

"Don't worry, she will stop when you start wheeling her. Don't cry, Devorah. You are going bye-bye! Rechel Chava, Yehudis, want to go to the park?"

"Yes!" They cry in unison as they both jump up from their puzzle.

"Come here, let me put on your jackets."

"I want to do it myself," Rechel Chava says.

"OK, but you need to leave now. Come, put it on, let's go."

Chana helps me carry the stroller down the stairs. Rechel Chava walks down the stairs by herself, and Chana runs back up the stairs to get Yehudis while I wait with Rechel Chava and Devorah.

"Myself! Myself!" Yehudis says.

"Sorry baby, it takes too long, maybe on the way up. Rosie is going to buy you a candy if you listen."

"I want a candy," Rechel Chava says.

"You too, but you have to listen."

"Rosie, look both ways before you cross the street. Don't talk to strangers. You will remember where the building is? There is a nice little park two blocks down; Yehudis likes to climb on the rocks there. You can let her. And here are crackers if they get hungry, just break it into pieces for Yehudis, I don't want her to choke, but Rechel Chava can eat it whole. Do you have a bottle of water? Oh no, I didn't give it to you. Wait here, let me get it."

I try to process everything she is telling me. Park, break up crackers, water. Devorah wails in the stroller and flails her arms. I stare at her. Her screams are making my brain buzz.

"I feel the same way, Devorah-poo," I say low, so Chana won't hear.

Chana comes back with the water. "OK, off you go, start wheeling her and she will be fine. Thank you so much! Girls, hold on to the carriage until you get to the park, OK? Bye, I love you, see you soon. Oh, here is some change, they can pick one candy from the store down the block."

Chana hands me change and turns and goes up the stairs. I start to wheel Devorah and at first, the girls hold on to the carriage as we make our way down the block, but the minute we turn the corner, Rechel Chava takes off running. Devorah is still screaming and Yehudis is lagging ten steps behind us. I feel frantic, how will I get them back together? I run with the stroller.

"Shhh, shhh, little Devorah," I say. She wails even louder. My heart pounds. Rechel Chava is at the corner with cars flying by and she jumps off the curb, then back on, and then jumps off again. A car comes too close to her and swerves. I take a frantic glance back at Yehudis who is ambling along, looking around with her thumb in her mouth. I make a split-second decision to leave her there. I run to Rechel Chava and grab her out of the street.

"I wanna jump!" she says.

My heart pounds. "You can jump in the park."

"I want to jump here!" she yells, and she wakes Devorah who had finally fallen asleep. The wailing starts again.

"Shh, Rechel Chava, you cannot jump in the street, it's dangerous! Want a candy?"

"Yes!"

"So then stop jumping."

She shrugs.

I have won this round. Yehudis finally catches up to us and we stand together by the curb and waited for the cars to stop. They don't. Everyone in the city looks like they have important places to go to, and fast. Devorah cries even louder, and my head feels all tangled from her whiny scream. I crane my neck and rock the carriage at the same time and finally, when the closest car seems far enough for us to cross without getting run over by it, I pick up Yehudis in one arm and balanced her on the carriage and take Rechel Chava with the other arm and give the carriage a big push across the street. When we finally get to the park, Yehudis and Rechel Chava start fighting over the metal slide in the middle. I pick them up and put them both on the swing. I push them and they look at each other and giggle.

By the time we get home I am exhausted. Chana says she will put Devorah down for a nap, and I say I will join her. I get into bed, and I fall right to sleep.

I wake up to a thumping noise. I get out of bed, wash my face, and go into the kitchen. Rechel Chava is standing on the table, and she proceeds to jump from the table to the chair. Then, with the skill of the acrobat I saw in the circus, she jumps nimbly back onto the table. Chana stands by the counter in front of a tray of chicken and lots of spices, ignoring her completely.

"Rosie!" Rechel Chava says. "Look at me jump!"

"Maybe you should join the circus," I say.

"Don't give her any ideas," Chana says. "How did you sleep?"

"Pretty good. Need help with the supper?"

"Not supper, but can you entertain the kids a little while I finish up here?"

"Sure."

"Thank you, Rosie, you are a lifesaver for me."

I may be Chana's lifesaver, but I am worn down to my bones. When we finally have supper there is more than enough chicken to go around and apple dumplings, too. I fill up my plate with the steaming food and we all eat together, and my stomach is full, but my heart is empty for missing my family.

The weeks continue like this. Chana keeps telling me what a help I am, but I secretly hate it there with all my heart. One day I stay home to babysit Devorah while Chana takes the girls to buy new shoes. The mail comes while they are gone and there is an envelope with familiar-looking handwriting on it. My heart speeds up as I gather the mail and put it on the kitchen table.

I pick up the envelope and touch the soft paper and almost cry at the thought of my Mama's soft fingers stuffing the paper in the envelope and addressing it to Chana. That is the problem, though. It is addressed to Chana, but it is from my Mama, and I do not want to wait to read it and find out how everyone is doing.

Before my conscience can talk me out of it, I rip the envelope open. Mama's warm curvy handwriting spills over the paper in my hand and my eyes want to devour it and hold it tight at the same time. She writes:

Dearest Chana,

Thank you for having Rosie for such a long time already. I am so happy she is comfortable with you. You are a doll, little sister. Things are going OK here. Yecheskel is getting so big, and he is really helping me around the house. We are getting by, although I won't hide it from you, it is hard. How are you doing? Send Mendel my regards and give all the children hugs and kisses from me. We miss you dearly. I know you can use more help, so although it is the time to send Rosie back to me, you can let her stay for another month if you need her. It would also be a help for me, although I hate to admit this, but it is still hard for me to put food in all their mouths, and I am so grateful to you and Mendel for having Rosie. Let me know if that is good for you, if not send her home next week. We miss her a lot here! Send her my love.

With all my love and appreciation,

Chaya Necha

Another month. My heart drops to my stomach. I look outside the tiny window at the rush of cars honking and zooming by, but instead I hear the excited little whistle of the stream lapping outside my window at home. I see Yecheskel running inside after a long day of school and making us all laugh no matter what kind of day we had. I see Leah in bed next to me. I see Mama by the fire making us her sweet milk drink. I hear birds singing gaily instead of cars honking rudely. I am not staying in this city one more minute than planned. Oh no, I am going home.

"I don't care if I have nothing to eat besides one piece of bread every day," I say out loud to the empty kitchen. "I am going home."

I rip the letter and the envelope up with quick moves of my fingers and bunch the pieces into my hands. I run to the bathroom. I throw it all into the fancy indoor toilet and yank on the flusher. I watch with satisfaction as the papers swirl and twirl and disappear into the sewer. No one is going to make me stay here even one extra minute. I will walk home if I have to.

My heart pounds a little when Chana comes home and rifles through the mail.

"I am waiting for a letter from your Mama," she says. "Maybe she got too busy to write?"

"The mail in Crasna is completely unpredictable," I say, and I try to keep my voice casual.

"Yes, I remember that. Small town problems," Chana smiles. "It is fine, you will see her in the flesh soon enough. Next Monday, in fact!"

And with that, all my guilt swirls and twirls and disappears into the sewer with the letter. I am going home!

27

AUSCHWITZ. NOVEMBER 1944.

"Let it come before you
The groan of the prisoner
As befits
The greatness of your might
Spare those condemned to die."

Psalm 79:11

The days go by in a blur. I cannot keep track of the days and nights anymore because each day feels like a thousand hours. I go to the bathroom to wash myself as often as I can, but I cannot get the stubborn lice to stop clinging to my body. They are everywhere. I watch them crawl into my bunkmate's mouth while she sleeps. I watch another girl crush them on her scalp. She bangs her head against the wood to stop the itching.

Each morning we get the same coffee, the black mud, and then stand for hours and hours in the cold while we are counted over and over again. We stand in wooden shoes that blister our feet and are as cold as the ground. More and more girls are pulled out of line, and they are never seen again. I feel a constant desire for food that is never given. There are no meals, just a sip of mud in the morning and a piece of bread or sometimes one slice of cheese in the evening, and that's it. My cravings are like a magnet that draws me to an empty well.

This morning, when Zeilappell is finally over, Eidy divides us up.

"All girls who work in the factory to this side!" she says.

Bailu and at least one hundred other girls move to one side.

"The rest of you, come here!" Eidy says and points to the other side.

We all walk over to the spot where she has pointed.

An SS guard stands before us. "Girls, all of you are going to get to take a shower today. Do not worry, it will be a nice, warm shower, and then we will let you rest in a warm room for a little while. Just do not make a fuss and follow me."

I am happy to have another shower. Maybe we will get new clothes this time that are not covered in lice. I feel bad for Bailu because she's not getting a shower today, but maybe the factory workers have a different shower schedule than us.

We walk behind the SS in a huge group until we get to a side of the camp I have never been to before. Maybe we are going to buildings where they have warm water for the showers! That would be nice. Suddenly, I freeze; there is music playing. I have not heard a note of music in over a year. Something inside of me comes alive but also stays completely calm. The music sings lies to me. It tells me that everything is going to be OK. We are a large group of girls. Several hundred of us probably. We walk five in a row, as if in a trance, to where the SS women are leading us. From the corner of my eye, I notice a small orchestra is set up. The musicians are prisoners, skinny and gaunt, like us. They play their cellos and harps like puppets on a string. I look down and see my second surprise of the day. Flowers line the pathway we are on. Fuchsia, yellow, and pink flowers stick out of beds of brown and green grass. They flap lightly in the wind to the music, and I smile at them.

"You are going to take a shower," says an SS lady in the front.

"It looks like it is going to be a proper hot one," I whisper to Leah.

"There is no need to worry about anything at all," continues the SS woman and we all nod. Some girls have glassy eyes. They are entranced by the music. They lead us to a large brick building. We file into a large room with benches lining the interior walls.

"Take off your clothing now," says the same SS woman. "Fold them neatly and put them in a pile on the benches. Don't worry. They will be waiting here for you when you are finished. Put your shoes under the benches. Remember where you put them so you can pick them up with ease when you are done."

Girls start to take off their uniforms and quickly fold them.

"Now line up by these doors and we will open them soon."

"You look like a responsible girl," an SS man says as he comes up to me.

I nod.

"I need you to look through all the clothing here, we are looking for gold, silver, or anything that looks of value. Here is a bag, fill it up with what you find and then give it to me."

"OK," I say. Then I decide to be brave and ask a question, "If you don't mind though, I really would love to have a shower. Will I still have a chance to go in?"

"Oh, don't worry," he laughs. "They'll wait for you."

Relieved, I get to work. I sit by the growing piles of clothing and pat each uniform down and check for anything of value, and then I fold each one up again, all perfect and neat. I pick up each dress and carefully pat it down and look through all the seams. The SS man stands over me, watching to see if I find anything. I know he does not want to touch the garments himself because of all the contamination they hold. I do not find anything.

"You can go in now before they close the doors," he says when I am done.

I run quickly toward the small, open door. As soon as I step in, it is shut behind me and I hear the lock turn with a big clank. I look around. This room is huge and made of gray cement. Hundreds of girls stand around, looking up at the shower heads. They are waiting for them to turn on. Some of us hug ourselves to keep warm. There are no windows except for one that looks like it opens on top of the ceiling.

I slip through the crowd to find Leah.

"Finally, a normal shower," I say.

She jumps.

"Didn't see you there."

"Yes, they gave me work to do."

"Lucky, I am freezing here waiting. I hope they turn these showers on soon and I hope it is hot."

Leah sticks her hand in mine. I clutch hers tight. I hate what is happening to us here but as Leah lays her head on my shoulder and looks up at the faucet, I know that no matter what happens I am so lucky to have her as my sister. I am blessed to have her with me through all of this. Together, we look up at the shower heads and we wait for them to turn on.

No water comes out of the faucets. Instead, there is a loud rapping on the door and the lock is pushed down with a crank and the door flies open. There is an SS man standing there and his face is red, and he is yelling at the SS women who stand near the door with him.

"I told you! We need more girls to work in the ammunition factory! What were you thinking? Just because there is tension, no one knows how to listen to simple directions anymore? You almost cost us 750 free, hard laborers; this is a disaster! Get them out, now!"

"What do you mean?" The SS woman yells back at him. "These girls were selected for the gas chambers."

"Do not argue with me, woman! We need more workers! Get them out now!"

The SS women turn to us and start pulling girls out with their hands.

"Louse! Louse!" they yell. They grab girls by their arms and pull them out of the shower room.

We all file out of the little door.

"Get your uniforms on! It doesn't have to be yours! Take the first one you see!"

I swallow with disappointment. I so badly wanted a nice shower. We all scrambled to grab a uniform and shoes and put them on.

Eidy stands with her back against the wall. She looks up in shock when she sees us coming out of the shower room.

"What? What is happening?" She blinks rapidly. Her voice shakes violently. "What are you doing?" Her eyes are huge. Eidy, who always looks like she is made of stone, suddenly looks like metal melting in a furnace. Her whole face changes and tears stream down her face.

We look at her in shock.

"They need us to work," someone says. "We can't take a shower because they need us to work somewhere."

"Children!" she sobs. She looks at us like we are ghosts. "Do you know what you just came out of? Do you know what you just escaped? Beautiful, young girls, beautiful young children." She sobs and then catches her breath. "You just came out from death. You are alive. Do you know where you just came from?"

We gape at her.

She touches some of our faces. "You just walked out from hell itself. You walked out. I have never seen that happen. You walked out of hell!"

I do not know what she is talking about. It is unnerving to see our Blockälteste who has never been moved by anything, now crying like a baby. I sense something big has just happened, but I do not understand what.

"I don't know where you are going, children. But don't you realize? You are going out from here!" She puts her face in her hands and she breaks down and cries a gasping sound.

"Beautiful children, you are alive. You are going out from here."

I squeeze Leah's hand. We are going out from here!

The SS line us up into rows of five again. "Louse! Run!"

We try to keep up with them. At first, I think we are going to march back to our barrack, but it soon becomes apparent that we are going somewhere else entirely. We march for hours. The SS push us forward. "Keep going!" they say. We walk and walk and walk. The hours turn to days. Like in a dream, I watch the sun go down and we still march. Then I watch the sun come up again. We have nothing to eat or drink. Finally, we get to a train station and the SS push us onto the train. I cannot think anymore. There is not enough energy in my body to use for thinking. I stand smothered between hundreds of girls and bob along, almost lifeless, with the train.

28

CRASNA. 1940–44.

"You made us
The target of strife to our neighbors
And our enemies
Mock us."

Psalm 80:6

When I come home from Chana's house, Mama looks different than how I have imagined her in my head all these months. I hug her tight and tell her never to let us go anywhere again.

"We need to get Leah home," I say when we are around Mama's table and eating a supper of sourdough bread and a small salad. I look at the room with our bed, and I cannot wait to get in it, but only with Leah. "Chana took me to visit Leah at Lipa's house one day, because he lives close by. All of Lipa's kids were at the table eating and Leah was in the back churning the water to make bubbles for their seltzer business. I do not want her stay in a house like that."

"*Mamashein*,"[1] says Mama. "I do not have anything to give her to eat."

"Mama. What we will eat, she will eat. She is coming home."

Mama nods and sits down right then and there to write a letter to

Tzadok. Leah comes home a week later, and our house is a home again.

Our house is a home, but then it is taken away from us.

One day, a Hungarian woman knocks on our door with official papers in her hand.

"This is the property of Hungary. This house is not yours anymore. You have to leave by tonight."

Mama just stares at her, nods, and then closes the door.

By the time I get home from work that day, Kokish Emma is helping my mother pack. She is crying but my mother's face is stoic.

"But how? How can they make you leave?" Kokish Emma asks. "It doesn't make any sense."

Mama doesn't answer. She folds our sweaters and places them into the suitcase.

"Rosie, go get Kokish Emma the basket of money from the closet."

"Oh, Chaya Necha, I don't want the money, I want my best friend to be my neighbor. I want my best friend to have her house."

I go to the closet to get a wicker basket that is overflowing with bills. Kokish Emma's husband owns the butcher shop, and he doesn't like banks, so we keep his money for him. We will not be able to do that anymore when we are all the way across town. Emma takes the basket out of my hands and puts it on the floor. She takes the sweater out of Mama's hands, and she folds it again.

We move to a small room across town. Leah and I get jobs from the old seamstress to help pay for our rent. It is never enough so we decide to eat as little as possible and save up our money for a sewing machine so we can start a business ourselves.

After a year of stuffing our bills into our own woven basket, we finally have enough.

Mama goes to the store, and we wait to see what she will bring home. She comes through the door with a sewing machine the size of half her body with a foot pedal attached to it. She sets it down on the table with a smile and we run to it.

"It is beautiful!" Leah says and she runs her hands over the ebony white curved top.

"It looks so professional," I say in wonder. I run my finger and thumb up and down the thin, silver needle.

"It is," Mama says. "They gave me a little discount; this is the best sewing machine around."

We celebrate with pickled cucumbers and a small cake. The room is small, but it feels perfect to us.

"To success we will have in the future," Mama says as she cut us pieces of her cake. It tastes sweet already. "You aren't girls anymore; you are young ladies," she adds as she hands us our cake. I look at Leah, she looks like a younger version of Mama, and she is becoming so beautiful with her sharp eyes, delicate but mature nose, and ribbon-red lips. I lean back and cross my hands over my chest and wonder how we got here so fast.

Leah gets clients right away. She quickly becomes a legend with her long, nimble fingers and arithmetic brain—and how she can take one look at the customer and a few weeks later a gorgeous, perfectly fitted dress is flowing from her hands. I am always around to help Leah with the measurements and ironing and some stitching when she is busy.

A new client walks into our apartment one day and says, "I want something to make me look *chinush*.[2] Leah, can you do that for me?"

Leah sizes up the woman.

"Do you have a specific fabric you want to use, or would you be interested in using one of ours? Because if you are, I have this gorgeous, mauve-colored fabric that I think would go beautifully with your complexion."

"I do have something with me . . ." says the lady, but she is already looking at the rolls of fabric behind Leah.

"OK, let me just show you what I had in mind and then you will have an easier time making the decision for yourself."

"Yes, that sounds like a good idea."

Leah nods to me, and I go to get the roll of fabric. I know which one Leah is talking about. It is soft and almost like velvet, very light, and not quite pink and not quite purple. I come back with the roll in my hands and Leah is already fluttering around the woman with a tape measure and muttering measurements under her breath.

"Here," Leah says as she takes the fabric from me. "Have a look."

She wraps the fabric around the woman's shoulders and brings her to the mirror. The woman's eyes brighten.

"You know, I could use a different kind of dress than my regular navy ones," she says.

"You absolutely can," agrees Leah. "You deserve something to make you feel really good when you put it on, you know? Now I just need to write down your measurements. It will be ready in three weeks."

The woman leaves with a flurry of thank-yous and instructions for the trimming, and I am left to wonder why there is a flurry of something unpleasant in me when I look at my sister. First in school, and now in work, she has always been better than me.

The woman comes back a few weeks later. Leah smiles at her and hands her the dress. I steamed and ironed it until late last night. It is perfect. There is not a shadow of a crease on the dress. At least I can iron well.

The woman disappears into the makeshift dressing room and comes out a few minutes later. She steps up in front of the mirror. She is a woman transformed. The dress curves and folds with her body and hugs her like a good friend, not too tight but nice and close and comforting.

"You look beautiful," I say. Leah bites her lips as we wait for a response.

The woman has her hands on her hips as she examines herself in the mirror.

"I must say, you did a wonderful job," she says, and for the first time since we met her, she smiles. "Thank you very much. Ah, and here is the pay for it." She pulls her wallet from her dowdy, black bag and counts out a few bills. I am glad for what Leah is doing for our family, even though it stings my pride.

The years pass and we continue our jobs as seamstresses for the town. Gitta gets engaged one day, and it is all Leah and I can talk about.

"We need to make dresses for her wedding, you have to look good! You are 18 already, time to get married!"

"Just because Gitta got engaged the day she turned 17, does not mean we all have to do the same."

"Ha! You are dying to get married, don't tell me you are not."

"I am not dying to get married." I blush. "I mean, it would be nice."

"I wonder who we are going to end up marrying. I just want someone who is really, really nice."

"I want someone nice, and really handsome."

"Ha! Handsome will not bother me either."

We walk up to our apartment.

Yecheskel sits at the table with his book. He looks up when he hears us come in. A bruise under his eye is a deep purple with swirling bits of yellow.

"Hi Cheskel," I say. "How are you feeling?"

"Oh, I'm fine. Just don't tell Mama that I have been coming home from school early."

Last week two older boys beat him up on the straight when he was walking home after dark. "Dirty Jew," they called him. Mama marched with us to court the next day, determined to take care of those two horrible boys who touched her son.

"You foolish Jew," the court told her. "You are looking for justice? What are you asking for? Go home lady! You are lucky we are even letting you go home."

Mama came home that night confused and worried, but by the time we all sat down to eat and Yecheskel was feeling better, she placed the salad firmly on the table and said, "I guess you will always have crazy people in the world; it won't happen again."

A few weeks ago, there was a man from Poland in town. The butcher's wife fed him at her house, and he wolfed down all the food that she put in front of him in a just three minutes. I saw him myself: he had a crazed look about him and wild, dirty hair and a half cut-off beard. He ranted about someone killing Jews in Poland. We had heard similar rumors, but rumors are rumors, and we were not about to start getting nervous about something a man who was clearly mentally unstable was saying. Anyways, this wasn't Poland; this was Hungary. Nothing was going to happen to us in this country.

"Rosie is getting married," Leah teases.

"He better be good to you, or he will have to answer to me," Yecheskel says.

"Ha! You do look threatening with that black eye," I say.

We laugh. Yes, nothing bad can happen to us here.

PART III

29

BERGEN-BELSEN. NOVEMBER 1944.

"He raised me
From the pit of raging waters
From mud which is slimy
He set me upon a rock
My feet firmly establishing my steps.
He put into my mouth
A new song
The multitudes shall see
And they will be awed
And they shall trust in God."

Psalm 40:2–3

It is pitch black outside when we get to our destination. When I climb down from the train, I shiver. The darkness all around seems to reach inside of me and suck out whatever joy I had left with a violent jerk. All that remains is a cold, gaping emptiness. The SS herd us over swampy land to a barn-like building. My feet grow more and more numb with each step. The wooden shoes are so hard and send shock wave after shock wave up through my whole body. When we get to the building the SS men order us to leave our shoes, then open the big doors and shove us in with their sticks. I tumble headfirst over the girl before me and Leah trips over me. We all move forward, but no one is on their feet. I reach up to my face and feel mud, and I struggle to stand. When I manage to stand up, the mud reaches my ankles. The darkness is so thick, I must push through it as I move forward. The horrible feeling inside of me intensifies. As my eyes adjust to the dark, I see we are in a swamp inside of a barn, with mud everywhere and no beds at all. Leah is right next to me, but I seem to have lost track of Chanky. The SS slam the doors shut and we realize this is our new lodging, and no one can stand anymore for the weight of the hunger in us. Suddenly we all cry at once as we lay down right there, one person on top of the other like we are already corpses. I am drained. I let my body fall to the swampy floor. The darkness closes in on me and I just want the muddy floor that I am laying on to swallow me up whole. The water is slimy in my ears and big clumps of mud and excrement swarm around my neck and my thighs. I am both freezing and starving. Cries and wails reverberate in the walls—the wailing of people who just want this to end. More mud creeps up my thighs and reaches my back. I am blanketed in it. Leah lays her head on mine. I close my eyes and join the cries of everyone else. This is the darkest place I have ever been in.

Suddenly there is a humming coming from the other side of the room. Slowly the cries subside into a shocked silence as the humming gets louder. Someone is singing. The voice gets louder, and everyone gets quieter, and suddenly I know who it is.

"Leah, that's *Faigy*[1] singing," I whisper. I would know that voice anywhere.

"It is," Leah whispers back.

We fall silent and listen to her singing.

My cousin Faigy always sang beautifully, like the bird she was named for. She has the most beautiful voice in the world. Back home when we would visit my father's parents in the country, she would always be there. As she showed us all the new changes on the farm, she would hum, which would fast turn into full-fledged singing. Her voice was like the little bells you hang up to sing with the wind. It was high and clear like fresh water from the stream. When she sang on the farm, the green grass and clear blue sky and wildflowers all came together to dance.

And now here she is lying in the mud with all of us, and I cannot believe my ears. She is singing. Faigy sings louder and the wailing stops completely. It is quiet in the thick, muddy barn. She sings:

"I'd like to ask of you a question,
tell me who knows,
With which dear possession does G-d bless everyone
It cannot be bought for no money;
it's given only for free
And when it is lost,
how many tears are shed.
A second is given nobody,
no cry can help,
Oy, he who has lost it,
he already knows what I mean.
A Yiddishe Mame
It doesn't get better on this earth
A Yiddishe Mame,
How bitter when she is missing.
How nice and bright it is at home,
when the Mame is here
How sad and dark it becomes,
when G-d takes her to Olam Haba
(the world to come)
In water, through fire,
she would have run for her child
Not to hold her dear,
is surely the greatest sin,
How lucky and rich is the one who has
Such a beautiful gift presented from G-d
Like an old Yiddishe Mame
My Yiddishe Mame!"

She sings *My Yiddishe Mame* by the great Cantor Rosenblatt. I miss my mother. I want her. I hope she is ok. "Please sing more," someone says. So, she does. She continues, singing all the songs we grew up with and soon, tucked into the mud and someone else's shoulder with thoughts of my mother, I fall right to sleep.

There is a huge creak, and the barn is filled with grayish light. The SS men stand at the door and wait for us to get up. Everyone wakes up quickly and barely tries to wipe the mud that cakes every inch of our bodies. I wait for the girls on top of me to unfold themselves, and when there is finally a little air and room, I lift my head and get up. I need to use the bathroom.

There is a crowd of girls outside and a big pit in the ground and an SS soldier sits on a chair at the top of a platform that overlooks the pit. He watches us. The stench in the air makes me gag. The pit is the bathroom. There are two beams over the pit to step on. I watch a girl next to me use the pit. She crouches down lightly and then jumps off quickly. Then the girl after her uses it. She sits down on the beams and suddenly with a whiny "crack" the beams give way, and she disappears into the feces. The SS man watches as she struggles for a minute and waves her hands above her head. He laughs and slaps his knees. The pit is too deep with feces for her to get out, and she drops her hands after a few moments and disappears and drowns. She dies! She just dies in the waste. I don't know what to think. I don't want to die, but I don't want to be here, either. Here, where living is worse than death and dying is entertainment for the SS. The sky is almost as dark and deep as the pit and there is nothing I can do. I could save that girl, and I cannot stand this. I cannot save myself. Why did Eidy seem happy that we were leaving the last camp? This is worse. There is screaming in my head. I need to get out of here. Horrible demons sift in and out of my brain. The hunger is beginning to rip my insides apart, piece by piece. I feel my stomach churning and grabbing onto something to try to devour it, but it is devouring itself. I turn around and find somewhere else to relieve myself. This is the worst place I have ever been in my life, and I can barely stand the agony inside of me.

The next night as we lay in the mud like pigs in a pen, Faigy sings to us again. I wonder what it sounds like to the SS soldiers standing outside the door. We are a few hundred girls with not one ounce of fat on our bodies, just skin and bones and a cave where our bellies used to be. We are a few hundred girls laying in a foot or more of mud and slime, in hell. Yet, there is a girl among us with the voice of an angel and she sings us to sleep like a mother to her children.

"Do you know where we are?" I ask the girl lying next to me.

"We are in Bergen-Belsen," she says. "I have heard they transferred us because the allies are winning the war. Not that we are going to make it out of here alive anyway."

"The allies are winning the war!" I repeat back to Leah. "I did not know someone was fighting for us. We are going to go home from here!"

"I hope so," Leah says, and she snuggles closer to me. More mud brushes up on my neck. Leah falls asleep on my shoulder.

In the morning we are given a little horse meat to eat and then we are taken back to the bathroom pit again. There is an SS soldier sitting up high in the sky in his chair on the platform again. He watches us all sit over the pit to relieve ourselves. I am careful not to the let the stick crack with me on it.

We do not work in Bergen-Belsen. We stand in Zeilappell for hours and then we are sent back to the muddy barracks. We do not have energy to talk to each other. We only sleep and when we are awake, we stare straight ahead.

30

CRASNA. 1943. AGE 17.

"By the rivers of Babylon
There we sat
And also we wept
When we remembered
Zion."

Psalm 137:1

Every summer since my father died, we have spent two months with our grandparents in the country. Even after we become seamstresses and are out of school, we still take summers off to be with our father's family.

We ride there by horse and buggy, and we spend the day in the carriage playing games and looking out the window at the apple and pear trees that stretch for miles.

When we get off the wagon near my grandparent's house, my aunt and uncle are waiting there to greet us. They live in the same house as my grandparents. My uncle helps Mama with the suitcases and my aunt Leah Mariam gives her a long hug. She is at least a head taller than my mother and strikingly beautiful, like a movie star from another world, and with the most gentle mannerisms.

"It has been too long, Chaya Necha," she says.

"I know, there is so much to catch up on," Mama says. "Oy, I missed you."

"Come, I will help you get settled," Leah Mariam says. "Ma and Ta are waiting in the living room. They have all the kids."

Mama laughs. Leah Mariam has a lot of kids. Every two years she has had twins. She has never had a singleton yet!

"Hi, my beautiful nieces and darling nephew!" she says to us warmly. "Yecheskel, you got so big!

"I am already Bar Mitzvah," he says.

"My goodness, where does the time go? And Rosie and Leah, you are both more beautiful every time I see you!"

We smile. This means so much coming from her.

We walk to the house together. It is bigger and grander than our house. My grandparents are in the living room sitting on the couch when we step in. It is a little too quiet in the room. Grandfather is nothing like Zaidy Greenstein. He smiles at us when we come to him and gives us hugs but there is already a baby in each of his arms so he cannot get too close. Mama and Leah Mariam go into the kitchen for tea and then upstairs to unpack our things. We watch the younger kids in the meantime and tell Bubbe and Zaidy all that has happened since the last time we saw them.

Mama comes down the stairs with Leah Mariam.

"Are the rooms OK for you?" Bubbe asks.

"They are fine, thank you."

Things are quiet again and then one of the twins starts crying and Leah Mariam scoops him up.

"I am going to change his diaper."

"Come outside with us!" Leah Mariam's five-year-old twins, Baila and Moshe, say.

We are happy to oblige. The warm summer sun and cool green grass are beckoning to us.

Once we get settled in, the summer with our grandparents is glorious. Leah and I had been growing sick of sitting indoors all day with a hot iron and tiny pins pricking our fingers. The field near our grandparents' home never seems to end. The sun is warm, but we don't get too hot because there are many trees to shade us. The air is fresh and smells of grass and sun. Each morning we wake up with an entire day stretched out before us and no work to do. All our cousins come to visit us. Faigy, our cousin who is our age, comes to visit us, too. We spend the whole week together. She sings like a bird with everything she does. She does not even realize she is singing. Her father has big wheat fields for his business and one day he takes us on a trip to go see them. We get out of his car near the fields, and we look in awe at the rows and rows of wheat stalks flowing in the wind. I cannot believe this is what they use to make *matzah*[1] for Pesach.[2] My other uncle owns a big vinegar factory. One night he comes over and tells us stories in his deep voice before we go to sleep. I wish he would tell us stories of what my father was like as a little boy, but no one speaks of him at all.

In August, *Tisha B'Av*[3] comes around. It is the fasting day to mourn the destruction of the Temple. Before the fast starts we sit on the floor and eat a meal of hard-boiled eggs with ashes on top and rye bread without any butter. The sun sets and the fast starts and Zaidy leaves the room. I hear him crying from the study and it is shocking to hear my quiet, gruff Zaidy like that.

Later, as we are going to sleep, I notice Yecheskel put a rock from outside on the floor of the room.

"What do you think you are doing?"

"It is Tisha B'Av. The one day a year that we take time to remember that life isn't the way it should be."

"OK, you are already fasting. You don't need a rock to do that."

"I don't want to sleep with a comfy pillow. I want to remember even in my sleep."

"So, sleep with your head on the floor. Why the rock?"

"Did you know that when Yaakov slept on the land where the Temple was to be built, he put 12 rocks under his head, and they all merged into one? They symbolized how although we are all separate, as the 12 tribes were, we really are one. I want to do the same. On the day we remember the temple we lost; I want to remember that."

"You are so sweet, Cheskel, but that's just crazy. You cannot sleep on a rock. Here, take your pillow."

"I don't want the pillow. Do you know why our Temple was destroyed? We destroyed it by destroying ourselves. We are all one, but we didn't know that, and we ripped each other apart and by doing so we ripped ourselves apart. We may seem different, but I am you and you are me and we are all part of each other. We are all part of God, living within Him. We have to know that!"

"What does Tisha B'Av have to do with that?"

"All destruction comes from thinking about others as different than you. To be cruel to someone, you cannot think of them as yourself. So, we make them a stranger in our eyes. As if we don't all have the same blood in our veins, as if we don't breathe the same air. No one can be cruel unless they really view someone as different but that rips the world apart. We cannot be different. We are all part of the same God. We are never alone."

"And that is why the temple was destroyed?"

"On Tisha B'Av, not only was the Temple destroyed. On Tisha B'Av it is the day that all evil came into this world. And yes, in the time of the Temple, we were destroying ourselves from the inside. We were like a baby trying to break free from our mother's womb because we couldn't be one with the mother. But we couldn't breathe on our own. Did you know that in the time that the Temple was destroyed, we were acting cruel to one another, and God was really supposed to kill us all, but He loves us so much that He let His Temple burn down instead? Now He has nowhere to go. I am not taking the pillow." And with that, he lays his head down on the rock and covers himself with a blanket.

"Tisha B'Av is going to be a holiday one day," he whispers as we all lay down to go to sleep. "We are going to learn; we are going to come together as one and it will be because of Tisha B'Av that we learn. We are going to dance together and eat a feast so delicious; you will not believe we ever fasted on this day. Believe me, we are going to celebrate on Tisha B'Av one day."

"He is so mature," Leah whispers to me as he falls asleep.

"Can you believe that's our baby brother?" I ask. We both look at the almost teenager laying on the rock.

"I hope he is right," Leah says.

We don't know what is coming. We don't know that we will soon be seen as strangers—not as humans—so that the cruelest acts in the world can be done to us. Everything that Yecheskel has said tonight will become reality in only one year. The entire world as we know it will fracture at its seams and explode into smithereens, causing destruction to everyone and everything in its wake. All because we haven't yet learned to view each other as ourselves . . . that we are the furthest thing from strangers . . . that we are all part of one whole. But some people will want to remain separate, and by pulling us apart, they will unravel the very essence of what keeps the world whole, until it has no choice but to explode. Like a cancer, splitting the body's own cells until every organ breaks down and the body, by doing to its own, dies.

The rest of the summer passes uneventfully. When September comes around and the tips of the trees start turning colors, we are sad to go. We hug our grandparents and aunts and uncles goodbye.

"See you next summer!" they say as they wave.

We wave back from the buggy. "See you then!"

31

DUDERSTADT AMMUNITION FACTORY. NOVEMBER 1944.

"When it fainted within me
Did my spirit
Inside me
My heart was appalled.
I recalled the days of old."

Psalm 143:4–5

A few weeks after our arrival at Bergen-Belsen, we are herded back onto trucks without a word of where we are going. I have no more energy to even think of what may lie ahead as we drift along, bumping up and down on the rocky road.

I wake up to the truck doors opening. They unload us from the trucks, and I can tell we are deep in the forest. There are thousands of trees surrounding us. Their branches umbrella us and keep us hidden. There are three barracks in front of me, surrounded by a tall barbed-wire fence. The SS women are all around and they are all wearing army uniforms and they have rifles on their shoulders. They yell at us and tell us to get into rows of five. We have not eaten anything the whole way here, so we are slow to form the lines. They hit us with their rifles to make us move faster. They walk us into the barrack where we will sleep. It looks like military tents I have read about. There are bunks piled one on top of the other.

"Go to sleep, you pigs!" an SS woman says. Then she closes the door to the barrack.

There is a shrill whistle, and an SS woman walks into the barrack to wake us up. With all my strength I pull my body out of the bunk. There is another SS at the front of the barrack with a pot. We pass the pot around and when it gets to me, I see it is barley. I put it to my mouth and gulp a little down. It tastes like poison.

"Schnell!" the SS woman says.

Some girls did not get the food yet.

"Come, hurry!"

We walk outside into the dark and cold night air. The moon is high in the sky. It must be three o'clock in the morning.

She leads us in rows of five down a long, snowy path.

We walk for around 20 minutes until we get to a big L-shaped building. We are silent as we enter the building, not knowing what to expect. It is a factory with long tables set up all around and gray, metal walls and tiny windows. There are lots of Polish-looking people already there, working at different stations. There are SS men walking all around. A young SS soldier stands in front of us.

"You will be working here in the Ammunition Factory. I am your manager. We will assign you to different jobs. Everyone stands where we tell you to. No one moves until we tell you to. You will do your job to perfection, or else we will shoot you with the weapons you clean or fix. You are going to help us make weapons to fight our enemies. Wait here until we position you."

He walks around and directs us where to go. I am placed in front of a big box of guns and cannons and a wooden basin filled with water. I want to drink from it like a horse.

A soldier comes up to me.

"You have to clean out the insides of these weapons and the cannon balls until they gleam brighter than the sun. Then pack them in the box behind you. Start now, what are you waiting for?" He kicks my shin.

I bend down over the basin and drop the cannon balls into it while everyone around me does different jobs. Chanky is at the station next to me. Leah is all the way across the room. We are all hard at work but while my hands are working, I feel dizzy and lightheaded. I look through the window. Between the tree branches I can see stars splattered across the velvet sky. I feel myself falling into them, but I steady myself and try to keep working. My vision blurs and then gets clear again. The factory comes in and out of focus in front of me. I don't have any food in my body; I am ebbing away. I focus on the wooden basin in front of me. I stare at its wooden slats, and they become almost familiar. Suddenly it becomes the wooden basin in my kitchen at home. The walls of the factory turn into the walls of our kitchen. The gray-cement floor has a turquoise rug on it. Our red door creaks open, and Uncle Duvid walks in.

"Look at you Rosie, washing all the dishes," he says. "Someone looks ready to get married."

"Hold your horses, Duvid," Mama says. "She's only 16 and she's been doing the dishes for me since she's been eight."

"Duvid is just one-track minded because all he can think of is Chanky, his kallah," I say.

"Chanky, Chanky, Chanky," Leah says. "Duvid can only think of Chanky."

"Stop teasing your uncle, that is not respectful," Mama says, but she is laughing and Duvid clanks his book on Leah's head.

"Chanky, Chanky, Chanky," Leah says again.

"I'm leaving," Duvid announces.

"OK, OK, we'll be quiet," Leah and I say quickly. "Stay."

"So, I will," Duvid says, and he settles himself on the couch and crosses his long legs. "But only for the aroma that is coming from that oven."

"Ah supper, you are finally here," Leah says. She pushes her chair back from the sewing machine and stretches her hands in the air.

"Rosie, get your hands out of that water basin and set the table already," says Mama. I stack my freshly dried plates and bring them to the table. I set one in front of each chair. One for Mama, one for me, one for Leah, one for Yecheskel, and one for Uncle Duvid. I put a knife and fork neatly on either side and fold the starched napkins and place them under each plate. Mama takes the bread from the stovetop, and we all sigh as we watch her cut it into slices, the steam rolls up to the ceiling like a dream. I pour the olive oil and salt in the small bowl and Mama scoops out the chickpea stew and puts it on a platter of sweet potatoes.

I open the door and stick my head out. "Yecheskel!" I yell, "Time for supper!"

"Very lady like," Duvid snorts.

"Not much like your girlfriend," I say, and I stick my tongue out.

"She is not my girlfriend, she is my bride," Duvid says.

"I am only serving you supper to make you all quiet for once," Mama says.

"I will tease them more if this is the result," says Duvid after he swallows his first bite of the stew. It is a good tactic of Mama's because we stay quiet now as we dip the steaming bread in the sweet and spicy stew and let the warmth fill up our bodies. We eat and eat until our bellies can stretch no more. Every cell in my body grabs on to the little pieces of energy from the stew. Every piece of me comes alive and full of energy. All the plates are scraped clean, so I gather them with Leah and put them in the water basin. I start washing and drying them but suddenly I am so tired. Gravity pulls me down. I cannot stand for one more minute. I take the box that I am supposed to put the plates away in and I turn it over and rest my head on it while I am still standing.

"I am going to hang you right here," says a voice close to my ear.

32

DUDERSTADT. NOVEMBER 1944.

"My days are like
A lengthening shadow
And I dry out
Like grass."

Psalm 102:11

I open my eyes and I am back in the cold factory. The young SS manager stands with his face an inch from mine. He takes a step back. His face is young, and his eyes are a cold blue. His hair is short, it is almost as bald as mine.

"See that pole over the ceiling?" he says, leaning in close to my face again. His breath smells like tobacco. It makes me think of my Zaidy. It makes me feel strong. "I will hang you from that pole. I will tie the rope around your neck, and I will carry you up the ladder myself and I will drop you until you hang like a puppet and die. Who do you think you are? Falling asleep in middle of your work? You will sleep, flying over all the girls. And I will leave you hanging there the whole time until your skin falls off onto the other workers' heads!"

From the corner of my eye, I see an old soldier. He steps close to the young manager to listen to him.

"Look at me!" the manager says. "Aren't you scared? You are going to rot from the ceiling and that is a promise!"

I look at him like he is a wall. He's going to hang me? He is not going to hang me. He circles around me. I look straight at his face as his eyes look at my shoulders, my chest, my hips, and my bare feet. When his eyes meet mine there is an eerie hunger in them.

"You don't understand, girl, do you?" he says, and he is inches away from my face, but he is scared to touch me for contamination. I see the white flecks in his eyes and the bumps on his clean-shaven cheeks. I smell his tobacco breath and see the saliva foaming slightly in his mouth. "I am going to hang you right there, and soon." I stand straight like a board. I breathe in and out. This man is not going to touch me, let alone hang me. Somehow, I know. The soldier snarls and then turns around and leaves me there. I start washing the insides of the gun. When the manager is far away the old soldier comes up to me.

He doesn't say anything for a few minutes, he just watches me turn the box back over and stack the dried cannon balls neatly into it.

"That is very good," he says, nodding at the box. Then he turns to me and gives me a sad smile. Shocked, I do not remember to smile back at him.

The hours pass and then we are led out from the ammunition factory in rows of fives. The sun is high in the sky. An SS woman blows her whistle and says, "You will be going now to help farmers in their fields! Remember, we only want girls who work, so work hard!"

We walk for a long time until we reach a long field. Little sugar canes peek up from the ground.

"You are to pull the sugar canes from the field and collect them for the farmers," the SS woman says. "Everyone take a shovel! Your time starts now!"

It is cold and we have no coats on. I bend down to the ground. It is hard and cold. The SS woman hands out shovels to us. I push it against the ground. The ground does not budge. I push again.

My fingers are as frozen as the ground. I push against the stalk. Finally, I pull one out and put it into the farmers' pile.

It is black outside when we are led back to the barracks.

Somewhere in the very back of my brain it registers that I am dying a slow death. I will either die from hunger or from exhaustion, but I am too tired to even think about that.

That night Leah slides in next to me on the bunk.

"They are using the ammunition we are working on here to help fight the Allies who are trying to save us. Can you imagine that? We wait all day for the Allies to come and save us, and while we wait, we wipe down the bullets that are used to shoot them." She lets out a deep sigh and we are quiet for a minute. "Who knows if it is true though," she shrugs, and she lays her head down on my shoulder and collapses into sleep.

We are woken up again to the shrill whistle of the SS woman. We get a little coffee and a few bites of poison-tasting barley, and then we are led through the frozen forest to the factory. I go to my station and there is a new shipment of dirty cannon balls. I stick my hands into the freezing water in the bucket and start washing them. Yecheskel appears next to me as I stick my hands again into the cold water. He watches as I pass a bullet from hand to hand and scrub it clean.

"What are you doing Rosie?" he asks.

"Oh, this is my job, sweetie. I wash and dry bullets for the factory. Then I put them away."

"And you are going to do that for them?"

"Do I have a choice?"

"You never listened to the rules."

I smile back at him. Then I slowly drop the bullets to the bottom of the basin. They land on the bottom with a slight thud and my heart thuds even louder, but no one seems to notice.

"Ha," Yecheskel says and then he is gone.

I suddenly feel reckless and wide awake. I take another pile of bullets and look around. The manager has his back to me, so I gently slide them all to the bottom of the basin. I look up and my heart skips a beat. I see the reflection of an SS uniform on the surface of the water. Someone is close enough to see me. I stand frozen with my head down to the basin; it is too deep to retrieve the bullets now. Then in the reflection of the water is the most beautiful thing: The old Nazi officer is smiling. I see his same sad eyes and drawn-down puffy cheeks, but he has a smile on his face, and he just caught me breaking the rules.

"Be careful please," he whispers. And then he shuffles away.

"Rosie, you are dropping all the forks to the bottom of the basin," Mama says. "We are not going to have any silverware left."

"Oh, am I? I must have been daydreaming too much, Mama, but it's fine, we can get them later."

"You are lucky Duvid isn't here to tease you today."

"But *I* am here," says a deep voice.

"Zaidy!" I say. "What are you doing here?"

"Can't I visit my favorite redhead?"

"But aren't you . . .?"

"Busy? Nah, never too busy to be with you. Never too busy to tell you what an amazing job you are doing. Never too busy to tell you how proud of you I am, no matter where I might be."

"Proud of me?"

"Of course, I am!" He ruffles my hair. "How can I not be? Keep it up Rosie, don't give up now, OK? We are all right here with you."

"OK, Zaidy." I smile and he goes to sit down at the table.

The water is warm on my hands and the house is perfectly toasty with a slight breeze of fresh air coming from the draft in the window. The bubbles slide up my sleeves as I massage each fork but somehow, I find it very important to drop each one to the bottom of the warm basin.

"That's my girl," Zaidy says with each thud.

"I finished another dress today," Leah says.

"Good job, Leah!" Mama says. "Did she like it?"

"She loved it," Leah says and puts the money in our basket.

I feel a little twinge of hatred for Leah. I am the older one, I am supposed to be the one dropping money in the basket. I cannot sew a dress to save my life. I am not as strong as everyone else. The lights go out in the house, and I find myself walking outside. Suddenly I am back in the forest. Leah is walking next to me, and she pulls on my arm. I shake my head and blink. I look at her, skin and bones but still beautiful. My heart free falls out of my chest.

"I love you so much." My voice is strong, as if I am trying to push all my emotions into those few words.

"I cannot do this anymore, Rosie."

"You have to. I am here. I will take care of you. We are going home soon." I pull Leah's hand into my own. We are led to the sugar fields. The sun is hot, even though the air is cold. My brain stops working. I watch my hands do their job but there is not enough energy in my cells to process what is happening. When the sun goes down, we are led straight to the barracks.

We walk to our barrack in a hazy world of exhaustion. We have three hours to sleep before we go back to work in the factory. I fall asleep as soon as my body is somewhat horizontal.

33

DUDERSTADT. DECEMBER 1944.

"Laid snares
Have the seekers of my life
And those who seek my harm
Speak treacheries and deceit
All day long
They contemplate.
But I am like a deaf man
I do not hear
And like a mute
Who does not open his mouth."

Psalm 38:12–13

We hear a shrill whistle too soon after we fall asleep, and my body protests the effort of waking up. I want to sleep for days. We gulp down the barley like crazed people and then we go out to the factory. We take our places at our stations with no talking. We do our jobs mechanically. I look around at the several hundred of us,[1] standing in rows at our stations, and each one of us doing a job to help the Nazis win. We are slaves to our enemy.

The Poles have their stations, too, but they do not have SS soldiers surrounding them like they are dangerous criminals.

The SS manager comes to my station as soon as I start working on the inside of a gun. "Are you ready for your hanging day?" he says.

I ignore him.

"Look at me when I talk to you!"

I look straight into his face, which is just inches away from mine and I stare back at him for five minutes as he breathes heavily. He has hunger in his eyes. He looks down into the basin where I dropped the bullets yesterday, but he cannot see anything in the murky water, and he does not dare to get his uniform wet by checking it.

"If I see even one bullet missing, I will hang you today," he says. "And I mean it. Just one thread out of place and I will hang you from this ceiling until the smell of your rotting body becomes too much for me to handle."

I am a wall, I think to myself, and when he leaves, I drop a few more bullets to the bottom of the basin. I am nauseous thinking of the bullets rusting on the bottom of the bucket and my body rotting from the ceiling. I swallow the thought and I get to work. I try not to fall asleep standing up; I am so tired that it is as if I am in a fog. Mama's face flits around me and she strokes my cheek as I work. Then I am home again.

"Rosie, please wash the cutlery," Mama says.

"OK, Mama." I stand in front of the wooden basin that is filled with water and I suds each fork down with soap. In my head I play a game that I always played as a child. Each piece of cutlery is a soldier in the army, and I am the nurse. I wash away their wounds and gently place them to sleep in the hospital bed.

"What are you muttering to yourself?" Mama asks.

"Nothing." I know she will laugh at my game. I am too old to be playing pretend.

"You are doing a good job on the dishes," she says as she walks away.

"Good night little soldier," I whisper to the fork as I gently pat it dry and put it to sleep in the drawer. "Get better soon, we need you." I pick up a plate. "You're the enemy, I am sorry; but I have to let you go," I say. I drop it to the bottom of the basin.

"What are you doing with your Mama's plates?" Zaidy asks. His voice is kind but then, right before my eyes, he turns into the old Nazi. I am scared when I see him but there is a smile in his eyes even as he frowns at the bullet sinking slowly to the bottom of the basin.

"I ..." I stammer.

"Be careful please," he says. "The soldier means what he says about hanging you. Do not test him. I think you are brave but don't risk your life. The Allies are winning. I am telling you. They are getting close."

"You think so?"

"It is all over the news, that is why the soldiers are getting so tense. We are losing." He smiles at that, and I have never seen a more gracious loser.

"I have to do my part."

"But take care of yourself."

I nod. "What is your name?"

"Ediger."

"Rosie."

"Nice to meet you," he smiles at me.

The young soldiers come back to do their rounds and when he spots them, he shuffles away quickly, and even though he doesn't see me, I smile back.

In this factory, deep in the forest, surrounded with barbed wire and horror, I have found a friend.

I can't listen to him though. I drop another bullet to the bottom of the deep, deep basin and then while still standing, I lay my head on the table and fall asleep.

"I see this really is a joke to you," the manager snarls in my ear. "You take naps? At work? You lazy pig!"

I jerk my head up and don't say anything.

"I am just waiting for a shipment of the finest ropes to tie tight around your ugly little neck."

Still, I keep quiet.

He leans his head to my ears without touching me and he says,

"You think just because you don't answer me, I think you can't hear me? You may be an ugly redhead, but you are not deaf."

I touch my head.

"Ha, you think I cannot see the tufts of red hair coming in?"

He reaches out to grab my head and stops short. He isn't allowed to touch me, and we both know it.

"When your body rots so much that it falls from the post you hang on, we are going to take your remains and feed them to the forest animals, you ugly, deaf, redheaded girl!"

I stare at him and want him to go away and leave me alone.

"Oh, and we are counting your quotas of bullets tomorrow morning while you work in the fields. Every single bullet had better be there."

I look down at the basin in dismay. It is bigger than me. There is no way I will be able to retrieve all of them. I hope he does not mean what he says.

The next night when I get to the factory the manager stands by my station and counts all the bullets that are in the box. My heart pounds heavily. I am doomed. Then I see in shock that all my bullets are lined up neatly, they are glistening and dry.

"They are all here," he says disdainfully. "But if I see any monkey business, we are hanging you today."

I can barely nod. I can't imagine how the bullet count could be correct. He leaves and after a few minutes Ediger is by my side. His sleeves are dark and wet.

"It was you!" I say.

He smiles at me. "I didn't say anything."

"But I know."

"Maybe."

"Thank you for doing that."

"I hoped you wouldn't be mad," he says, "but the young soldier was catching on. It is not worth risking your life." He speaks from the corner of his mouth, so it barely looks like he is talking to me. "You must miss your family very much; I know I do."

I nod.

"I have a granddaughter around your age, I think of her every day.

I hope she is going to be OK, you know? There is nothing I love more in my life than her." He sighs and the wrinkles on his face soften.

"I had a grandfather who I loved more than anything. I still miss him every day. I always think about him."

"I am sure he was very proud to be your grandpa."

I open my mouth to answer but then I see the manager turning a corner in the factory and I freeze. My old friend shuffles slightly away. The manager walks toward me with straight, purposeful steps and stops when he is inches from my chest. He takes a quick glance at my bullets, stacked in their boxes, and then takes a not so quick glance at me, and then he walks away.

I go back home. I am standing in my kitchen and wash the dishes that are streaked with the remains of a hearty dinner. I wipe off lines of tomato sauce and oil that are left from the fish. Zaidy comes in.

"There's nothing I love more than you children," Zaidy says as he hugs me. "Rosie, you are so beautiful, especially your golden-strawberry, sun-stroked hair. Oh! Look at your hands, you must be freezing. What have you been doing?"

He takes my little hands in his huge, strong hands and rubs them until some of the circulation comes back. Now they are warm and toasty. It is so good to be back home.

"Zaidy? How can some people be so good, and some people be so bad? Aren't we all the same people?"

"That's a good question, my little philosopher. That is the power of free choice. You choose what you want to be."

"So, someone who is cruel, chose to be that way?"

"Yes of course, maybe not all at once, but with the everyday decisions he made he molded himself into the person he is today."

"It scares me sometimes, though, that I have the right to decide."

"Think of it as the greatest gift of all. You don't wait to see what kind of life you lived or what kind of person you became, you choose for yourself no matter what you are going through. You don't wait for life to happen to you, you happen to life. With every move you make you can choose to make it what you want, what you believe in, even if it is the harder choice."

"Zaidy, sometimes it is easier to surrender."

"It is," he nods. "But if I know my beautiful granddaughter, which I may be so bold as to say I do, then I know the choices you like to make. Choose life, my Rosie, choose life."

"What do you think you are doing?" says a voice in my ear. I jump. I have fallen asleep on the floor with my head resting on an upside-down crate. The steel-blue eyes of the manager blur and then focus in my vision. I see every pore on his face.

"Trying to hasten your hanging day, aren't you? You've had enough of this miserable existence? Get to work now or we will get this over with tonight. I will tie your arms behind your back with the rope and then wrap it tight around your neck and we will watch you float on the ceiling."

I get up and start washing the bullets as he watches over my shoulder.

I have just as much choice as you do, I think, and I wait until he walks away.

34

DUDERSTADT. FEBRUARY 1945.

"Favor me God
For feeble am I
Heal me God
For shudder with terror
Do my bones.
My soul is terrified utterly
And you God,
Until when?
Desist God
Release my soul
Save me
As befits your kindness.
For there is no mention of you in death
In the grave
Who will praise you?"

Psalm 6:2–5

The days and nights pass slowly in a blurry streak. There are often the sounds of planes flying overhead and distant bombing. There are rumors circulating that the planes are the Allies, coming to redeem us. I wake up in the middle of the night and there are two lumps on my chest and one under my arm. They are slightly hard; they feel like rubber, and they move beneath my skin.

"Do you know what these are?" I ask the girl who sleeps next to me.

She has been in this war longer than I have. "Tumors," she says simply. "I have seen them on other girls who were in Auschwitz with us. I think it is because they put bromine in the food to make us not get our periods and the medication causes these tumors."

"What did the other girls do?"

She gives me a plain look. "They are not bothered by anything now."

"What can I do about them?"

She shrugs. "Maybe try the doctor here?"

"Yes, that is what I will do."

Before the SS women come with the food I crawl out of bed and go straight to the doctor. I've heard a doctor named Rivka has a little triage set up on the side of the barrack in a small hut. I walk into the bare hut and sit there and wait until an old-looking woman walks down the path toward me.

"I have these bumps all over my body," I say as she walks in. "I need you to get them out of me."

She has a very tired looking face, and she nods when I say I have bumps. Like she has seen them too many times before.

"Let me have a look at you." She opens my uniform. "I don't believe this! Oh, my goodness!" She begins to spit out Polish phrases.

I am worried that she is alarmed by the size of the lumps.

"Look at you, in this hellhole, with all these atrocities, you actually make sure to keep yourself clean like this? You are sparkling! You are doing a great thing."

I smile and she pats me on my bald scalp. But then she looks sad again and she shakes her head. "These tumors will kill you, but look what they give me, only this rusty blunt knife. No anesthesia, no medication, the only thing I have is this knife. But if you leave the tumors alone, you for sure will die; if I try to take them out maybe you will live, maybe you will die."

"Take them out," I say, without hesitation.

She shakes her head. "Look at this knife. Look at what I have. Just this knife. They call me a doctor, but it is a joke. I am nothing without my equipment. No medication, no alcohol, not even a simple numbing cream. How can I do this with just a knife?"

I look straight into her eyes. "Kind doctor, please, I want to go home, please, take them out."

She nods slowly. "There is no other way."

"This is what we have to do, so we will do it," I say. I am not scared. I just want the tumors gone.

"Come sit down on this chair and hold on to the sides of it."

I do what she says. I close my eyes. She opens my uniform and holds one hand on my skin. Her hand is cold, but it is firm and still, and it steadies the beating of my heart.

"I am so sorry," she says as she takes her knife and slices it across my skin.

At first, I feel nothing at all as I watch my skin get slit open and blood run wild as if it is a prisoner being set free after years of confinement. Then I gasp as I feel the searing pain and I cannot breathe. She sticks her fingers through the wound and opens my flesh wider. Then she takes the knife again and twists it inside me. The pain intensifies to a level I have never felt before in my life. All the vessels in my chest are being twisted. I put my arm in my mouth to muffle my screams. She pulls out a tumor the size of a grape and puts in on the table. She takes a cloth and presses it to the wound and my blood pounds at the wound site, angry that it is being blocked from coming out. Finally, slowly, the pain begins to subside.

"Raise your arm now," she says, and she has tears in her eyes.

I raise my arm above my head and close my eyes and there is a flash of pain all over again. Cut, cut, cut; she hacks away at my underarm. I feel my eyes roll back in my head and vomit piles up in my throat and I faint. She slaps my face and I wake up as she is bandaging me again.

"You are doing great, my brave, clean girl," she says and suddenly my mother stands there next to me, and she wipes my forehead with a cold washcloth like she did when I was sick as a little girl. "Here, drink the orange juice, Mamale."

"I can't Mama, it hurts too much to drink."

"Drink my baby." She places the cup to my lips.

"But I am going to throw up. It hurts too much."

"I know baby, I know, but you have to drink."

"I am nauseous, I don't want to drink, Mama. It hurts so much. It just really hurts me."

"Shh, come open your mouth, it will help. I know, my baby, I know."

She lets me collapse into her arms and she drops the orange juice on my tongue. Then she holds me while I lean over and vomit all over the floor.

"You did the right thing," she says when I am done. "I am so sorry you are sick my baby. You are going to feel better soon. I just know." Then she is gone.

The doctor wraps me with white gauze pads. "You did great. No more tumors."

"Thank you, doctor."

"Don't thank me. I am going to write you a note of mercy for the SS women, you can't go to work until your wounds heal, OK?"

"That is more than OK." I hold on to the chair to steady myself.

"You are going to be healthy now," she says. "Go back to your barrack."

I walk slowly through the snowy path. My whole body throbs but it is all worth it. I am going to be OK!

The next morning the SS finds me still in bed when she comes into the barrack. "What are you doing lazy pig?" she yells at me. "I am going to kill you! What are you doing still in bed?"

I shove the note out to her and she takes it. She reads the doctor's order that says I need mercy from work until my wounds heal.

"OK, you can stay in here, but only until you recover. You had better be grateful."

I am grateful but my heart tugs when I see Leah walk out with the rest of the girls. Her head is low, and her arms hang limply at her sides. She is not going to make it if she continues to work so hard.

When she comes in late that night, she is grayer than ever and so skinny she is almost translucent.

"Are you OK? How was it today?" I ask.

She sighs and lays her head on my shoulder for a second. "I cannot do this anymore."

I want to hug her and hold her but just then the SS walks in and we all scamper apart to our beds.

The next morning the SS woman barges through the door of our barrack to find two girls left behind instead of one. "You, you!" She points a disgusted finger at me. "I know why you are here, you have 'mercy' because of your wounds. But what is she . . ." She swivels her finger to Leah, whom I had tucked into her bed with the scratchy blanket covered tightly over her whole body up to her nose. ". . . What is she doing in here?"

Leah looks like a mummy, lying straight as a board with the blanket tightly wrapped around her body. Her big, brown eyes are the only part of her that is visible. They are wide with fear.

The SS woman stealthily advances closer to her, hand up in the air ready to whip off her blanket. If she doesn't find any bandages or boils, we will both be shot.

"She is sick," I say quickly.

Leah's huge brown eyes stick out from the top of the blanket wide and unblinking.

"Can't you see?" I say. My voice is strong and clear. I hardly recognize it, but I must convince the SS to let Leah stay with me today. "What can't you see? This girl is sick, she has boils all over her skin, contagious boils. Do you want to be the one answering to why she isn't working in the factory next week because she was sick and forced to work this week?"

"She has boils on her body?" The SS woman asks, narrowing her eyes.

"Oh yes, she does." I cross my arms and look straight at her.

She looks at me and says, "I will see you both in the factory right on time next week!" and then she turns around and walks out. I wait until she is out of earshot and then I turn to Leah and with a laugh I pull her covers off.

"Not a boil on your body but she didn't even check, and that old cow just walked straight out of here." I put Leah's cover back on her and march around her bed. "Ah, these boils on you are bad," I say and peer at Leah's arms. "So bad you should have mercy always. Maybe, just maybe, if I didn't smell like a horse your boils would be better. Maybe if the warts on my face would go away you would have a chance of getting better, perhaps. Do you think I should leave?"

I march to the door in an exaggerated way and then I hear a weird sound. I freeze. It's a sound I haven't heard in what feels like a million years. I slowly turn around. Leah is giggling. I look at her in shock and then laughter pours like seltzer from my throat. I climb into bed with her, and we both laugh and laugh.

"I don't know if I can do this anymore, Rosie," she says mid-laugh and I quickly sober up.

"Of course, you can, it's almost over. Don't you hear the planes? It's the Allies coming. What do you think we are here for? To make bullets to fight the Allies because they are strong, and the Nazis know that."

"Yes, and the Allies will bomb us before anyone can liberate us. We are working in the factory that is hindering their victory."

"They won't find it; we are so well hidden."

"Lose-lose; they won't bomb us, but they'll never find us, and we will be stuck making the ammunition to fight them forever."

"Leah! Stop this talk, you are so strong. You can do this. You don't have a choice. Come with me, we have not washed ourselves in a while, and we have to keep clean to stay healthy."

"Oh, leave me alone. I am so tired."

"Don't you even think about it. I got you out of work, so now I can tell you what to do."

"Bossy," she says. But she smiles and she lets me lead her to the bathroom.

35

DUDERSTADT. MARCH–APRIL 1945.

"Hungry
As well as thirsty
Their soul wrapped itself
In them."

Psalm 107:5

My wounds heal, as do Leah's fictitious boils. We start working in the factory again, arriving at our stations every day before the sun comes up and then we are taken straight from there to pick sugar canes in the freezing cold. I feel myself slipping further and further away from reality. I cannot help it; my brain does not want to stay in the factory or the fields, so it goes back to where it most loves to be: home.

One day there is whispering from the table next to mine and they are pointing to something and then the whole factory is buzzing slightly. Everyone seems to be looking up. I look in the same direction, up to the window, and I see a newspaper pressed to the glass.

"AMERICAN AND RUSSIAN ARMIES ADVANCING. END OF WAR IMMINENT" the post reads. The rest of the article is too small to make out.

"The war is almost over!" I hear a girl whisper from the booth next to me, but I am too tired to care. I look up at the paper again and it rustles and moves, and I see the telltale face of Ediger behind it as his hands struggle to hold it up for us to see. It is raining and the newspaper smacks on the window from the wind.

I am home again suddenly, and it is raining outside and big leaves smack onto the window as they rustle and whip in the wind. Yecheskel sits by the table with his book, deep in concentration as he sways back and forth and sings with his learning. He looks like he has been transported to another world. It is cold and rainy outside but inside we have a fire, and it is toasty and warm. We have nothing to do besides lay on the couch and rest. We eat chestnuts, lazily cracking each one open and slowly popping the pieces into our mouths and rolling them around on our tongues.

BOOM! The factory shakes.

"What was that?" yells an SS.

BOOM! SWOOSH! SWOOSH!

Some girls scream.

"Shut up you idiots!" the SS says. "We need to see what is happening!"

"It is those damn American jets! They are getting closer!"

Suddenly it is quiet.

"They didn't see us," says another SS. "Idiots, missed us again."

"They could bomb us any day. We need to get out of here. Let us just leave the girls here and go."

We all look around shaking.

"We are not going anywhere just yet," says the manager. "We can always run into the trucks and go to the city. We will leave the girls here."

The sounds of the planes fade into the distance. I hope the Americans do not find us and bomb us to smithereens.

A few hours later, as we work, Ediger puts another newspaper in the window, but I am too tired to try to squint and see what it says.

The sounds of army planes get louder every day. The SS become agitated and even more hostile. As we work, we hear snippets of their conversations. The SS women stand in their own corners. The men look just as panicked as the women. There is one SS woman who we gossip about at night. We call her *Katalin Karády*[1] because when we first arrived here, she looked just like the famous singer and movie star. But now she doesn't look anything like a movie star, she looks nervous and ragged. She doesn't wear lipstick anymore; she no longer smiles at the other SS women. Her fingernails were always perfectly polished but now they are ragged.

One night as I wash the bullets, there is a loud BOOM and the entire factory rattles.

"What was that?" an SS yells.

"They are bombing us you idiot!" the manager yells. "To the doors!" The SS all make a beeline for the door. They rush out and lock us in before any of us can leave.

We gather around. First it is silent as we hear the whistling of bombs falling from overhead.

"The Nazis have been out there a while, maybe they were hit by a bomb?" one girl finally says.

"I do not think they can do that without hitting us," someone else says.

I feel the walls close in on me.

Soon the booming stops and the soldiers walk back in. They have snow falling from their jackets like a dog shedding hair. Their faces are red and chapped looking. They move stiffly as though their limbs are blocks of ice. They must have laid down in the snow to hide from the bombs.

We do not disband back to our stations. Someone starts to giggle at the soldiers. They do look funny, like frozen statues covered in white powder trying to walk. Suddenly we are all laughing. The soldiers are still terrified; they ignore us. We laugh out of exhaustion, out of the hurt and pain and hunger. We look at the frozen snowmen Nazis. The more we look at them, the more we giggle. The Nazis are frozen and so are we, tiny skeleton girls without even a sweater in the dead of winter. But there is laughter glowing in our bellies. We are together, so we are warm enough.

The planes come close a few times each week. The Nazis always run out of the factory. As we listen to the swoosh and roar of the planes overhead, I imagine bombs falling and an explosion blowing up the factory until we are strewn over the whole forest. Mama, Zaidy, Yecheskel and sometimes even my father come to visit me, and they smile as they wash the dishes with me in the warm and quiet kitchen. After an hour of circling planes, the sound fades and then the SS come back into the factory and stroll around as if nothing has happened.

Then it gets worse. BAM! SWOOSH. BANG! BANG! This noise is different than all the others. This noise sounds like it is right above our heads.

The SS yell and run out of the factory like scared little boys.

I am shaking.

"We have to do something with the girls!" an SS says. The SS women are already outside. Three SS stay behind and herd us into a little room with no windows. Their rifles are out and pointed at us. They stuff us into the room in quick succession and lock the big metal door. We all scramble over each other to get on solid ground. We are silent as we hear their boots banging further away and the planes sound like they are even closer. We are trapped but I am not staying here. I run to the door and shake it hard. It does not budge.

"We have to get out of here!" I scream to the girl standing next to me.

She looks at me.

"Help me open the door!"

She pulls it hard.

It does not move. It is made of iron.

"We are stuck!" she says.

BOOM! The whole room shakes.

I hear a splintering of glass.

A colossal shattering. These bombs are different. These bombs are right here.

We both grasp the door and try to pull it together.

"Help us!" I yell to the other ones.

Two girls come to our side and start pulling with us.

"What is the matter with you all?" I yell to everyone else. "Come help us get this door open!"

A tall girl stands in the middle of the room. She is skinny; her dress flows on her like a tent and her shaven head sticks out from it. She smiles at me serenely. "Come sit." She points to the floor next to her. "Do you need a good recipe for kokosh cake?" she asks as she turns to the group of girls surrounding her.

I gape at her.

"Oh yes," a small girl sitting next to her says. "I am no good at baking, but I would love to get that right. Do you think I can use the dough from my challah for that?"

"No way, too airy. Kokosh cake dough must be thick and moist enough to hold the oozing chocolate. I will give you a good, sweet recipe for the dough and then all you will have to do is mix cocoa powder with powdered sugar. Roll the sweet dough out thinly and pour oil on it lightly and smear the cocoa mixture all over it. Twist the dough into a long snake and then into a figure 8. It should be soft and stretchy in your hands. Then bake for 35 minutes. It is divine."

"You must give us the recipe," another girl says.

My heart races and I pull harder at the door.

"Give it up," says Leah softly and she pulls at my hand. I push her away and yank harder at the door.

"The bombs!"

"I know," she says. "There is nothing we can do."

"I have a really good recipe for cream of chicken soup," says another girl as she sits in the circle with her legs folded like stacked sticks on top of each other.

"How do you get a chicken soup creamy?" asks the girl on her right.

"It is the root vegetables. I pull them from my garden right before I make the soup. To get the flavor, first boil the chicken bones in a pot of water for at least an hour. Then, add in celery root, parsnip, parsley root, potatoes, and celery. Flavor it with parsley and ginger. When it is finished cooking, pound down the vegetables and then put the soup through a strainer. The soup will have a rich chicken flavor combined with the smooth creaminess and earthiness of the vegetables."

"Mmm," says another girl in response. "I am going to try that tomorrow. I can never seem to give my soup enough flavor.

"Oh, heavenly."

"I have a great recipe for *yapchik,*"[2] says another girl. She is so skinny; her thighs are as narrow as her wrists. Her eyes bulge out of her tiny face. "You should really try this, too. You grate the potatoes as fine as you can get them, almost to a dust..."

There is a massive explosion. The ground shakes and feels like it is trying to hold itself together. I am as stiff as a board with fright.

I see Chanky standing absolutely frozen.

"Please, someone get me out of here!" I scream.

"We have to get out of here!" the girl next to me repeats.

Everyone else ignores us.

Tears rush to my eyes. If we don't get out of this room, we will be trapped here with no one looking for us until we all rot to death.

"... then add five eggs," the girl continues, as if nothing has happened, "and a cup of oil. Oh, and don't forget the onion, grate that up finely, too. Then add the meat. Make sure it's the real fatty kind, the kind that gets soft. Bake the yapchik overnight in a very low heat oven. You won't be able to sleep all night with the smell of that yapchik cooking. But don't take it out; when you eat it in the morning you will feel like you are in Gan Eden."

"I must try that! My husband will love it. Maybe I will make it for Pesach, it is coming up soon."

"Who can wait for Pesach? I want to make it tonight."

Everyone laughs. Another smashing bang: the room is closing in on me.

"For dessert, you can make meringues, there's no flour in them so they are perfect for Pesach. They taste like a cloud. The trick is to whip up lots of egg whites until they look like the mountains in the winter. Then pour in lots and lots of sugar, but pour it in slowly, make the sugar drizzle in. Keep whipping it until your arm feels like it is going to fall off. Then put dollops of the whip on a baking sheet and bake for only seven minutes."

"Oh goodness, flour or no flour, I am going to make that tonight."

There is another deafening smashing sound and I want to tear out whatever hair I have on my head.

"I just made an incredible roast chicken the other day," says the girl who looks like a willow. "I was reading this book and in it they were eating the most amazing fish; I knew I had to make it into a chicken recipe."

"Ha! That always happens to me!" says the short girl at her side. "That's the worst part about reading a book with food in it when you are hungry! Suddenly you are craving the black, shriveled, deeply mysterious olive, when you have never even tasted one before!"

"Yes, all the time! This book had me running to the kitchen to cook before I could even finish the chapter!"

"What is the recipe?" someone else calls from the other side of the circle.

"It is called orange-fennel chicken. Mix olive oil, the juice from two oranges, the juice from two lemons, two big spoonfuls of whole-grain mustard, and salt and pepper. Take a full chicken, plucked and cleaned, and sprinkle it with salt and pepper. Quarter a fennel bulb and place the pieces around the chicken. Pour the sauce over everything and then sprinkle thyme on top of it all. Let it marinade for two hours and then roast it, uncovered, in the oven for 45 minutes. My goodness, that aroma that will come from the oven and send you over the edge! When it is done the chicken should be bubbling and crispy and the fennel soft like butter. Dip a bite of that moist chicken into the sweet, thick sauce and add a piece of fennel, put it in your mouth and close your eyes, and you will thank me again and again."

I watch the girls around her close their eyes and smile as if they could taste the chicken right then. My stomach rumbles but no time for that. I am about to be crushed or blown apart; I need to get this door opened.

"We all are mad!" I tell the girl next to me. I know I hallucinate here, but this is different. "We all are crazy, stupid mad!" I continue. "We are a bunch of starved girls trapped in a room with bombs about to fall on us and blow us apart, and we are trading recipes!"

Another smashing boom and my heart hammers. The door still won't budge. I start to cry, and I sit myself down among the cooking girls and wait to die. But I don't die yet. Soon the smashing and booming stops and a few hours later an SS opens the door. As I file out of our tiny tomb, stretching my cramped legs, I finally take my first normal breath in hours.

"What are you waiting for?" The SS bellows at us.

No one laughs now.

"Get to work!"

We walk to our stations and continue to work as if nothing has happened.

36

ON THE WAY FROM GERMANY TO PRAGUE.
APRIL 5–12, 1945.

"I am poured out like water
and all my bones are out of joint
my heart is become like wax
it is melted in mine innermost parts."

Psalm 22:15

"This is the last time I have to wake you up," a voice says in my ear.

I open my eyes and my heart jumps. The manager stands in front of me again; I must have fallen asleep. I can't help it. It is a torture to keep my eyes open. I count the dry flakes of skin between his eyebrows.

"Tomorrow night is the night," he says, and he looks up at the ceiling. He studies it for a few minutes as he cocks his head to the side. "Do you reckon that ceiling is strong enough to hold your weight? It should be. Everything is ready, I even got permission from higher authorities, they agreed you would be a good example to the other girls. And the rope came, and it is strong and tomorrow night is the perfect night to do it. So that will be that. And if you do not come to work tomorrow, I will hunt you down—and I will torture all of your friends." I look at his face and don't answer him. Ediger passes by us and shakes his head sadly. I know he will not do anything to me. I am going home from here.

I walk into the factory the next night, keeping an eye out for my unmerciful bully. When I get to my station Ediger comes over to me with a smile that lights up his whole face.

"Did you hear?" he says. "The manager is gone! They moved him to the front. To the front! He will never bother you again!"

My whole body exhales with relief. The front. I beam at my old friend; we know what happens to people who fight in the front.

"Can you believe it?" Tears are in his eyes, but he laughs. All the lines on his face seem to lift upward.

I have never seen someone so joyful in my life.

"He's fighting in the front!" I say and I start laughing.

He smacks his hands down on his knees and laughs even louder and I join with him and we laugh.

Other SS men pass by us and stare, but no one tries to stop us.

The Allies are close. We all know it. More and more SS disappear to go to the front lines and the planes fly overhead more frequently. The SS men have darting eyes and huddle together often to whisper to each other. Some girls like seeing them scared, but I feel just as trapped as they do. If they are bombed, we are bombed along with them. Plus, with their fear they get more violent. A girl drops her weapon and the soldier doing rounds jumps and ducks from the sound. He turns red when he sees her crouching on the floor next to the fallen gun. He masks his embarrassment with rage, and he picks up the gun and brings it down hard onto her head. She cries out once and he brings it down again, harder. He is not a soldier anymore; he is an animal. She is silent. The rest of us look straight ahead.

Finally, he is done, and he walks away. Someone helps her up and there is blood running from her head. She stands by her table, picks up the gun and wipes the blood off it. Then she dunks it into the water.

"I cannot see anything," she whispers.

We are all in shock.

"Do not let them know that," I say. "They only want you if you can work."

"I will help you," someone else says and moves closer to her station.

"They will be defeated soon," a girl says to make us feel better, "the Allies are so close. The SS are scared."

"They haven't found us yet," another girl says.

"They are close though," the first girl says, "even the soldiers know it. Yesterday one of them asked me if I had a white sheet. A white sheet, can you imagine? I don't have a single pair of underwear and he wants a white sheet!" She shakes her head.

"What would he want a white sheet for?" I ask, placing the last dry bullet into a wooden box.

"Probably to spread it out like a flag of surrender."

They know they are losing, and they want to save themselves.

"So, what did you say when he asked you?"

"I said, 'Sure I have a white sheet, let me just get it down from my armoire. I will get my lady to iron it for you, so it is nice and crisp.'"

"Did you really say that?"

"No," she smiles. "But I would have liked to."

She lifts the wooden box I have just filled with bullets and puts it on the shelf behind her. She takes the next box of dirty bullets and together we dump it into the water basin.

"Can you imagine?" she says. "Can you imagine if they surrender and this will all be over, and we get out of this place?"

I nod my head slightly, but I am too tired to imagine. The only thing I can imagine comes into my head without me summoning it. I am in the kitchen in my house, and it is warm. My grandfather dries the dishes I have washed. Leah sits by the sewing machine. Mama makes another rug. There is a caramelized onion and carrot soup bubbling on the stove. Zaidy smiles and dries every dripping dish I pass to him. Cheskel sings his learning in the background, his voice is still sweet and uncorrupted by adulthood.

"Good going, Cheskel," Zaidy says.

Cheskel sings louder. Zaidy keeps taking the dishes from my hands. He puts them away neatly in the wooden box.

"My beautiful family," he says, and I want to stay in the kitchen forever, but Leah is standing up from the sewing machine. She folds the fabric and places it on the side of the table and comes to me and lifts my hands from the water basin. I try to protest but I cannot talk, and she dries my hands on her dress and leads me outside, to the barrack, to the bed, and she whispers *Shema*[1] as I drift off to sleep.

The next morning, we arrive at the factory and there is an SS waiting for us in the front. He leads us to a side room.

"You can all wait here," he says and then turns and walks away. He closes the door and turns the lock. We huddle there without saying a word; something is happening, but we do not dare to think of what it could be. After what feels like half a day a soldier turns the lock and opens the door. We follow him outside and see two trucks waiting there. He herds us onto them. Leah climbs in first and she turns around and takes my hand and pulls me up. I lean against her, and she pulls me back as the rest of the girls are pushed into the truck. They fill and fill and fill the truck with girls. Someone's head is pressed up against my right cheek, and another's is tight against my shoulder. The truck jerks to a start and then rumbles upwards. Through a slit in the tarp, I can see dark green and brown blend together. It seems like we are going up a very steep hill. The truck turns and all the girls collectively lean into me. There is now a big gray wall and then houses and steel gates and cars. Everything turns gray and then black, and I somehow fall asleep.

The light in our cramped space slowly turns from pink to pale yellow and then bright white. I wake up as we jostle along. My stomach pines for food, coffee, anything. I am starving.

The light turns from gray to navy and then to black again. Pink and yellow and white. Gray and navy and black. Pink, yellow and white. Time stops and I do not know how many days pass as we jostle in the truck.

My stomach turns on itself. My knees won't hold me up. I am suspended by the pile of bodies around me. We are cargo and nothing else.

Suddenly, the truck pulls to a stop and the doors open and a few SS are standing there and in the back of my mind I register that they are screaming. A soldier pulls out a sleeping girl. She falls to the ground onto her head, as if she is dreaming. She doesn't get up. That makes us all move. We untangle ourselves from each other and I watch as spidery limbs unravel, and blank bald faces blink themselves awake. My face mirrors theirs.

"Your Allies are great!" says the SS who opens the door. "They came to liberate you a day after you left the factory." He slaps his uniform and laughs. "Can you imagine? If you had stayed there one more day you would all be free now."

I follow the girl ahead of me off the truck and Leah stays close behind. I see Chanky emerge from the other truck. I see that we are at a train station and a red train is waiting for us.

"Too bad for you now," the SS says. "A matter of timing of a few hours and now you are all going to die. This is your death journey! Schnell, what are you waiting for? Get on the train!!"

The soldiers throw us into the train cars. I get in the second one, some of us go into the third and fourth. There is no space for air to circulate. I am weak and dizzy and now air is hard to come by. The train lurches forward and we all lurch forward with it. The good thing about being packed like a sardine is that there is no space to fall down. The bodies around me hold me up. I fall asleep standing up with another face pinned against mine, like we are hugging or dueling with our hands locked to our sides. The train chugs ahead. I drift into sleep.

BOOM! I am rattled awake. The train screeches angrily to a stop and the train car behind us smashes into our car. We all fly forward together. There is another boom and a smashing sound and the telltale swoosh of a jet flying away. A piece of metal from the ceiling of our car comes loose. For a moment it stubbornly swings on its hinge but then it gives way and falls straight on to a girl's head. It hits her with a dull thud. She looks around shocked and then her eyes go wide.

"I can see! Magda, I can see!" she says.

In the back of my brain, I register her as the girl who was beaten by the SS in the factory. The train is shaking but I see her eyes tear up through the commotion. Blood trickles down her face and mixes with her tears until it becomes a milky pink. She can see again. Our train car shakes and shakes.

When the train stops shaking an SS officer slides the door open. There is a wild look of fear in his usually expressionless eyes.

"Your allies are bombing you!" he yells. "Even your Allies want you dead! Get out now so they can see who you are and stop bombing us! Get out and climb on top of the train, there are more planes coming!"

He picks up the girl closest to the door and flings her to the top of the train like a rag doll. A plane flies low overhead, but then its sound grows distant and I hear it fly away. We all climb off the train.

"Stupid Americans!" the SS man says. "Now they bombed you all."

I look at the train car in front of ours. He is right. It is completely flattened on one side and the back wall has been thrown off and only a skeleton of it remains. A few girls limp out from the carnage and there is blood flowing and there are girls on the car floor who are not moving. I see an arm, ripped from a shoulder, strewn to the side. I try to find the body it belongs to but there is nothing there except raw, gaping flesh. My stomach lurches but there is nothing to come up. The nausea is overwhelming. I turn around and lean on Leah.

"Don't look back," she says.

I don't.

37

THE DEATH MARCH. APRIL 12–26, 1945.

"For His Angels
He will command to watch over you
in all your journeys.
On their palms,
they will carry you,
lest a stone strike against your foot."

Psalm 91:11–12

We stand in middle of the train tracks. There is a mountain to the left of us and a mountain to the right. There is a mutilated train behind us that looks like the skeletons we are: twisted and broken. The soldiers stand in front of us with their strong thighs and high boots and straight faces. They begin to walk with their hands on their rifles. We are whispers of people. We are thin and white and bent over. Skin stretched over bones.

"What are you waiting for?" an SS in the front says. "They bombed your train so now you have to walk!"

"Now walk!" another SS says.

We stare at him blankly.

"You heard me you idiots! March!"

We hold each other's arms and fall into rows of five. Leah is on my right; someone I don't know is on my left. We hold each other up and we march.

We walk and walk and walk. The mountains to my right turn into plains and we still walk. There is a small town with people on the roadsides who gape at us. Dusk sets in and still we walk. There is some grass on the side of the road. I watch as the girl in front of me runs to the side and pulls up some grass with her bony fingers and stuffs it into her mouth. There is a shot, and she falls sideways and blood flows from her head like a stream. The soldier who shot her sticks his rifle back on his side and we continue to march. Someone drops to the ground a few rows in front of me. She is a figure of twisted branches. She puts her head on her knees and she closes her eyes. There is a bullet whizzing past us and straight to her head in a split second. Her body crumples forward. Now we all know what will happen if we dare to take a break.

There is nothing worse than this gnawing hunger. I am starving. My stomach turns in on itself and my heart beats fast, then slow. Then, like a dream, there are rotting potatoes on the side of the road. The girl in front of me sees them first. She runs to them and lays on her stomach and stuffs the potatoes in her mouth with both hands. Her mouth is so full of potatoes it looks like she will swallow them without chewing. She stuffs another potato in her mouth and in a split second there is an SS man besides her. He slams his rifle into the back of her head and her neck. Then he flips her over and smashes her chest and stomach. She convulses and shakes, and we march on, and she is left in that field to die all alone. Somehow, in my starving stupor, I remember to look out for Chanky. It is hard to find her because we all look the same now. I finally spot her a few rows ahead, dragging her once beautiful legs.

My feet are slow, but the SS do not slow down. Leah pulls me forward. We walk and walk and walk and I slip further away. We march on with no sound except for the steady *click-clack* of the soldiers' boots and the *thump-thump* of our wooden shoes. There is still snow on the ground and the wood on our shoes picks up every bit of it until we can barely walk. I hear shots and someone cries out, but I can't turn my head to see who has fallen. The sky slowly turns colors. First lilac, then gray, then dark navy, then black. There are a million stars around me, and I am slipping, and they become a kaleidoscope of a million twisting lights. There is no more grass or mountains or small towns. I am completely hidden. I am nothing at all. The air is thick, and it is an exhausting effort to lift my legs through it. The sun comes up and we make our way through a few more towns. When the sun is already high in the sky, we pass through a new town, and I notice there are people standing by the road. I look up and see their backs retreating. The backs of men and women and little children with aprons and plaid shirts and little brown knickers. There is bread thrown to our feet and then the people are running away because there are shots, but some still throw the bread over their shoulders as the shots ring out. Anyone who lays on the ground with bread in their hands, halfway to stuffing it into their face, is shot. We walk over the bread and the girls to continue to march.

"Schnell! Schnell!" the SS scream. We are just a long line of emaciated girls walking over loaves of forbidden bread. We walk on.

I am so hungry, but I do not feel it in my stomach anymore. I feel the hunger in my heart, in the way it flaps wildly. I feel it in the cells in every inch of my body; they yearn for energy, for the buzz that food gives them. My cells have been drained of everything they ever had. I am gutted and hollow. I am so tired I cannot take another step.

"Louse! Louse!" the SS soldiers yell. They walk past us and hit us with their sticks. "You need to move faster!"

Faster? I cannot stand one moment longer.

Leah feels me falling. She squeezes my hand and straightens me.

I was strong the entire time I was in the war, but now there is not an ounce of strength left in my body. I want to be strong, but strength is nowhere to be found. "Leah," I say. "I cannot do this anymore. I cannot take another step."

Another girl drops to the side of the road. An SS comes over to her and slams his rifle on her chest. She does not move, and he leaves her there to die slowly. But she can lay down now. I do not pity her.

Leah grips my arm with a strength I did not know she possessed. "You have to Rosie," she says.

I have not eaten a morsel of food in days. My bones feel like lead in my body. Every time I put my foot down it is a struggle to lift it up again. My muscles are slack. I am overcome with nausea. Empty bile and air rumble in my stomach.

"I cannot take another step, Leah. I give up."

"Rosie, I do not care, you have to march."

"I am so tired. Please let me lay down. It will be over before I know it and then I won't feel anything."

"They will shoot you, or worse just beat you so you will die slowly; you are not laying down!"

"I don't care, I just need to lay down. Leah, I really cannot do this anymore. I don't want to die but I can't do this, I can't." I fall slowly forward. The stars in the sky become blurry and they beckon me to join them. Leah pinches my hand hard, and the stars come back into focus again.

"Listen to me now, Rosie," she says forcefully, "and listen to me good. You are not laying down now. This is almost over. We are going to be free. You did not make me live through this whole thing so you could give up now. If you wanted to sleep, you should have let me sleep months ago. Not now. Now, you march."

I look at the road in front of me. Past the bent-over girls who drag their feet. Past the SS soldiers who still walk straight and proud. The road is endless and black, and the thought of taking another step feels like climbing a whole mountain. I want to scream but I am too tired, so I let out a whimper. A tear comes to the corner of my eye, and I am surprised there is enough water in me to produce it.

"I cannot do this anymore."

"Rosie, yes you can."

"I can't."

"Well, don't you know? You have to."

I whimper again, and then with a strength I didn't know I had I lift up my right foot. I feel as if I am picking up a thousand boulders of stone. I feel as if I am balancing the weight of the world on my skinny knee.

I take the step.

Suddenly, I feel someone come up to me on my right and another on my left. I look, but no one is there. There is no mistaking it, though: there is a presence around me. I feel my right side lifted and then my left. I look right and left but still, no one is there. This isn't like when I hallucinated in the ammunition factory. I knew I was dreaming then, escaping. This is different. The beings on my right and left feel strong and sure. They lift me off the ground with a steady strength. I am gliding in the air with them. My feet don't touch the ground. They hold me up, firm and sure, and I am enveloped by their goodness. I am calm and I let them hold me. They don't put me down until we get there.

38

THERESIENSTADT. APRIL 26–MAY 8, 1945.

"That you showed me great evils and troubles
You will revive me once again
And from the depths of the earth
You will again raise me up."

Psalm 71:20

We arrive at the gates of another camp. We stand there and wait to go in. The ground is pounding but not from the thud of bombs. It comes from the steady walk of hundreds of prisoners who look just like us, their wooden shoes hitting the ground. *Boom, boom, boom, boom. Boom, boom, boom, boom. Boom, boom, boom, boom.* Skeletons putting one step in front of the other. There are now thousands of them. They have sunken cheeks and hollow eyes and their ripped uniforms float over their skin and bones.

We walk along with the thousands of other prisoners, into the camp. We are led to a fortress deep inside the ground. The SS open the heavy wooden door and we are pushed underground. Inside is a bunker and we all fall onto the thin beds. The SS closes the door, and we are pitched into darkness. We are buried alive.

We lay there for days. We do not move from our beds, only to get food that is sometimes pushed through the door.

Some girls speak from their beds.

"They only want to gas us. Do you know? They will gas us too."

"They just want us dead."

"That is what we are waiting for."

I do not have enough energy to add to the conversation. I lay there, still.

One night there is bombing and shooting for hours and hours.

BOOM! Our sunken bunker shakes.

"Maybe it is the Russians trying to liberate us."

"Maybe it is the Americans."

"Maybe it is the Germans, and they are winning."

We fall silent. We are already buried. We are already dead.

We hear the bullets whistle through the air, we hear bombs exploding in the distance, we hear shots repeatedly.

That night, the booms continue nonstop. Then, as a slight ray of sunshine mixed with dust that pushes through a tiny crack in the door. All the noise stops.

We do not move from our beds.

Hours later someone opens the door. He climbs down to us. "Girls!" he says.

No one moves.

"Don't you know? You are free!"

We stare blankly at him.

"Children, children," he says. "You are free. The Russians liberated us. You are all free."

"He went crazy," someone says. "What is he talking about?"

We look at each other from our hard, wooden planks.

"No, no, children, it is true. You are free," he says again.

"Free?" Leah says. "Free? We are free?"

"Free?" Someone else repeats. "What do you mean we are free?"

"Yes, children," he says. "You are free."

"Do you mean to say we are free?" We are incredulous. We cannot wrap our brains around that word.

To show us, he climbs up and pushes against the heavy door. It opens all the way and blinding sunlight fills our bunker. Mud and dust swirl with it. I make the first move. I run toward the door and lift myself up. I climb out of the bunker. I rise from my grave and come alive again. We are free and I am still alive. Me? I am alive? I almost want to laugh.

I pull more girls out of the bunker, and they climb around me until they are above the ground. I watch more girls pull themselves out, alive, from our grave. Their skin is tight against their bones; they have no flesh on their bodies. They are covered in dust and rags. But they are alive.

We blink for a few moments in the sunlight. No one moves. Then I look around. The ground is lush and bursting with green grass and bushes everywhere, growing on top of the bunker that we laid in. I blink and then everything in front of me comes into focus. I cannot believe what I see. There are flowers all around us. Tears spring to my eyes. There are tiny blue flowers growing from the grass. They are a purplish blue with a perfect light-yellow circle in the middle of them. They spring from the ground in miniature bouquets of three. Next to the blue flowers are orange flowers shaped like a bell. They hang upside down in perfect, sweet humbleness. There are pink flowers on a stem, straight then slowly unfurling. There are white flowers that drape over each other. There are long stalks of green, as straight as rifles. Brilliant yellow sunshine bursts all around us. It has been months since I have seen color. I do not know how long we laid in the bunker but while we were there, these flowers were only seeds, disintegrating underground just as we were until they became something new and pushed their heads through the earth. We sit down among the flowers and my tears blur them into a watercolor of soft and bright hues. I am alive. All the time I was buried underground, there were flowers growing on top of me.

"Leah, we are alive. Just look at these flowers."

Leah looks at them. A soft smile forms on her face.

"Look what God is doing," I say.

I said I was going to go home, but when I was buried underground, I was not sure I believed it anymore. I was tired and breaking apart. Now I sit here among the flowers, and I know there is a God and there is life still to be had. I am going to go home. I am going to live. I am going to have a family. The flowers sway in a light breeze. I never believed I would see a sight like this again in my life.

"We are going to go home, we are going to be OK," I say in an awed whisper. "Leah, this is never going to happen again."

Leah squeezes my hand.

I look at the skeleton girls around me and I know that we have a long road ahead of us. But right now, we are surrounded by flowers. There is beauty in the world we thought did not exist anymore. We are alive again and the flowers tell us there is a life still waiting for us. We rise like the flowers and push our heads into the world. I breathe in the sweet perfume of grass and lavender.

"Leah," I say.

"Yes, Rosie?"

"Let's go home."

39

THE WAY HOME. MAY 1945.

"They will be planted in God's house
And bloom in the courtyard of our God.
In old age they will still be fruitful,
They will be robust and fresh."

Psalm 92:13–14

Getting home is easier said than done. Theresienstadt is infected with typhus. The grounds are covered with sick people who are too weak to move. They lay in groups, moaning and shivering and then laying still. Russian women come in to clean the place up. I have never seen women clean up a mess as efficiently as they do.

The man who told us we are free comes down to our bunker the night after we are liberated.

"We are looking for volunteers," he says.

"For what?" someone asks.

"We need girls to work."

I do not wait for him to say what kind of work they need. I knew in Auschwitz that work would kill me. I know that here, work will keep me alive.

"I volunteer!" I say.

He assigns me to work in the nursing home.

"Why is there a nursing home here?" I ask as he walks me there the next morning. We walk over people laying on the ground, waiting for death. He shakes his head.

"Sick Nazi propaganda," he says. "The Germans invited the Red Cross to come see this camp as if it were an example of all the camps. They even made films here. When the Red Cross came, they had an orchestra of Jews playing and people watching and enjoying it. When the Red Cross left, they killed every last Jew in the orchestra."

"So, they kept an old age home just to show the Red Cross?" I ask.

"Yes, and some children too."

I do not have anything else to say.

We reach the old age home, and he sends me inside.

"I am going to go recruit more volunteers," he says. "We have so much to do."

I walk into the nursing home by myself. There are rows of beds with ancient looking people laying on them. They look like they are waiting for death to come and claim them already.

"Who is here?" An old lady says from her bed. She sits up. Her skin is translucent.

"My name is Rosie Greenstein," I say. "I have come to help."

More people sit up in their beds.

I gulp nervously as they all watch me.

"Rosie, thank you for coming," says another lady. "Step closer so we can see you."

I spend the day talking to them, feeding them, washing them, and then I go back to the bunker to go to sleep.

I go to the old age home every day. The elderly people there love me. They direct me to the attic where there are suitcases of forgotten clothing. They tell me I can take what I want. I bring back a suitcase full of beautiful floral dresses to the bunker. Each of us picks out a pretty dress. When I get dressed the next morning to go to work, I start feeling better about myself already.

My cousin Faigy and I take walks every evening when I get back from the old age home. A boy from Faigy's town joins us. His name is Pinchas Hershcovitz. It is clear to me that Faigy is falling in love with him. She looks up at him while he talks, her face in a rapture from his every word. But slowly I realize with a horrible guilt that he isn't falling in love with Faigy, but rather, he is falling in love with me. I will not be the one to get in the way of my cousin. Anyway, it is time to find my mother.

When I get back to the bunker that night, I speak to Leah about going home.

She is starting to look better already, and wearing a green floral dress that is tied with a ribbon at her waist. Her hair has grown in short, and it almost looks stylish. The rice that they feed us here has added some shape to her cheeks. "We need to go home," I say. "Mama and Yecheskel might be there already."

Leah nods. "How are we going to get home?"

"There are trains of soldiers going toward Hungary. I heard the soldiers talking about them. We can get on board. There is one leaving tomorrow morning."

"I met a boy," Leah says. "Can he come with us?"

"A boy?" Here?" I try to keep the annoyance out of my voice. "We need to go to Mama." Now is hardly the time for boyfriends.

Leah blushes. "His name is Avrumi Frankel. He saw me through a window and came down to meet me. He says he knew right away he wants to marry me."

"Leah, this is not how we do things. We must go see Mama first. What will she say if we come home with a boy? She won't be happy."

Leah's face falls. She knows I am right.

"I'll tell him he can't come home with us then."

The next morning, we find a group of girls and boys going toward the train. Chanky, Leah, and I walk along with them.

"Leah!" a man's voice says.

Leah blushes. A dark and handsome man comes toward us.

"This is Avrumi," Leah says.

"You must be Leah's sister and aunt," he says. He looks at Leah like she is a movie star, not an emaciated girl.

"You cannot come home with us," I say. "Our mother will not be happy."

"I know," he says. He smiles at Leah. "I will find you afterwards."

We find the platform and wait in huddled groups as the train steams toward us. The train is full of soldiers, but the conductor is kind and lets us ride on top. The ride is exhilarating. We hold onto bars on the rooftop and feel the sweet wind on our faces as the train chugs closer to our mother and our home. The soldiers from the train start to come up to the top. One soldier takes my hand and spins me around. I am bewildered but he is so much stronger than me that I let him lead me as I twirl. He says something in Russian. He spins me around some more and we are dancing on top of the train, then he goes back down to his seat.

"He said he is going to marry you," a girl says in a broken Romanian. She starts laughing. "He said he has a farm at home with a chicken and a hen and he will take you there and make you his wife."

"Oh no, he won't!" I say.

"See if you can stop him," the girl laughs.

More soldiers come up, but these ones do not talk of marriage like the other soldiers did. They start assaulting girls before my eyes. The girls whimper and cry like pitiful baby birds as the soldiers do whatever they want to them. The soldiers act like the girls are objects that they are entitled to. I avert my eyes. It reminds me of *War and Peace,* and I feel like I read that book a million years ago, rather than just a few. Suddenly, a soldier comes toward Chanky and starts touching her. She whimpers. I do not cry like a baby bird. I screech like a wild animal.

"Stop it! Let go of her!" I scream.

The soldier ignores me and carries on. Another soldier starts walking toward me.

God, I whisper to myself. *You let me come home from Auschwitz and no one touched me. Let me go home the way I came here. We need our dignity. Now God, take care again of me because they are not going to touch me or Chanky.*

The soldier comes even closer.

"Ahhhhhhh!" I scream like a wild animal. I let all my anger power my scream. I will still have some control over my life. Everyone must stop doing whatever they want to us like we are not people. I scream so loud, my own ears hurt.

In a second the train stops, and the conductor comes flying up to the top. The soldier backs away from Chanky. The one that was on his way toward me takes an abrupt turn.

"Who is screaming like that?" the conductor asks.

Someone points to me.

"These soldiers are bothering us," I say.

The conductor sees the look of despair in my eyes. His face turns to rage. He bellows at the soldiers. "Get down! Get down now or I will kick all of you off the train! I don't care what you say. Not a single soldier will remain on my train if you continue this behavior!"

The soldiers don't look at us as they follow the conductor down. They do not come up again.

We get off the train in Budapest and there are Russian soldiers everywhere. I do not want to have the same problem as we had on the train, so I put my arm around the first poor boy I see walking. He looks at me bewildered.

"What are you doing with your hand around me, Miss?" he asks.

"Shhh. You are my husband. If the soldiers see I am with a man, they won't bother me."

"Okay," he agrees. And he walks us all the way to the train station on the other side of town.

On the next train we meet Avrumi again. Leah's face lights up. We climb up on top of the train together.

"You cannot come home with us," I remind him.

"I know," he says. "I am going to my hometown, Dej, it is very near to Crasna."

Leah and Avrumi spend the whole train ride talking.

Suddenly there is a Russian soldier next to us. "Come with me," he says to Leah. Leah shrugs him away. The soldier walks away and then turns around and comes back. He walks up to Leah and starts to pull open her blouse.

"Get off of her!" Avrumi says.

The soldier ignores him and sticks his hand up Leah's shirt. I am about to scream but Avrumi is fast. He pulls the soldier back and in the blink of an eye, Avrumi lifts him by the back of his shirt and hauls him over the side. We are going through a tunnel and the soldier disappears down into the darkness. The other soldiers look at Avrumi in shock. I let him travel with us for as long as he wants.

Chanky is depressed. She keeps crying about Duvid and her baby.

"They are OK, Chanky," I say as I try to reassure her.

"You do not understand," Chanky says. "You are just a girl. You do not have a husband; you do not have a child. This is agony for me."

Someone finds Chanky the next day on the train.

"Duvid is alive!! I saw Duvid! He is on the way to Satu Mare."

Chanky shrieks. "Are you sure?"

"Yes!" the man says. "Go to Satu Mare. He is looking for you! He talks about nothing but you!"

Chanky is ecstatic. "I am going to Satu Mare! Duvid is alive! Come with me!"

"We need to go home, Chanky," I say. "Our mother is waiting for us."

Chanky hugs us and gets off the train to transfer to Satu Mare.

Avrumi gets off by Dej and promises to find Leah as soon as he locates his family.

We finally reach Crasna. I hold Leah's hand as we get off the train. It has only been 13 months since we were last here but as I look at my town, it feels like I have been gone for a million years. We walk slowly to our one-room apartment. I stand next to Leah as we look up at our small building. Maybe our mother is already there, preparing a meal for us. Suddenly someone comes to the window. It is the window where I used to look out at the stream every day and listen to it sing. This was my home. A lady opens the window and sticks her head out, out of my window.

"Oh, look who showed up," she says with a laugh that makes the blood in my body stop cold. "You little girls came home, did you?" Her ugly face contorts. She speaks to us like one speaks to a child, but worse, in a mocking voice. "Oh, you little girls came home?"

There is a big rock on the ground next to the building and I pick it up in my hand. I am ready to hurl it at her and smash her into pieces.

"Put down that rock," Leah says through her teeth. "Do you want to get put into to jail after all we have been through?" She nudges the rock from my hand, and I let it go.

I see the reflection of the stream through the window. The birds do not sing. The trees do not whisper. The stream does not trickle along the colorful rocks.

"Get out of here!" the lady says. "This is not your house anymore."

40

CRASNA. MAY 1945.

"He is the healer
Of the broken-hearted
And the one who bandages
Their sorrows."

Psalm 147:3

Raizy Waldman opens her home to all of us who have come back.
Her house is the biggest and there are enough rooms for everyone.
We wait and wait for Mama and Yecheskel, but they do not come. We
wait for weeks. More and more people stagger into Raizy's house.
They bring rumors, stories, and horrors, one after the next.

Herschel Frankel is one of us, living in Raizy's house. He is
waiting for word of his wife and three children.

One day Hershel asks to speak to me. "Rosie, they aren't coming
back," he says. His words hit me colder than the ice-cold shower I
took in Auschwitz.

"No," I shake my head. "Don't say that."

"Rosie, look at me."

"No, no, no," I say. "I don't want to."

"Rosie, listen to me! My sweet wife, my two daughters, my son . . .

they aren't coming back either. Your Mama, Yecheskel, they are gone. When we got to Auschwitz, they sent them straight to the gas chambers. They put hundreds of people in there at once and poured in poisonous gas that suffocated them."

"No, no, no, no," I say again but I know his words are true. I am cold all over and then my heart is ripped open. It is bleeding inside of me. My whole body is being washed with the blood.

"Mama!" I wail. "Cheskel! Where are you?"

Leah wails too. I want to hug her, but I cannot move. I am dying. It feels like I am ejecting my soul out from my body. From the first moment we come to this earth, we cry, and it is our mothers who soothe us. Even if we don't realize it, every time we sob, we think of our mothers. It is the most primal part of us that cries to our mothers. But what do I do when the very thing I am crying for is my mother? I wail and cry, but I do not have even the knowledge of my mother out there somewhere to hold me when every bit of me shatters into a million little pieces.

"No, no, no! Come back! Yecheskel, come take care of us. Mama, where are you?"

I think about what the people in Raizy's house have been talking about. I think about the revelation that we were being gassed and burned. I try not to think about it, but the image of Yecheskel and Mama gasping for air like fish flopping around, frantically gasping, keeps burning in my mind. I know now why Eidy the Blockälteste cried when we walked out of that gas chamber, bewildered over not having a shower. Eidy was used to opening the gas chamber and helping to transfer the bodies of hundreds of dead girls. Girls with their mouths open, the agony of needing air that will not come etched on their faces forever. I'm told that they kept trucks rumbling next to the gas chambers so the Germans would not have to hear the desperate cries of human beings who pined for air that would keep them alive.

Hershel stays with me the whole time as I cry.

I cry for a week straight. Hershel must force me to eat between my tears. I feel full from my tears but he spoon-feeds me anyway. After a full week, I finally stop crying.

"They aren't coming back," I say to Leah and Hershel.

"No, they are not," Hershel says back.

"And Raizy Waldman is sick," Leah whispers. "She has TB."

"Take me to her," I say.

"She is contagious," Hershel says. "You cannot go near her."

We ignore him and I follow Leah to Raizy's room. She lays in her bed and breathes heavily. Leah and I sit on her bed and do not leave it, except to go to sleep. Raizy was the richest girl in our town, and you never met a more giving person than her. All she wanted was to make her friends and family happy. When I didn't have skates, she insisted I use hers, saying that she liked skating with just her shoes, too. When she brought food to school, she always shared with all of us, leaving herself the smallest piece.

"Raizy, we are here," I whisper over and over to her. She is still a muselmann from Auschwitz and her body can't seem to fight the disease. We are both in her bed with her when she dies.

Hershel Frankel says maybe we can start over again together. I tell him no. I do not want someone who had a wife and children already. I do not want someone who lost even more than me.

We wait for more news of our loved ones. Aunt Chana went straight to the gas chamber with her five children. Yaakov her husband is still alive. Leah Mariam went to the gas chamber too. I know this because her husband's brother, Mr. Schwartz, knocks on the door to Raizy's house one day and asks for me.

"Rosie," he says when I come to the door. He has two children beside him. They are the dirtiest children I have ever seen. Their hair is matted to their faces, they are barefoot, and their hands and feet are black, there is a rash covering their necks, faces, and legs.

"Mr. Schwartz, who are these children?" They hide shyly behind his back.

"Rosie, I don't know what to do with them. It's Baila and Moshe. They came to me today. I just don't know what to do with them. They are your first cousins. Can you help me?"

"Baila, Moshe, come inside," I say. I sit them down at the table and give them each a cup of milk that goes down in an instant. I bring their uncle to the other side of the room. "How did they find you?"

"They were in Auschwitz. A madman, Dr. Mengele, did experiments on them. He had this obsession with twins. He did unspeakable experiments, he tied them together, he starved them. Leah Mariam's other sets of twins died from the experiments, but somehow these two seven-year-olds survived. They were brought to the children's home right after the war, and someone recognized them and brought them to me."

"What do you know about their rashes?" I cannot let myself think about my vivacious little cousins, dead from experiments. I can only focus on what's right here in front of me: two seven-year-old twins sitting at the table, my flesh and blood, swinging their legs and trying to get the last drops of milk out of their cups.

"They cannot stop scratching themselves. It's probably contagious but I cannot bathe them, you're their cousin, can you take care of them?"

I do not mention that he is their uncle, too. "Of course," I say.

The first thing I do is go to the pharmacy and get a cream for their rashes. Then I heat the bath for them. I let them soak in the bath for over an hour while I sing to them. They still don't say a word to me. Then I wash them like I have never washed anything in my life. They have a year's worth of grime, lice, and mud on them. *Leah Mariam will have a heart attack when she sees them,* I think to myself. Then I remember she will never see them again. I pull the lice out, bug by bug. I wash down the grime, I scrub off the mud. After their bath I smear the cream on them and dress them in old clothing that I find in Raizy's house. I bring two very different children back to their uncle.

Of course, my skin breaks out in a rash two days later, but I have kept some of the cream for myself, just in case.

Every night more and more people come to eat at Raizy's house. Men and boys come in, women and girls. We are all like driftwood on the ocean. Once we were trees, but we were uprooted and taken apart —and now we have nowhere to go, and we don't know who we are. Someone plays music after the meals, and everyone gets up, and there is dancing. Leah gets up to dance with the boys and girls, but I don't. Leah is 18 and I am 19. Just a year ago, we weren't all living together like this. A year ago, we were all home, safe, each in our own place. I look around at the men dancing. They call to me to dance with them, but I refuse. There is no one here for me that I want to marry, and I do want to get married—I want to have a family. This town holds nothing for me anymore. Everywhere I go and everything I see puts more pain in my heart. The pain stabs me. When I go to the market, I see my mother. When I walk past my grandfather's house, I see his big frame leaning on the front door. When I pass the old yeshiva, I see Yecheskel running in. I cannot pass by our old apartment; it would kill me to see it now that my mother will never again be inside of it. I cannot stay here a moment more. The town that I loved with all my heart is now ripping me to pieces.

"Let us go to Satu Mare to see Uncle Duvid and Chanky," I say to Leah.

"I can't leave now. I am waiting for Avrumi."

I think of staying with her, but I have no one I am waiting for. It breaks my heart, but I leave without her.

41

SATU MARE. JUNE 1945.

"They will be sated
From the abundance of your house
And from the stream
Of your delights
You give them to drink.
For with you
Is the source of life
By your light
May we see light."

Psalm 36:8–9

I get off the train in Satu Mare and I find Duvid right away. The first person I ask points me to a restaurant in the middle of town. Duvid is so happy to see me. Chanky and Duvid have started the restaurant. Everyone who comes home is so hungry, and there was no one here to feed them. They had a little money hidden and there are some organizations giving out money for the survivors to buy food and start small businesses. They rent a room with a kitchen in the middle of the town. Chanky is a master cook. Everyone who comes to Satu

Mare looking for family flocks to her restaurant, and her food nourishes their bodies and broken hearts.

I stay in Chanky and Duvid's one-room apartment. Chanky teaches me to make fresh pasta. I make the flour into a little mountain on the table, then I make a valley in the middle and crack eggs into it, sprinkle some salt and add a splash of oil. I mix the eggs in the valley, careful not to mix in the flour. Then I mix everything together, knead the dough, and then roll it out as thin as it can possibly go.

Eventually I realize Chanky is pregnant again. The pregnancy seems to remind her of the son she lost so she spends most of the day in bed, except for when she is cooking in the restaurant.

Finally, after a few weeks Leah gives up on waiting for Avrumi. She comes to Satu Mare and joins us in the one-room apartment.

There is a cousin that keeps coming to Duvid to discuss business that they are doing together. His name is Yitzchak Heilbrun and I realize he was engaged to Rivka. He said she never came home. He is handsome. His hair is blonde, and his eyes are blue. He exudes confidence and a sure, business-like manner. I cannot help that my heart speeds up when I see him. He is so full of life.

"Were you in Auschwitz, too?" I ask him as we all sit down together for dinner in the restaurant.

"I got papers," he says. "There was a drunk laying on the platform at the train station and he looked like me and before I could stop myself, I asked him for his papers in an official voice and he handed them right over."

"Wow, so you avoided everything?"

He shook his head. "I watched everyone I love go to the ghetto. They starved before my eyes. I knew where they were headed, I had heard about Auschwitz. I tried to get them to escape with me, but they told me to stop being such a troublemaker, to put my head down and follow the rules. So, I let them stay there. I let them die. And I went about with my papers."

He looks haunted when he says this, as if he wishes he had gone along with them.

"Did anyone figure out who you were?"

"I moved around every few weeks. But my roommate was shot while I was at work. I came home and the land lady told me that he was really a Jew. She said it with such disgust."

"Let us talk about something else," Duvid says because Chanky is beginning to get that hollow look in her eyes.

So, Yitzchak tells us about his father, my Zaidy's brother. He tells us how he loves to learn. He tells us about his family. They sound just like mine.

"I have a house in Csenger," he says after the meal. "A few of our cousins are living there. Come with me?"

"Of course, you should go," say Duvid and Chanky. It is clear that they want their privacy. It must not be easy having two nieces staying with them in a one-room apartment.

I look at Leah.

She nods.

"Of course, we'll come," I say.

When we get to his house in Csenger, the first thing I notice is the mess. There are four girls sitting on the couch in the middle of the room. Yitzchak introduces us to our distant cousins. There is dust everywhere, dirty clothing on the floor, and nothing on the stove. For some reason the mess fills me with a sense of purpose. I find a broom and start cleaning right away. Then I take the clothing to the laundry lady.

Yitchak leaves to go do his work, importing salt. When he comes home that night the house is clean, and the table is set.

His house is in Hungary, on the border of Romania, so all the survivors who stumble across, scrounging for loved ones, come to his house first. They all look like they are starving, and I want to cook for them, but I do not know how. My mother never let me in the kitchen with her. She was as fast as lightening, and I just slowed her down and got in her way. I wish she had taught me at least the basics, though, because now I have no idea what to do.

Yocheved, one of the cousins living in the house, tells me about a gentile woman who used to work in a Jewish home and knows how to cook and make everything kosher. She takes me to meet her. Her name is Wiig Nani, and she gives me a warm hug when I ask her to

243

teach me to cook so I can feed all the survivors who come to Yitzchak's house.

"Of course, you beautiful girl," she says to me. She wraps her steady arm around my shoulder, and I hold back my tears. "Come," she says, "let's go to the market."

Yitzchak makes good money from his salt business, so I can buy a chicken, some vegetables, a duck, and some eggs. My instructor shows me how to make the chicken kosher, how to make the cholent, how to make the *letcho*[1] and how to make the kugel. I go to her every day to learn. Soon enough I am cooking huge pots of food for all the people coming in. I watch them as they gulp it all down with appreciation.

One day, I get a long letter in the mail. It is from Uncle Duvid. He writes that I should marry Yitzchak. He writes that Yitzchak comes from a fine family; he is smart and learned and Duvid thinks he would make a great husband for me. I think he is right. Yitzchak is self-assured and so manly. He is away all day working but at night we go out on walks, we scrub the big pots together and sometimes he sings while he dries the dishes. He reminds me of my family. I didn't think I would ever feel anything again, but then I realize that I am (quite quickly) falling in love. A few weeks later he asks me to marry him. For the first time since I got home, I feel a true joy. I say yes.

One night on our walk Yitzchak looks at the faded, floral dress I am wearing and says, "My bride should have beautiful clothing to wear. You like nice clothing, right? Will that make you happy?" He reminds me of Yecheskel, with the way he wants to take care of me. The way he wants me to have fine things.

"I don't think that is on the agenda for right now," I say. We are just coming out of a war. No one is thinking about beautiful new clothing right now. But the next day Yitzchak brings home rolls and rolls of different kinds of fabric. He tries to hide his pride as he gruffly plops it all down on the table.

Leah's eyes light up at the sight of the material. "Oh Rosie," she says touching the cloth, "I'll make you the dresses."

She sits in front of an old sewing machine, day and night, for hours on end. She spins together the most beautiful suits and dresses for me. It warms my heart to see my baby sister hard at work making clothing for me and asking for nothing in return.

Then, it is Leah's turn to get a letter. "It is from Duvid!" she says. "Avrumi is there! He is asking for me! Come with me to see him, Rosie!"

"Let us go tomorrow," I say. "I need to wait until Yitzchak comes home so I can tell him."

When we get back to Satu Mare, Avrumi is waiting for us at the train station. Leah falls right into his arms.

Just a few days later Leah walks down the aisle to Avrumi. She looks beautiful. Her hair is long enough to wear in a low bun, she is wearing a white silk dress, and carrying a small bouquet of flowers. Chanky and Duvid cook a beautiful meal and we eat it in their restaurant after the chuppah. Leah's eyes are brighter than I have ever seen them. She leans into Avrumi and whispers to him the whole night through. It is their wedding, and I am so happy for her, but I cannot help that my heart stings because I know my sister will not be only mine anymore.

"We are going to Romania," Avrumi says a few days after the wedding.

"We have to see if Avrumi's grandmother is still alive," Leah says.

"The war didn't hit certain parts of Romania," Avrumi explains.

I swallow my tears and they slide down my throat in a lump of acid. "Of course, you should go," I say.

I don't know what I am thinking when I tell her to go. I will have no way to contact them while they are in Romania, but Leah promises to write to me. We are about to do the one thing that we promised our mother, in the last moments that we ever saw her, that we would not do. After all we have been through together, we are letting each other out of our sight.

After Leah and Avrumi leave, I move back to Csenger with Yitzchak. We stay there for a few more months and I still cook for all the straggling survivors coming through. Then, the Russians take over Romania, they bring in their communism and Yitzchak's business is banned. With no source of income and the growing hostile environment, we realize we must leave our home. The worst part of leaving is knowing that Leah won't be able to write to me. In the chaos, however, I don't have a choice.

We move to a displaced person's camp called The Agudah. Jewish organizations have put together these camps for people like us. People with no homes, no country and nothing to call our own. We move there while we work on making more permanent arrangements for our lives that have once again unraveled at the seams.

Funnily enough, it is in the displaced persons camp where I start to find my place again. The people are nice, and they quickly become like family. The organization provides us with all our basic needs so we can focus our energy on moving on and not merely surviving. We spend Shabbos together with the people from our camp and sometimes we sing the Shabbos songs late into the night, just like we used to.

Our new family offers to put together a wedding for Yitzchak and me.

I go to a store and rent a wedding dress. It is not the gown I always dreamed of, but it is beautiful. I do not have enough money to buy a veil, so I get my hands on some lace and I sew one myself.

Everyone in the camp comes to the wedding. My heart aches for Leah, we haven't heard from them in so long. I write to Duvid when we can get ahold of stamps, but he hasn't heard from her either. I can only hope that they are OK.

Yitzchak stands under the chuppah waiting for me. As a young boy plays the flute, a kind older couple from the camp walk me down the aisle. Yitzchak looks nervous. I think it is hard for him to let himself be happy. He feels it is his fault that his parents died. I know he wishes they were here now under the chuppah with him. Still, as I walk down the aisle to him, and into our life together, I feel nothing but pure joy in my heart. After we are married, I look around at the group of strangers I've grown to love, and I watch them dance for us.

My Zaidy does not take my hand and spin me around like he promised he would. My mother does not fix my hair and bring me a drink when I need it. Yecheskel does not tell my husband to be good to me. I look around my wedding celebration and suddenly I feel a sadness that threatens to pull me down into the empty spaces of everyone who is not here. But then someone opens a window, and the room fills up with more guests. I hear the faint sound of birds singing outside, I hear the slight ripple of a stream lapping over colorful rocks, I hear frogs croaking in unison. I am home. I am alive. And slowly, so slowly, I feel my heart open to let the music enter, and I take my new husband's hand, and we dance.

EPILOGUE

My grandmother Rosie spent the first few weeks as a new wife worried sick about her sister, Leah. She asked everyone she knew if they had any idea of her whereabouts. She couldn't believe she hadn't kept her promise to their mother, not to let Leah out of her sight. Like the other survivors, they were just drifting people, frantic to put down some roots so they could feel at least slightly steady again, but in the mayhem of it all, they lost each other. Then one day in the DP camp, when my grandparents were sitting outside together, a charming couple (who also lived in the camp) came to talk with them.

"I am from Dej," the husband said.

"I have a brother-in-law from Dej," my grandmother said quickly. "Do you know him? He married my sister, and I don't know where they are. His name is Avrumi, Avrumi Frankel."

"Avrumi Frankel!" said the man "He is my best friend! I will write to him tomorrow!"

My grandmother thought she would faint to the ground. The man wrote to Avrumi, telling him of his sister-in-law's whereabouts. Leah wrote back and she and Rosie were connected once again. In her letter, Leah explained that they had gotten permission to move to Israel. They were preparing for the boat ride as she wrote. My grandmother and grandfather applied for visas to Israel so they could live near Leah and Avrumi. Much to her dismay, they were denied access to Israel because my grandmother's blood test showed she had latent tuberculosis. My grandmother speculated years later that perhaps it was the bacteria in the moldy cheese she ate in Auschwitz that stopped the tuberculosis from activating.

Most of the people from the Agudah were applying to go to America. With the destination of her sister being denied to her, they decided on the destination of America. My grandmother had always wondered if her red hair would get more positive attention there. With the entire world recovering from war, there was an arduous wait to receive the necessary paperwork. Meanwhile they were transferred to another DP camp in Italy, where they had their first child, my aunt Necha. When Necha was two years old, they finally received approval to travel to America. They traveled by ship, eventually docking in St. Paul, Minnesota, where they lived for a few years, before moving to Brooklyn, New York (where my grandmother lives to this day).

Many years passed before my grandmother was able to see her sister again; but once they were reunited, she went to visit Leah in Israel every year, even as she was reaching 90. They spoke on the phone every day and then face-to-face via Skype, which made them feel so close despite the thousands of miles between them. Leah and Avrumi enjoyed a beautiful marriage and had three beautiful children together. Leah died on the last night of Hannukah 2014 at the age of 87. Heartbroken, my grandmother threw away the computer in her living room because she couldn't bear to see it without Leah's face calling in.

When she was 41 with 4 children, my grandmother unexpectedly got pregnant again. Due to complications, the doctor told her that it was unlikely that her pregnancy could be successful.

"If you have this baby, I will eat my hat," he said.

"Dr.," said Rosie, in her trademark stubborn fashion, "you better start chewing." She put herself into bed and a few months later she gave birth to a beautiful, redheaded baby girl. That daughter grew up to have nine children, the third of which is me.

As I write this now, the redhead who promised herself that she was going home has 5 children, 28 grandchildren, 120 great grandchildren and 7 great, great grandchildren. Each one of these children is a world in themselves. Each one laughs, loves, and has revelations of their own. For each, it is as if the world was created just for them. If you are reading this now, you are alive, and for you, too, the world was created for you alone. All the beauty of the world was created just for you, and for each one of us.

When I look at my own two girls, I see the spark of life from my grandmother who promised herself, "I am going home." When they dance, when they learn something new, when they look at the flowers in bloom, when they play on the beach and laugh with excitement as the sand sinks beneath their feet and the waves come to tickle their toes; I think of a redheaded girl who pushed with all her might to live. I am so happy and grateful that she did. Above all, I am grateful to God for letting us live this beautiful life, because while there is hardship, pain, and sadness, there is also beauty, happiness, and love. We cannot always prevent the bad, but we also cannot let it overshadow the good.

My grandmother is 95 years old as I finish the last lines of this book. She did not have an easy life, or a happily ever after, even when she got home. The Holocaust ruined many more years than the one year she lived through. There were nightmares and trauma, and irreparably shattered people. As immigrants, they struggled to find themselves, to restore their culture, and to make a living. My grandmother fought paranoia for her entire life, and my grandfather was racked with guilt because he survived while his family didn't. My mother said she used to watch her father rock back and forth with his face in his hands, as he bore the responsibility of so much sorrow on his shoulders. Actually, as I write this, it is the day before the anniversary of his death. I know his soul is at peace and I hope he knows how much I love him. My grandmother lived a hard life, like King David did. There wasn't a day in her life that she forgot what happened to her. But somehow, like the 11-year-old girl she once was, she still opens the window and sings. The world sings back to her and tells her that everything is going to be OK.

And my grandmother is still singing. She sings while she does the dishes, while she sweeps the floor, while she irons her own blouse to perfection (she insists no dry cleaner can do it as well as her), and while she puts her makeup on. She is a small 95-year-old woman with a red wig, blue eyes that radiate love, and the most infectious laugh you will ever hear. She is the one who knows me the most. She warms my heart with sunshine and lights up my world.

But lately her song has adopted a sort of sadness. She is scared. She knows that there will not be many more years in which this world will have living testimony of what happened. She is saddened by antisemitism—especially by the extreme rise in it now. She is bewildered by the number of people who have no idea of what the Holocaust was. Most of all she is in agony over the way people treat one and other.

People speak of forgiveness, but it is not for us to forgive. Forgiveness belongs to the six million Jews who gasped for air, who were shot into mass graves, who were shot into rivers, who were abused, violated, and embarrassed—it is their choice to forgive, but they are forever silenced. While they cannot speak, we can speak for them. Instead of speaking of forgiveness, we can speak of remembrance and revenge. The greatest revenge we can inflict is to have tolerance and kindness for ALL peoples, all those that Hitler so strongly stood against. Hitler, who did not kill six million Jews by himself. Evil does not only happen when a person is abnormally bad. Evil happens when good people do not see the good in other people. Evil happens when we judge each other. Evil happens when we put ourselves higher than others. Evil happens when we stand by someone else's evil and do not speak up.

I did not want to write this book. It was painful to hear the horrors of what my grandmother went through. It was hard to deal with the biggest of all questions, "How did God let this happen?" I wanted to let the past stay buried with the past. But I know that knowledge is power. My grandmother always told me, "They can take everything away from you, but they can never take away what is in your head."

I know the past shapes the future and I also know, *"Those who do not remember the past are condemned to repeat it."*

My grandmother wants you to know what she went through so you can change the way our future looks. She wants you to know you can never let this happen again. She wants you to know that it doesn't matter what race you are, or the color of your skin, or what religion you practice; we are all one. She wants you to treat others with respect and she wants you to stand up for those who are being treated unjustly, no matter who they are. She wants you to remember, so you can stand up for peace.

So, remember. Remember a redhead who was just skin and bones who said she was going to live. Remember, and make it a world worth living in.

ACKNOWLEDGMENTS

First, I would like to thank my brother-in-law, Dani Machlis. Writing this book has always been my dream but he was the one to turn it into a reality. He spearheaded the project and made it happen by spending hours videotaping my grandmother telling her whole story. This book would not be here without him.

Liesbeth Heenk of Amsterdam Publishers, I am blown away by you. If only the world had more people like you in it, we wouldn't need this book in the first place. It is only thanks to you that my grandmother's story became this book that will now be shared with the world. Each time I work on it I am astounded anew at the suffering my grandmother was put through. All she wants is to give some meaning to her suffering and make the world a better place by telling her story. You gave her a voice and a platform. You have brought comfort to our whole family. I cannot imagine a work more meaningful than yours. Thank you will never be enough.

Thank you Shawn Richardson for being the most amazing editor a writer could dream of. You ironed this book out better than my grandmother could have ironed a dress.

Gideon Summerfield not only are you a talented artist, you are a wonderful person. You reached out and joined me in this project without asking for any return for your work. Your soul shines through to your work. No matter if we are supposed to or not, we do judge a book by its cover and thank you for giving this book a perfect one.

Eli Tabak, thank you for taking this project under your wing and introducing it to so many people. It would not be the same without you.

Thank you to all my early readers: Bubbe Bodner, Babi Birnbaum, Babi Friedman, Mom Birnbaum, Rena Baldinger, Shira Perl, Gila Bodner, Tatty Bodner, Ita Bodner, Michal Tabak, and Nechama Tendler. Not only did you take the time to read it and critique it, but you also constantly encouraged me. You did more for me than you know.

Thank you, Rena Baldinger, for selflessly editing the entire book before it was a book at all.

Thank you to my parents, Meyer and Fagie Bodner, for encouraging and inspiring me to follow my dreams.

Thank you to my parents-in-law, Moshe and Alisa Birnbaum. Thank you for getting me help so that I could actually have time to write. A special thank you to my mom-in-law for proudly talking about the book, because that is how I got the connection with the publisher.

On that note, thank you to Penina (Kallus) Fischer, who thought of me and connected me with her cousin who also wrote a Holocaust book. Thank you Zvi Wiesenfeld for taking the time to talk to me and connect me to Amsterdam Publishers.

Thank you to my daughters Ita and Rivka. You sure made it hard to write this book, but you sure made it easy to have a reason for writing it. You are my greatest joys.

Thank you, Benny, for *everything.* Thank you for supporting me exactly the way I need it and for making me laugh louder than I ever did in my life. You make everything better. It is an honor to be your life partner and a wonderful thing to have you as mine.

Thank you, *Bubbe,* for telling your story even though it was painful to relive it. Thank you for being my best friend and greatest fan.

Most of all, thank you God. Every time I sat down to write, I asked you to please use me to tell this story. I only hope I did you proud.

AFTERWORD

We interviewed Rosie (now known to most as Rachel) over the course of more than two years, from March 2016 to June 2018. It wasn't always consistent. Sometimes we'd do interviews once a week and sometimes months would go by without a single interview. I would drive in from my home in Queens to her home in Brooklyn to set up a camera and some lights. Occasionally I'd be joined by one of Rosie's daughters, but sometimes it was just me, armed with a list of questions prepared by Nechama (the author of this book), who was living abroad at the time. In classic Rosie fashion, she always wanted advance notice so she could look nice for the camera. When I'd arrive, she'd be dressed to the nines, as though she were about to head out to a wedding. Sometimes, I would drive all the way in only to find out that it "wasn't a good day"; talking about the Holocaust is hard. Often, she'd detour to discuss modern politics and, while she had some great insights, I'd struggle somewhat to bring her back to talk about her experience of her youth. She was always proud of this project as she felt it was her duty to tell her story to the world.

My wife Sara is Rosie's granddaughter and the author of this book's older sister, the eldest of nine children. These days, Sara and I have been driving our young children to visit her in the Rehabilitation Center as Rosie has been having health issues lately. I sometimes feel bad for my children as I'm pretty sure they'd rather be spending their Sundays jumping on a bouncy house somewhere instead of visiting a stuffy old age home. But I know that their lives will forever be impacted positively by having intimately known a strong Holocaust Survivor, and not just any, but the Redhead.

— Daniel Machlis, the author's brother-in-law.

ABOUT THE AUTHOR

Nechama Birnbaum knew since she was a little girl that she would write her grandmother's story. Her friend's grandmas brought them presents. Hers brought her stories, and stories were her favorite thing of all. When her grandmother told her how she would rip petals off flowers to see if the boy she liked, liked her back, and how she would crumple up the flower that landed on "he loves me not," and start again until it landed on "he loves me"; that was when Nechama knew for sure she would write her stubborn, determined grandma's story. She knew her grandma's tenacity started long before she told her friends in Auschwitz that she was going home from there.

Nechama lives in Brooklyn NY with her husband and daughters and nearby her redhead grandma. She is currently finishing her master's degree in nutrition.

Dear Reader,

If you have enjoyed reading my book,
please do leave a review on Amazon or Goodreads. A few kind words
would be enough. This would be greatly appreciated.

Alternatively, if you have read my book as Kindle eBook
you could leave a rating.
That is just one simple click,
indicating how many stars of five you think this book deserves.
This will only cost you a split second.
Thank you very much in advance!

**To see pictures and hear messages from the redhead herself,
follow her on instagram:**

@thereheadofauschwitz

NOTES

Chapter 1

1. *Yeshiva:* An Orthodox Jewish school, traditionally with a male-only student body.
2. *Mamale:* Affectionate Yiddish term meaning "Little Mama."

Chapter 2

1. *Zaidy:* Grandfather.
2. *Talmid Chacham:* Smart scholar.
3. *Bubbe:* Grandmother.
4. *Rebbe:* Teacher.

Chapter 4

1. *Tatty:* The Yiddish word for father.
2. *Shul:* Synagogue.
3. *Sefer:* Holy book.

Chapter 5

1. *Dobosh:* A Hungarian sponge cake, usually layered with chocolate filling, coated on the sides with chopped nuts, and topped with caramel.
2. *Rugelach:* A thin, yeasty dough smeared with chocolate, or sometimes vanilla, then rolled into a crescent-moon shape and baked.

Chapter 7

1. *Schnell:* Fast.

Chapter 8

1. *Bris:* Circumcision ceremony.
2. *Bimah:* A raised altar in a synagogue from which the Torah is read.
3. *Kugel:* A baked dish made from any kind of ground-up vegetable.

Chapter 11

1. *Shabbos:* Sabbath.
2. *Blockälteste:* Literal meaning is "block elder." Nazi prisoner charged with keeping order in a concentration camp.

Chapter 12

1. *Zeeskeit:* Sweetness.
2. *Blech:* Cover placed over the cooking area of a stove on the Sabbath.
3. *Kiddush:* A prayer recited over wine on *Shabbos* and Jewish holidays.
4. *Chrein:* A relish for gefilte fish that is made of ground beets and horseradish.

Chapter 14

1. *Kokosh: Like a rugelach, but better. Made with a sweet, yeasty dough that is rolled out in a rectangle, smeared with sugar and chocolate, rolled up into a long snake-like shape, twisted into a figure eight, then baked. When sliced the chocolate oozes over the sweet dough and you find yourself in heaven for a few good minutes until the entire thing is gone.*
2. *Tante:* Aunt.
3. *L'chaim!* To life!
4. *Peyos:* Sidelocks. All male Orthodox Jews have sidelocks. Usually, they are sideburns under the temple. In Hasidic Jews, they may be longer strips of hair that are curled into one bottle curl on each side of the head.
5. *Mazel Tov:* Literal meaning, "good luck," but also used as congratulations.
6. *Kallah:* Bride.
7. *Chuppah:* Wedding canopy.

Chapter 15

1. *Zeilappell:* Daily, often cruel, and always grueling, manual head count of all concentration camp prisoners.
2. *Muselmann:* Slang term for Nazi concentration camp prisoners who were suffering from both starvation and exhaustion.

Chapter 16

1. *Leu:* Romanian currency.

Chapter 18

1. *Amar Abaya:* literally translated as "Abaya said." Abaya was a Rabbi in the Talmudic era, and his teachings are often quoted in the Talmud.

Chapter 19

1. *Chossen:* Groom.

Chapter 20

1. *Sheifala:* Affectionate term that means "Little Lamb."

Chapter 24

1. *Shochet:* One who is certified to perform *shechita,* or the slaughtering of certain cattle or poultry, in accordance with Jewish law, for kosher consumption.
2. *Gan Eden:* Garden of Eden.
3. *Cholent:* A traditional Jewish stew.

Chapter 25

1. *Jetzt:* Now.
2. *Häftling:* prisoner, detainee.

Chapter 28

1. *Mamashein:* My good mama.
2. *Chinush:* Somewhere between chic and slim.

Chapter 29

1. *Faigy:* Yiddish name that means bird.

Chapter 30

1. *Matzah:* The unleavened bread that commemorates the Jews redemption from slavery in Egypt. The Israelites had to leave Egypt so quickly they did not have time to let their bread rise.

2. *Pesach:* Passover. The holiday to remember the redemption of the Israelites from slavery.
3. *Tisha B'Av:* "The ninth of Av." A day of fasting, observed annually, in the Jewish month AV. It commemorates the day on which the temple was destroyed and usually falls in July or August.

Chapter 33

1. Seven hundred girls from Auschwitz were transported to the Duderstadt Ammunition Factory from the gas chambers.

Chapter 35

1. *Katalin Karády:* While the Katalin Karády "look-alike" was in the factory, in charge of Jewish prisoners, the real Katalin Karády was doing everything in her power to help the Jews. She was arrested by the Nazis on allegations that she spied for the allied forces. She was held for three months, tortured, and nearly beaten to death. When she got out of jail, she saved Jewish families who were about to be shot on the banks of the Danube. She bribed the Arrow Cross police with her belongings and gold to get families safely out of there. She even took children home with her and cared for them until after the war.
2. *Yapchik:* Potato kugel (ground potatoes with onions and oil) baked together with a layer of meat over the top.

Chapter 36

1. *Shema:* The Jewish proclamation of faith.

Chapter 41

1. *Letcho:* A Hungarian peasant dish made with bell peppers.

HOLOCAUST SURVIVOR MEMOIRS

The Series **Holocaust Survivor Memoirs World War II** by Amsterdam Publishers consists of the following autobiographies of survivors:

1. Outcry - Holocaust Memoirs, by Manny Steinberg

2. Hank Brodt Holocaust Memoirs. A Candle and a Promise, by Deborah Donnelly

3. The Dead Years. Holocaust Memoirs, by Joseph Schupack

4. Rescued from the Ashes. The Diary of Leokadia Schmidt, Survivor of the Warsaw Ghetto, by Leokadia Schmidt

5. My Lvov. Holocaust Memoir of a twelve-year-old Girl, by Janina Hescheles

6. Remembering Ravensbrück. From Holocaust to Healing, by Natalie Hess

7. Wolf. A Story of Hate, by Zeev Scheinwald with Ella Scheinwald

HOLOCAUST SURVIVOR TRUE STORIES

The Series **Holocaust Survivor True Stories WWII** by Amsterdam Publishers consists of the following biographies:

1. Among the Reeds. The true story of how a family survived the Holocaust, by Tammy Bottner

2. A Holocaust Memoir of Love & Resilience. Mama's Survival from Lithuania to America, by Ettie Zilber

3. Living among the Dead. My Grandmother's Holocaust Survival Story of Love and Strength, by Adena Bernstein Astrowsky

4. Heart Songs - A Holocaust Memoir, by Barbara Gilford

5. Shoes of the Shoah. The Tomorrow of Yesterday, by Dorothy Pierce

6. Hidden in Berlin - A Holocaust Memoir, by Evelyn Joseph Grossman

7. Separated Together. The Incredible True WWII Story of Soulmates Stranded an Ocean Apart, by Kenneth P. Price, Ph.D.

20. Painful Joy. A Holocaust Family Memoir, by Max J. Friedman

JEWISH CHILDREN IN THE HOLOCAUST

The Series **Jewish Children in the Holocaust** by Amsterdam Publishers consists of the following autobiographies of Jewish children hidden during WWII in the Netherlands.

1. Searching for Home. The Impact of WWII on a Hidden Child, by Joseph Gosler

2. See You Tonight and Promise to be a Good Boy! War memories, by Salo Muller

3. Sounds from Silence. Reflections of a Child Holocaust Survivor, Psychiatrist and Teacher, by Robert Krell

---

The Series **New Jewish Fiction**, by Amsterdam Publishers, consists of the following novels, written by Jewish authors. All novels are set in the time during or after the Holocaust.

1. Escaping the Whale. The Holocaust is over. But is it ever over for the next generation? by Ruth Rotkowitz

2. When the Music Stopped. Willy Rosen's Holocaust, by Casey Hayes

3. Hands of Gold. One Man's Quest to Find the Silver Lining in Misfortune, by Roni Robbins

4. The Corset Maker. A Novel, by Annette Libeskind Berkovits

5. There was a garden in Nuremberg. A Novel, by Navina Michal Clemerson